D0139555

Bombing the Marshall Islands

During the Cold War, the United States conducted atmospheric tests of nuclear weapons in the Marshall Islands of the Pacific. The total explosive yield of these tests was 108 megatons, equivalent to the detonation of one Hiroshima bomb per day over nineteen years. These tests, particularly Castle Bravo, the largest one, had tragic consequences, including the irradiation of innocent people and the permanent displacement of many native Marshallese. Keith M. Parsons and Robert A. Zaballa tell the story of the development and testing of thermonuclear weapons and the effects of these tests on their victims and on the popular and intellectual culture. These events are also situated in their Cold War context and explained in terms of the prevailing hopes, fears, and beliefs of that age. In particular, the narrative highlights the obsessions and priorities of top American officials, such as Lewis L. Strauss, Chairman of the Atomic Energy Commission.

Keith M. Parsons, Professor of Philosophy at the University of Houston-Clear Lake, has won awards for both teaching and research. He has published in diverse fields, including the philosophy of science, the history of science, the philosophy of religion, and logic and critical thinking.

Robert A. Zaballa is a physicist specializing in nuclear physics. His areas of research include models of excited nuclei and high-energy heavy ion collisions. In addition to teaching physics at the college level, he is currently employed as a radiographer at Grady Memorial Hospital.

Bombing the Marshall Islands

A Cold War Tragedy

KEITH M. PARSONS
University of Houston-Clear Lake

ROBERT A. ZABALLA
Grady Memorial Hospital

CAMBRIDGE
UNIVERSITY PRESS

CAMBRIDGE
UNIVERSITY PRESS

University Printing House, Cambridge CB2 8BS, United Kingdom

One Liberty Plaza, 20th Floor, New York, NY 10006, USA

477 Williamstown Road, Port Melbourne, VIC 3207, Australia

4843/24, 2nd Floor, Ansari Road, Daryaganj, Delhi – 110002, India

79 Anson Road, #06-04/06, Singapore 079906

Cambridge University Press is part of the University of Cambridge.

It furthers the University's mission by disseminating knowledge in the pursuit of education, learning, and research at the highest international levels of excellence.

www.cambridge.org
Information on this title: www.cambridge.org/9781107697904
DOI: 10.1017/9781107239036

© Keith M. Parsons and Robert A. Zaballa 2017

This publication is in copyright. Subject to statutory exception and to the provisions of relevant collective licensing agreements, no reproduction of any part may take place without the written permission of Cambridge University Press.

First published 2017

Printed in the United States of America by Sheridan Books, Inc.

A catalogue record for this publication is available from the British Library.

Library of Congress Cataloging-in-Publication Data
Names: Parsons, Keith M., 1952– author. | Zaballa, Robert A., author.
Title: Bombing the Marshall Islands: a Cold War tragedy / Keith M. Parsons, University of Houston-Clear Lake, Robert A. Zaballa, Grady Memorial Hospital.
Other titles: Nuclear testing and the Cold War, bombing the Marshall Islands
Description: Cambridge University Press: Cambridge, New York, NY, [2017] | Includes bibliographical references and index.
Identifiers: LCCN 2017006124 | ISBN 9781107047327 (hardback) | ISBN 9781107697904 (pbk.)
Subjects: LCSH: Nuclear weapons – Marshall Islands – Testing. | Nuclear weapons – United States – Testing – History. | Nuclear weapons testing victims – Marshall Islands. | Nuclear weapons – Testing – Political aspects. | Cold War.
Classification: LCC DU710.P39 2017 | DDC 623.4/51190287–dc23
LC record available at https://lccn.loc.gov/2017006124

ISBN 978-1-107-04732-7 Hardback
ISBN 978-1-107-69790-4 Paperback

Cambridge University Press has no responsibility for the persistence or accuracy of URLs for external or third-party internet websites referred to in this publication and does not guarantee that any content on such websites is, or will remain, accurate or appropriate.

This book is dedicated to the faculty and graduate students of the Department of History and Philosophy of Science, the University of Pittsburgh, 1990–1996. Thank you for sharing your intelligence, your knowledge, and your friendship.

– Keith M. Parsons

I would like to dedicate this book to the memory of Dr. David Finkelstein (1929–2016), of the Georgia Institute of Technology, who I am proud to call my mentor from a young age and with whom I had the honor of being a colleague in physics for almost twenty years.

– Robert A. Zaballa

Contents

Illustrations

Acknowledgments

We would like to thank Mr. Lew Bateman, recently retired from Cambridge University Press. He worked with us in initiating the project and guided it through until its final stages. Ms. Debbie Gershenowitz took over as Senior Editor for History, and she and her editorial assistant, Ms. Kristina Deusch, guided the project to its completion. The unfailing professionalism and efficiency of the Cambridge University Press personnel was always appreciated. The expert handling of the copy editing and indexing process by the people of Newgen Knowledge Works was similarly appreciated.

We would also like to thank an outstanding and widely published historian, who has requested not to be identified by name, but who kindly but critically read the original manuscript and made numerous suggestions for its improvement. Also, four anonymous reviewers of the original and revised prospectus and the book manuscript pointed out serious lacunae in the project while applauding its strengths and encouraging its development.

Thanks to Mr. Spencer Howard and the staff of the Herbert Hoover Presidential Library in West Branch, Iowa. Their aid in accessing the Lewis Strauss archives was very helpful and most appreciated.

We had originally planned to conduct our own interviews with Marshallese survivors of the tests and to include these in the book. However, repeated attempts to contact Marshallese officials, both in the Marshall Islands and in the United States, got no responses whatsoever. We suspect that at this point, when the survivors are now quite elderly and have been through so much, perhaps there is an understandable desire to spare them from reliving painful memories.

Last but certainly not least, we would like to thank Ms. Rebecca Ruiz, who, along with her many other duties as suite secretary, gave unstinting aid in putting this project into acceptable format for submission.

The authors would each like to offer their own thanks individually.

Keith M. Parsons

Thanks to my university, the University of Houston-Clear Lake, for granting a Faculty Research Support Fellowship that was very helpful in completing the research. I would like to thank my Dean, Dr. Rick Short; Associate Dean, Dr. Samuel L. Gladden; my Department Chair, Dr. Shreerekha Subramanian; and numerous colleagues for their support and encouragement of this project. I would like to thank my wife, Carol Molina, for driving me through the beautiful state of Iowa to the Hoover Presidential Library. Her companionship made a working trip into a pleasure trip as well.

Robert A. Zaballa

I would like to thank my wife, Erin, for being so supportive as I worked on this project. I would also like to thank my parents, brother, and sister for their support as well, and to thank Dr. John Wood, of the Georgia Institute of Technology, who has been a great mentor and research collaborator in nuclear physics.

Introduction

Sunrise in the West; Snow in the Tropics

In the early morning hours of March 1, 1954, the *Daigo Fukuryū Maru (Lucky Dragon #5)*, a Japanese tuna boat with a displacement of 141 tons and a crew of twenty-three, was fishing the waters of the Marshall Islands about seventy-five miles east of Bikini. The ship had been at sea for over a month, and food and fuel were starting to run low. The ship's master decided to cast out lines one more time before heading home. After the long lines were let out, the tired crew took a break.

Young fisherman Ōishi Matashichi was resting in his bunk when, at 6:45 a.m., he was startled by a bright yellow flash. He jumped up and ran on deck to join the other alarmed crewmen who saw what looked like the sun rising in the west. He records their reaction:

"Over there!" A spot on the horizon of the ship's port side was giving off a brighter light, forming in the shape of an umbrella. "What is it?" "Huh?" Other crewmen had followed me onto the deck, and when they saw the strange light, they too were struck dumb and stood rooted on the spot. It lasted three or four minutes, perhaps longer. The light turned a bit pale yellow, reddish-yellow, orange, red and purple, slowly faded, and the calm sea went dark again.[1]

A few minutes later, they heard a tremendous noise:

The rumbling sound engulfed the sea, came up from the ocean floor like an earthquake. Caught by surprise, those of us on deck threw ourselves down. It was just as if a bomb had been dropped ... In the dark people speculated in subdued voices: "An explosion on the ocean floor?" "No – maybe an asteroid." "An American military exercise?"[2]

It was not an asteroid or an earthquake. It was a scientific experiment. American scientists and engineers had exploded a thermonuclear device

1

at Bikini Atoll. The glowing object of umbrella shape was the expanding mushroom cloud, and the reverberating boom was the sound of the bomb. The event witnessed by the crew of the *Lucky Dragon* was called "Castle Bravo." This was a stupendous blast of fifteen megatons – the equivalent of the simultaneous detonation of fifteen million tons of conventional high explosive. The fireball reached four miles in diameter and excavated a crater 250 feet deep and 6,500 feet across. The mushroom cloud rose to a height of over sixty miles in less than ten minutes. The power of the blast greatly exceeded expectations. It had been predicted to explode with a yield of "only" about six megatons; instead, it "ran away" to fifteen.

Castle Bravo was just one of a series of nuclear tests code-named "Operation Castle," which was just one series among several such testing operations conducted in the Marshall Islands from 1946 to 1958. During that time, the United States conducted sixty-seven nuclear tests on and in the vicinity of Bikini. The combined explosive yield of these events was 108 megatons – the equivalent of one Hiroshima-sized bomb detonated daily for nineteen years. As a result, some of these islands were grossly polluted with radioactive fallout and rendered uninhabitable.

So far that morning, the crew of the *Lucky Dragon* had only suffered an unpleasant surprise. Much worse was to follow. About two hours later, white flakes began to fall, like snow in the tropics. It was not snow but intensely radioactive bits of pulverized coral that had been sucked into the mushroom cloud and now were falling out over 7,000 square miles of ocean, an area including the ironically named *Lucky Dragon*. This white ash covered the crew as they worked. It was irritating but did not seem dangerous. Ōishi even tasted a bit of it and found it to be gritty but without flavor.[3]

After working for several hours in the falling ash, the crew cleaned the ship and washed themselves. Apparently, no harm had been done. Later that evening, however, everyone aboard began to suffer distressing symptoms of nausea, dizziness, headache, and diarrhea. Blisters began to appear on their skin, especially on their hands and where the ash had settled under their clothes. Soon their hair began to fall out in batches. They were exhibiting all of the classic signs of acute radiation sickness.

Once they had returned to port, radiation sickness was quickly diagnosed. A Geiger counter showed that both the boat and the crew were still highly radioactive. The story of the *Lucky Dragon* and its crew soon reached the newspapers, provoking a reaction in Japan that was a combination of panic and outrage. Fear of radiation poisoning swept the country after it was learned that some contaminated fish had made it to market. The sense of outrage was intensified by the fact that Japan was, and still is, the only nation to have undergone atomic attack. The injury of more Japanese citizens by a US nuclear explosion was like salt rubbed into unhealed wounds. It was, after all, not even nine years since Hiroshima and Nagasaki.

The fate of the *Lucky Dragon #5* and its crew is movingly told by Ōishi in his book, *The Day the Sun Rose in the West*. Within months, the ship's radioman, Kuboyama Aikichi, died of complications related to the radiation poisoning. Other crew members survived longer, suffering varying health problems throughout their lives. They were not the only victims of the radioactive fallout from Castle Bravo. Various islands to the east and south of the test site also got a dusting of the "death ash." A number of islanders also suffered from the immediate effects of radiation sickness as well as long-term problems such as cancer.

Castle Bravo soon became an international incident, prompting widespread condemnation of atmospheric testing of nuclear weapons and stimulating the burgeoning nuclear disarmament movement. "Ban the bomb" demonstrations became much larger and more frequent. Eventually, the Castle Bravo event was to have widespread political, social, and cultural repercussions. Even popular entertainment was affected as movie monsters came to symbolize the nuclear threat.

This book will be a succinct narrative history of the nuclear tests in the Marshall Islands – and of the Castle Bravo event in particular. It is a fascinating story that deals with big science, big issues, and big egos. The narrative of the Bravo test and its consequences will focus on the events as experienced by the participants.

Yet merely telling the story of Castle Bravo and the other nuclear tests leaves many questions unanswered, and the goal of this book is not merely to recount the events but to understand them as causes and effects of events of their time. Although these things took place merely sixty (or so) years ago, they are already strange and distant to us. Open-air testing of multi-megaton thermonuclear devices, even in supposedly "remote" areas, now seems unaccountably risky, even reckless. These days, with our greater sensitivity to environmental issues and the exploitation of indigenous peoples, the actions of the US government at the Pacific Proving Grounds might seem grossly irresponsible. Yet such impressions, when unsupported by deep and detailed examination of the historical context, inevitably lead to facile judgments.

Each nuclear test pushed the limits of scientific knowledge. As the Castle Bravo test made starkly clear, atmospheric testing of cutting-edge weapons posed dangers that were hard to predict and harder to control. On the other hand, the Soviet Union was a formidable adversary that was proceeding at full speed to develop its own thermonuclear weapons. Clearly, this was a threat that had to be faced. This book will, therefore, aim to understand these events in terms of what was believed, hoped, and feared at the time. What was the frame of mind of the protagonists toward the Soviet threat and possibilities of nuclear conflict? To what extent were the dangers of atmospheric testing recognized, and what steps were taken to minimize them? In the final analysis, and given the very real threat of Soviet weapons development, were atmospheric tests unavoidable and were they conducted with sufficient attention to the safety of innocent persons? This book will address such questions.

The history of nuclear weapons is fascinating precisely because it encompasses so many contrasting elements. The beauty of basic physics is part of the story, but so are terror, suffering, and death. Likewise, the story glitters with the allure of scientific brilliance, but the offspring of that brilliance was a competition to build ever-more terrifying weapons. The story of atmospheric nuclear testing is a story of science and how it unleashed destructive forces that it could not control. It is also a story of two superpowers that were acquiring the means of mutual annihilation and struggling to find ways to deal with an unprecedented situation. Finally, it is an account of the ongoing ordeal of those who had long lived on Bikini and other atolls. The establishment of the Pacific Proving Grounds required the relocation of hundreds of indigenous Marshallese from their ancestral homes. This book will tell their story in some detail.

Chapter 1, "Operation Crossroads: The World's First Nuclear Disaster," concerns the first of those tests, Operation Crossroads, in 1946. Operation Crossroads was not only the first but was the most unusual of the test operations. Later tests in the Pacific were conducted under a tight net of secrecy and security, but Crossroads was a media spectacular. Surrendered German and Japanese warships, as well as retired American vessels, were assembled in Bikini Lagoon and subjected to nuclear blasts. The spectacle was witnessed by a boatload of journalists and by many others, including observers from the Soviet Union. The ostensible purpose of the tests was to see how warships might fare under atomic attack, but the whole operation looked so much like a publicity stunt that officials hastened to deny that it was. One very serious consequence of Crossroads was that the native Bikinians were evicted – temporarily, they were told; permanently as it turned out.

Crossroads has also been called "the world's first nuclear disaster" because it showed how badly things can get out of hand when nuclear tests take an unexpected turn. Though scientists had given plenty of warning ahead of time, the military officials in charge of Crossroads were unpleasantly surprised when the second of the tests, Test Baker, released vast quantities of radiation into Bikini Lagoon. Baker was an underwater test, and the fission products, instead of dissipating in the air, were concentrated in the waters of the lagoon. The surviving target ships were made intensely radioactive, and American sailors attempting to decontaminate them were exposed to high levels of radiation.

Chapter 2, "The Coming of the 'Super'," begins with an account of Operations Sandstone and Greenhouse, the next nuclear tests to be held in the Marshall Islands. The object of these tests was the development of new and more powerful weapons, and they were quite successful in that respect. Chapter 2 also tells the story of the decision to develop thermonuclear weapons. In 1950, President Harry S. Truman decided that the thermonuclear, or hydrogen, bomb would be developed. The hydrogen bomb is an ultimate weapon. One bomb can yield more explosive energy than was expended by all of the weapons on all fronts of the Second World War. We tell about the decision to develop these bombs, noting especially the opposition of prominent scientists, including many of those who played leading roles in developing the atomic bomb.

Chapter 2 ends with an account of the first test of a thermonuclear device, the Ivy Mike test of November 1, 1952. Mike was an experiment, not a prototype of a deliverable bomb. It was a test of the design of physicist Edward Teller and mathematician Stanislaw Ulam. The result, an explosion of over ten megatons that dwarfed every other previous detonation, confirmed the validity of the design and prepared for the tests leading to deliverable weapons.

By the way, one great advantage of living in the Internet Age is that you can actually see many things that previously could only be imagined. Ivy Mike and almost all of the tests we describe can be viewed on YouTube. We strongly encourage readers to look at the actual films of these tests, since only the visual experience can truly convey both their horrifying power and eerie beauty.

Chapter 3, "Runaway Bomb," tells the story of the Castle Bravo detonation and the immediately following events. The Castle tests were intended to provide the information needed to develop a deliverable thermonuclear bomb and, toward that end, they were completely successful. However, the unexpected size of the explosion caught everyone off-guard and endangered the crew that fired the bomb even though they were hunkered in a steel-reinforced concrete bunker twenty miles away. The really unpleasant surprise came when, contrary to predictions, fallout began to occur due east of the shot.

Chapter 3 also considers the enduring question of just what made the cloud of radiation move in an unexpected direction, that is, in the direction of the *Lucky Dragon* and inhabited atolls. At that time and later, people blamed an unexpected wind shift for the occurrence. We examine this theory but also an alternative theory that suggests that most of the fallout precipitated from the stratosphere. At the time, it was expected that any radioactive material injected into the stratosphere would be trapped there for some time (see Appendix 1). Yet with Castle Bravo this expectation may have been another thing that went wrong.

In Chapter 4, we follow the story of the *Lucky Dragon* crew and of their illness and continuing travails once they had returned to Japan. We also tell about the fallout on the inhabited islands and its effects. Here we enter into territory that is still highly controversial. Some writers take up the cause of the Marshallese victims of Bravo and frankly advocate on their behalf, expressing outrage at the perceived callousness (or worse) of the US government. Other writers, while admitting that the Bravo events were tragic and terrible, address what they consider to be hyperbole and distortion by critics of the tests.

Because we cannot settle these issues here, we attempt to tread lightly. We do not adopt either the role of advocates for the victims or of apologists for the testers. Rather, we attempt to give credit where we think it is due and do justice to the arguments of both sides. We are as appalled as anyone about the harm done by Bravo and, to a lesser extent, by other tests. However, we equally do not wish to condemn those who, in conducting the tests, were guided by what they took to be reasonable and humane precautions. Our goal, then, is to present the contrasting claims and to endorse the ones that seem most reasonable to us. In seeking the most reliable information about the fallout and some of its consequences, we have cited a paper by Steven L. Simon and his colleagues published in 2010 in a leading peer-reviewed journal, *Health Physics*.

We end Chapter 4 with a brief account of the Redwing and Hardtack tests in the Marshalls following Operation Castle. These tests, many with yields of over one megaton, continued until 1958 when the testing at Bikini finally ended.

After telling the stories of the tests themselves in the first four chapters, we look at the international response to those events. Because of its victims, the Castle Bravo test became the shot heard round the world and made people aware of the dangers of atmospheric testing. In Chapter 5, "Monsters and Movements: The Cultural 'Fallout' of Nuclear Testing," we trace the impact of the nuclear tests on the broader cultural milieu. We feel that it is as important to understand how these tests, and Castle Bravo in particular, changed the way people thought and felt about nuclear weapons.

Popular film is a reliable indicator of collective anxieties and obsessions. We focus on two films, one American and the other Japanese, that were produced in the immediate aftermath of Castle Bravo. The Japanese film, *Gojira*, was explicitly intended as a response to Castle Bravo and contains unmistakable references to that event. Unfortunately, because *Gojira* was the origin of the iconic pop-culture monster Godzilla, and because the screen was soon overrun with images of radiation-spawned creatures running amok, the film was never taken as seriously as it should have been. Actually, it is a powerful statement of the terror and anxiety caused by nuclear weapons and their testing.

The American film, *Strategic Air Command*, was produced with the aim of justifying the policy of preventing nuclear war by constantly preparing for one. The film celebrates nuclear warriors and their wives, emphasizing that it is their dedication and sacrifice that maintains peace and freedom. These two films show plainly that by the mid-1950s two antithetical attitudes had emerged concerning nuclear weapons. One view was that these weapons were purely evil and their eradication was the only hope for humanity. The opposed view held that eradication was impossible, at least at that time, and that deterrence was the best way to avoid a nuclear catastrophe.

The nuclear tests in the Pacific also got the attention of one of the most remarkable minds of the twentieth century. At the time of Castle Bravo, Bertrand Russell was probably the world's most distinguished and best-known philosopher and public intellectual. The tests, particularly Castle Bravo, motivated him to dedicate the rest of his life to the prevention of nuclear war, and he became the living symbol of the antinuclear movement. With other recognized and distinguished figures, he founded the Campaign for Nuclear Disarmament, perhaps the most prominent of the antinuclear groups. In his 1955 speech "Man's Peril," he argued with characteristic eloquence against what he saw as a head-long descent into jingoism and belligerence that endangered all of humanity. One of the most important effects of Castle Bravo was, therefore, the stimulus it gave to the antinuclear movement.

The nuclear testing program obviously had a scientific purpose, but it also communicated to allies and enemies the depth of the American commitment to weapons development. There were some, including Bertrand Russell, who expressed the hope that the awesome destructive potential revealed by the American tests might make the Soviets more amenable to a slowing of the arms race. Actually, if anything, they had just the opposite effect, acting as an accelerant of the arms race. The Soviet program proceeded at full speed, and, in 1955, the USSR acquired thermonuclear weapons. We conclude with a brief account of the Russian "Castle Bravo," the first Soviet test of a "true" two-stage thermonuclear bomb. Like the American test, the Soviet bomb also caused tragic and unintended results.

Chapter 6, "Bikini Postmortem, Part I: Public Perceptions and Official Obsessions," seeks a historically sensitive understanding of Castle Bravo. Why did it happen? How could an event that looks outrageously risky from sixty years' distance have appeared rational and responsible to sober-minded people at the time?

We begin with a rather basic exposition of some important principles of historiography, namely why it is important to avoid writing "Whig history" that judges the past by the standards of today. We also indicate why historians cannot moralize or sermonize but must set aside such judgments in the attempt to offer an account of past events as they were understood by people at that time. This is a particularly important point when historical events remain controversial, as do the nuclear tests in the Marshall Islands. Our exposition may seem somewhat elementary to professional historians, but our book is not just for such professionals. Our genre is what might be called "scholarly popular history." We are, therefore, addressing a broader audience that we think will include undergraduate students and the educated general public.

How do you understand an incident that was meticulously planned, with an earnest effort to anticipate every contingency, but which, in the event, led to disaster? One must first understand the tenor of the times. The mid-1950s in the United States was a period obsessed by the fear of communism and especially of the Soviet Union. This fear was so strong that people were motivated to take risks that in less perilous times would have seemed foolish. Nuclear tests in the United States as well as in the Pacific unleashed vast quantities of radiation into the atmosphere. Yet, most people saw this as a tolerable price to pay for nuclear preparedness.

The pervasive fears and obsessions of the time provide the explanatory background for the Marshall Island tests. By the way, during this period, in the Soviet Union there was also a fear of the United States amounting to paranoia, and this led them to take the same sorts of risks.

Also, to understand disastrous events caused by large, complex organizations – such as the massive 2010 oil spill in the Gulf of Mexico caused by British Petroleum – you have to look at the "corporate culture," the attitudes, beliefs, and intentions of the people at the very top. The people at the top set the tone, agendas, and the priorities for everyone in the organization. It is true of large corporations, and it is also true of large governmental operations, like the nuclear tests in the Pacific.

In particular, we look closely, and in considerable detail, at the published memoirs and archival records of Lewis L. Strauss, the Chairman of the Atomic Energy Commission at the time of the Castle tests. We find that, for Strauss, the success of the testing program was of such paramount urgency that safety was relegated to an afterthought, and that the well-being of the victims of Castle Bravo became important to him only after they became a public relations problem. Had a greater concern for safety originated from the top, plans could have been made that were more proactive than merely reactive, and perhaps disaster could have been avoided, or at least mitigated. We do not condemn Strauss but understand him as a dedicated public servant, charged with huge responsibilities in a world situation of unprecedented gravity. He was deeply frightened, as was every sensible person at the time, and he was charged with making crucial decisions in a situation of many uncertainties.

In Chapter 7, "Bikini Postmortem, Part II: Nuclear Policy and Nuclear Tests," we cast the explanatory net more widely. The program of atmospheric testing was just one aspect of American nuclear policy – the comprehensive set of accepted doctrines about every aspect of the manufacture, military use, and diplomatic significance of nuclear weapons. Here we sketch the evolution of US military doctrine during the period roughly corresponding to the period of testing in the Marshall Islands, 1946–1958. We begin with the decision to use the bomb at the end of the Second World War. After a brief period of idealism, when the United States proposed international control of atomic weapons, the question quickly settled on how best to employ these weapons to win wars.

We will emphasize that, during the period of our study, many military and civilian leaders and nuclear strategists saw the atomic bomb as the winning weapon, the knockout blow that would assure victory. Before the development of the intercontinental ballistic missile, the only way to deliver an atomic bomb was by airplane, and so the era that depended upon nuclear-armed bombers is known as the "air atomic" era. In the air atomic era, nuclear war was widely regarded as winnable. With a decisive qualitative and quantitative advantage in bombers and bombs, the United States could annihilate any enemy nation while suffering horrendous but survivable losses. Only with the later development of the doctrine of Mutual Assured Destruction (MAD) did the goal become stability rather than victory, that is, nuclear weapons became tools of deterrence, not victory. Before MAD, nuclear war was not only thinkable but was actively planned as a winning strategy.

The lesson we draw is straightforward: When nuclear war is not only conceived as possible but is planned as a basic element of policy, then the risks run during the period of nuclear testing are completely unsurprising. When individuals or nations are stressed, crucial decisions tend to be based upon a cold, utilitarian calculus that puts the premium on survival and tolerates risks to self or others to the extent that these are calculated as necessary. Later, when the immediacy of the threat has apparently subsided, a more reflective tendency will emerge that evaluates actions more in the light of moral categories such as rights and justice. At the time, the development of nuclear weapons was seen as a matter of survival, and risks were run that would seem excessive, even unconscionable to later, more reflective generations.

In "Epilogue: Back to Bikini?," we consider the impact of the nuclear tests upon the group that constitutes the vast majority of the victims – the Marshallese people. We begin by briefly considering the claim that the events of Castle Bravo were not accidental but were planned as part of a nefarious conspiracy that intentionally exposed native Marshallese to radioactive fallout. We criticize these claims as counterproductive, implausible in the extreme, and unsupported by the documentary evidence. We see this unsubstantiated charge as an inflammatory distraction from the real issues.

Finally, we consider the deleterious effects that the tests have had on the people, their culture, and their way of living. What were the long-term effects on the lives and culture of the victims? We note especially how the continuing alienation from ancestral lands has made life difficult for the Marshallese who, though they appreciate the compensation that has been paid to them, can never forget how they used to live and the self-sufficiency and happiness they had previously enjoyed.

In the end, we see that the Marshallese and the other victims of nuclear testing were casualties of the Cold War. Putting it this way may make the sufferings of the victims seem to be due to impersonal forces rather than human choice. However, history always presents a double aspect. Looked at in one way, past events appear destined, driven by events and forces no one can control. Surely, it was unavoidable that the United States and the Soviet Union would come into sharp conflict with the close of the Second World War. On the other hand, when looked at another way, the course of history seems deeply contingent, highly subject to human choice and the vagaries of chance. We try to show both how these events were parts of a larger historical picture and how they were shaped by the actions and culpable inactions of the people involved.

To understand the significance of nuclear weapons and why they are so uniquely dangerous, you have to know something about how and why they work. What are these primal energies hidden in the depths of matter? How do nuclear weapons use these energies to produce their tremendous effects? Considered purely as scientific and technological achievements, nuclear weapons are among the most remarkable products of human intelligence. They are dreadful, yet they derive from beautiful theories and elegant experiments. Also, the complex process of turning theory into weaponry required technological and engineering expertise of the highest order.

To acquaint readers with the basic physics, technology, and effects of nuclear weapons is the purpose of Appendix 1, "Ultimate Weapons." As such, this section will begin with a primer of the basic physics of matter and energy. Readers familiar with the basic physics may skip this section, of course, but those who are fuzzy on concepts such as "isotope" and "binding energy," or the difference between fission and fusion, are *strongly* encouraged to read these sections. Much that is said in previous chapters will be incomprehensible or misunderstood without this knowledge. The remainder of the appendix will outline the nature of nuclear weapons and their effects. There will be some repetition here of information given in the earlier chapters. This redundancy is intentional. The chapters were written to provide readers with some knowledge of physics with a narrative that does not have to be frequently interrupted by reference to the appendices, where that information is elaborated.

Appendix 2, "Radiation Exposure, Dosage, and Its Biomedical Effects," fills in the details about how exposure to radiation is measured and the effects of exposure to radiation. This information is complex and is often confusing to laypersons because of the different measures and the technical terms employed. The terms are explained clearly as are the dangers posed to living things by radiation. Also included in this appendix is information about the worldwide exposure to radiation caused by the nuclear tests. Note once again that much of the material in the narrative is much more easily understood with reference to this appendix.

There is occasionally some uncertainty in the sources with respect to precise numbers, such as distances, numbers of people, and even the yields of the Hiroshima and Nagasaki bombs. Distances are made more uncertain by the fact that many sources report distances in miles and do not make it clear whether they are nautical or statute miles. It would probably be best to assume that distances between islands are given in nautical miles and distances over land in statute miles. For most purposes, an approximate value is all that is needed. As for the numbers of people, we have reported any discrepancies in the accounts, but these are small. We have accepted the value of fifteen kilotons for the Hiroshima explosion and twenty-one kilotons for Nagasaki. These are the values given in the 1985 report by John Malik for the Los Alamos National Laboratory, "The Yields of the Hiroshima and Nagasaki Nuclear Explosions."[4] All times and dates mentioned are local. Finally, different sources present very different spellings of the names of atolls and their constituent islands. We try to use the spellings that seem most widespread or familiar.

NOTES

1 Ōishi, *The Day the Sun Rose in the West*, pp. 18–19.
2 Ōishi, *The Day the Sun Rose in the West*, p. 19.
3 Ōishi, *The Day the Sun Rose in the West*, p. 20.
4 Malik, "The Yields of the Hiroshima and Nagasaki Nuclear Explosions." Atomic Archive site.

I

Operation Crossroads

The World's First Nuclear Disaster

On August 9, 1945, Major Charles W. "Chuck" Sweeney piloted the mission to drop the atomic bomb on Nagasaki. When bombardier Kermit Beahan released the "Fat Man" bomb at 11:01 a.m., he dropped the only nuclear weapon then in existence. Other than the bomb that fell on Nagasaki, there had been only two other nuclear bombs, and they had already been detonated. One was the "Little Boy" gun-design uranium bomb that had destroyed Hiroshima three days previously. The other was an implosion-design plutonium bomb, like Fat Man, that had been tested in the New Mexico desert three weeks before Hiroshima.

In those three weeks the world had entered the Atomic Age, but the instrument of that momentous change – the atomic bomb itself – was still largely an unknown quantity. The Trinity Test in the New Mexico desert on July 16 was the climax of the Manhattan Project, the all-out, super-secret effort to develop the atomic bomb during the Second World War. At the time of the test, many of the attending scientists had little confidence in their creation. They took bets on the bomb's yield, and J. Robert Oppenheimer, the scientific director of the Manhattan Project, bet on a low-yield fizzle. It did not fizzle. When the light "brighter than a thousand suns" blazed in the New Mexico desert, all those assembled knew that they had something extraordinary on their hands. But what exactly?

Any new and complex technology presents many significant unknowns, even to those who devise it. There are always unintended and unforeseeable effects of any such technology. Now we are aided by sophisticated computer models, but in the 1940s computers were still in their early infancy. Research on nuclear weapons would proceed by trial and error, and it was hoped that the "error" part would not be too catastrophic. So, atomic bombs would need to be tested, but how and where?

The first postwar atomic tests were Test Able and Test Baker of Operation Crossroads, conducted in July 1946, just eleven months after Hiroshima and Nagasaki. These tests had nothing to do with weapons development. The bombs used were identical in design to the Nagasaki Fat Man. Crossroads was a military exercise, or, at least, that was what it was alleged to be. The stated object of the tests was to determine the effect of nuclear weapons on warships. So, a sizable fleet of captured German and Japanese warships, and retired US ships, was anchored in Bikini Lagoon, where they were to be subjected to atomic blasts. The tests took place under the direction of Joint Task Force One, created by the Joint Chiefs of Staff.[1] Though it was not a purely naval project, Vice Admiral William H. P. "Spike" Blandy of the US Navy was placed in charge.

Bikini is part of the Marshall Islands, a group of low-lying coral atolls in the northern tropics of the Pacific at approximately the same longitude as New Zealand. In many ways, the Marshall Islands seemed ideal for nuclear tests. The climate is warm but not subject to violent storms. The islands are remote from continental landmasses, so that radioactive fall-out would supposedly drop harmlessly into the surrounding ocean. The islands were under US control, and in fact ruled by a military governor, Commodore Ben H. Wyatt of the US Navy. There were few built-up structures to be damaged by a bomb blast, and, best of all, the islands were lightly populated. However, "lightly populated" does not mean "uninhabited." In fact, the Marshall Islands had been continuously inhabited by Micronesian people since the second millennium BCE. At the time of the Crossroads tests, there were 162–167 (precise numbers vary in the accounts) inhabitants of Bikini who would have to be evacuated.

In general, what was the attitude of American military and civilian officials toward the Marshallese during the period of nuclear testing in the Marshall Islands? A good indication is found in a booklet "Operation Castle" produced by Joint Task Force Seven, which conducted the Castle tests in 1954. The booklet was given to all of the official observers of Castle tests, and along with other helpful information, contained this account of "the natives:"

The native inhabitants of Eniwetok and Bikini were relocated to new homes in the Marshalls when their homeland became the site for the atomic weapon proving ground. The Marshallese are an indolent, care-free, and friendly brown-skinned people whose existence has undergone few changes in spite of the advent of western influence. They still subsist primarily on fish, tropical roots, and fruits, although domestic animals such as pigs, goats, and cattle have been introduced to the area. Peace and happiness keynote their existence as they spend their days fishing, fruit-gathering, visiting and singing and dancing. They are passionately fond of tobacco and during the war acquired a taste for beer and other beverages common to the west, notably gin. They are born with a remarkable gift for navigation and frequently undertake long voyages between atolls with the utmost confidence and skill. Many of their ancient tribal customs have been retained to the present day, but they remain warm and friendly toward people from other lands.[2]

While the sociability and navigation skill of the islanders are admired, there is an unmistakable note of condescension. We have the familiar stereotype of childlike islanders; they are an indolent lot who enjoy lives of ease supported by the bounty of tropical nature. With few responsibilities, and few notable achievements other than their feats of navigation, they are free to spend their time socializing, singing, dancing, smoking, and drinking. The implied inference from this account seems to be that, being simple and carefree (and perhaps inebriated), these people do not mind too much if they are removed from their ancestral homes or have some big bombs go off in their vicinity.

Nevertheless, the removal of indigenous people from their ancestral homes was a touchy subject. Some of the darkest blots on US history had involved incidents such as the Trail of Tears, whereby the Cherokees and other Native American nations were forcibly removed from their homelands. The testing of nuclear weapons in the atmosphere was a controversial policy right from the beginning. Distressing accounts of distraught natives being forced into exile would make things much worse. Ever sensitive to bad publicity, the Navy therefore put its version of events on film. The well-being of the Native Marshallese became a primary concern only when it threatened to become a public relations problem.

In the film we see Commodore Wyatt addressing the assembled Bikinians and assuring them of the goodness of American intentions and that the tests are necessary to turn the power of the atomic bomb to unspecified beneficial uses. The Bikinians are depicted as cheerfully cooperative and are evacuated waving and singing on a Navy LST. The film's narrator offers glib assurance that the natives of Bikini are a nomadic people who do not mind a change of scenery at all, and actually appreciate the "Yanks" for adding a bit of variety to their lives. Needless to say, the film is a rather shameless piece of self-justifying propaganda, and the reality was darker and more complex.

Operation Crossroads was a huge news story at the time, but is largely forgotten today. To understand its origin and put it in proper perspective, one must consider the condition of the US Navy at the end of the Second World War. On September 2, 1945, when the official surrender ceremony took place in Tokyo Harbor on board the battleship the *USS Missouri*, the astonishing might of the US Navy was on display. At that time, the United States possessed what was by far the largest, most formidable naval force the world had seen. It arose from the devastation of Pearl Harbor and, in less than four years, had ravaged the Imperial Japanese Navy, the armed force that had inflicted that humiliation. It accomplished this feat while simultaneously conducting a separate campaign in the Atlantic.

In 1946, fresh from its triumphs in the War, the Navy abruptly faced a world with atomic weapons. Other weapons had changed the nature of warfare – the composite bow, gunpowder, tanks, battleships, the machine gun, submarines, and aircraft – but none so suddenly or so comprehensively as nuclear weapons. The Second World War had shown that the massive deployment of conventional weapons could do catastrophic damage, as the firestorms at Hamburg, Dresden, and Tokyo had made terribly clear. But nuclear weapons promised to make mass destruction easy, quick, and – ironically, considering the eventual cost of the arms race – cheap. Army Air Force Head General Henry Arnold noted these factors of economy in 1945:

It [the atomic bomb] made airpower more efficient by decreasing the "cost of destruction." General Arnold calculated that substituting atomic for conventional would make a given amount of destruction "at least six times more economical." Fewer aircraft would be needed; the dropping of a single atomic bomb by a B-29 on Hiroshima caused "as much damage as 300 planes would have done. Not only would fewer planes be required but also effective range would be increased, as an atom bomb would represent a lighter load than a full complement of conventional explosives."[3]

In general, the arrival of the atomic bomb seemed to be a vindication and consummation of the claims of air power advocates.[4]

Things appeared differently to the Navy. It could not promise economy to the Congressional budget hawks in the postwar era of tighter military budgets. On the contrary:

The Navy was particularly anxious to secure support for its own expensive investment program, for "super carriers," and felt it had little choice but to oppose the Air Force and its atomic strategy head-on. Admirals warned of the unreality of expectations of quick and easy victory, the need to prepare for a wide variety of contingencies and the affront to American values represented by strategies based on mass destruction … The Navy was seen as parochial and backward-looking, desperate to justify its existence in a world in which the reach of airpower was being extended all the time.[5]

Was the mighty Navy, the irresistible force so shortly ago, now a sitting duck? If one atomic bomb could destroy a city, surely it could sink the mightiest fleet. What the Japanese Navy could not do with hundreds of planes, a single, nuclear-armed aircraft might accomplish. The existence of the atomic bomb inevitably suggested an unsettling question: Was the Navy obsolete?

Since the Navy obviously had a vested interest in showing that it still had relevance in the Atomic Age, many politicians, scientists, and journalists suspected that the proposed test would be mostly a publicity stunt. As reported by Jonathan M. Weisgall in his thorough history of Operation Crossroads, the Congressional debate over the proposed tests grew raucous.[6] Influential congressmen could see no point in staging such an "experiment." Leading scientists were also very dubious of the value of such tests, concluding that if the bombed ships suffered sustainable damage, this would create a dangerous sense of complacency about the perils of atomic weapons. Further, one scientist noted that nobody would waste an atomic bomb to destroy a few ships but would hit cities and harbors instead.[7]

For many persons, then, Crossroads seemed to have no serious scientific or military purpose. They suspected that the whole scheme was a piece of theater staged by the Navy to pressure Congress for more lavish appropriations. One magazine article had a picture of Admiral Blandy and other Navy and Army officers and the picture caption read, "High command of 'Operation Crossroads,' officially known as Joint Task Force One, unofficially known as 'The Great Boondoggle.'"[8] The criticism stung and the Navy's responses were somewhat defensive. Some attacks got personal; one prompted a testy riposte from Admiral Blandy: "I am not an atomic playboy, as one of my critics labeled me, exploding these bombs for my personal whim."[9]

When *Bombs at Bikini* by W. A. Shurcliff, the official report on Operation Crossroads, came out in 1947, the entire first chapter addressed the question "Why Operation Crossroads?" Shurcliff responds:

The general answer is, of course, well known: It was imperative to find how to improve our Navy. As long as we have a Navy – and we will have one as long as the possibility of war remains – we want to have one of highest possible quality. We want ships which are tough, even when threatened by atomic bombs we want to keep the ships afloat, propellers turning, guns firing; we want to protect the crews so that, if fighting is necessary, they can fight well today and return home unharmed tomorrow.[10]

In addition to this general requirement, says Shurcliff, a long list of questions needs to be addressed, and these questions are made urgent by the unprecedented power of the bomb:

If the list seems long, it is because of the unequalled importance of the atomic bomb. This new bomb is no mere creator of dazzling light and peach-colored clouds; it shakes the very foundation of military strategy. The questions are many; they are highly technical and eminently practical. They are not easily separated and cataloged. Years may be required to answer them, but answers must be found.[11]

If the Navy seemed overwhelmed with questions, they were not alone. Probably never had so many people felt suddenly propelled into a new stage of history, one in which old certainties were suddenly defunct, as at the beginning of the Atomic Age. Historian Paul Boyer puts it like this:

How does a people react when the entire basis of its existence is fundamentally altered? Most such changes occur gradually; they are more discernible to historians than to the individuals living through them. The nuclear era was different. It burst upon the world with terrifying suddenness. From the earliest moments, the American people recognized that things would never be the same again.[12]

Actually, it was not just the American people that were aware of entering a new age; as Boyer says when Hiroshima was bombed, "the whole world gasped."[13] When people perceive that they have entered a new age, old verities, like the need for a large surface fleet, have to be questioned.

The international situation also made the timing of the Crossroads tests controversial. With the end of the Second World War, the alliance between the United States and the Soviet Union ended, and relations between the two countries quickly deteriorated. This, of course, was the beginning of the decades-long confrontation that came to be known as the Cold War. The fact that the United States had a monopoly on nuclear weapons certainly heightened Soviet anxiety, and they began a crash program to develop their own bomb. Over twenty million Soviet citizens had been killed in The Great Patriotic War against Nazi Germany. Now the country was suddenly faced by a new opponent wielding a new type of weapon that could kill millions in a day. A public demonstration of the power of nuclear weapons could only look like a chest-thumping and saber-rattling display aimed at the Soviets.

From a diplomatic perspective, the timing of the proposed tests could hardly have been worse. The initial plan was for the first test to take place on May 15 and the second on July 1. Yet late April or May was to be the time for the meeting of the Paris Council of Foreign Ministers which was to prepare for a peace conference to be held later that summer.[14] To say the least, for the United States to set off nuclear explosions while involved in planning a major peace conference would be to send mixed signals. Ultimately, because the Navy had powerful friends in Congress and the support of President Truman, Crossroads was approved, though with a six week delay so as not to interfere with the Paris meeting.

The planning for the operation was meticulous and vast in scale. Whatever the successes or failure of Crossroads, nobody could charge that it had been a haphazard undertaking. The operation plan for Crossroads was immensely complicated and no relevant detail was overlooked. Eight task groups were charged with essential jobs, from maintaining radiological safety to ensuring that the photographic equipment was ready to record the momentous events.[15] The photographic requirements were stupendous. Crossroads was to be the most documented event in history and consumed literally miles of film.

Whatever else Crossroads was, it was also a media extravaganza. An entire ship, the *Appalachian*, was assigned to ferry 117 newspaper reporters from the United States to Bikini. Numerous observers were invited, including some from the Soviet Union. This was in remarkable contrast with the absolute secrecy that had surrounded the Manhattan Project. Whereas the development of the atomic bomb had been shrouded by the most stringent security measures, the Crossroads tests were publicized and documented like no other military event.

One very sensitive and unpleasant detail was the evacuation of the Bikinians. As Weisgall reports it, this was not quite the rosy scenario depicted in the propaganda film.[16] On Sunday, February 10, Commodore Wyatt spoke to the assembled islanders after church services. Wyatt, clearly a man of natural eloquence, invoked biblical metaphor and the goodness of American intentions. He likened his audience to the Children of Israel who had to wander before entering their Promised Land. As Weisgall notes, this was an odd comparison since the Bikinians were not being freed from bondage in a foreign land but were being evicted from their ancestral home. Although he was no Moses, Wyatt's biblical rhetoric was effective. He also assured the Bikinians that their island was needed for the benefit of humanity.

The Bikinians quickly decided to accede to the American plan to evacuate, even before they knew where they would be going. Why did they decide so quickly? Wyatt may have been an eloquent and persuasive speaker, and he may have made "one hell of a good sales job," as one official said at the time, but the quick decision has a more obvious explanation: The people of Bikini recognized that they had no choice.[17] The propaganda film speaks condescendingly of the natives' "simplicity." They may have seemed "simple" in their lifestyle, but they could hardly have been so ignorant as not to know that when the mighty make a request of the powerless, it is tantamount to a demand.

Cartoonists often depict reality more accurately than reporters. A *New Yorker* cartoon of the era shows a barefoot, shirtless, "simple" native leader addressing American officers while a huge landing ship discharges sailors and cargo and battleships patrol offshore. The caption reads "The residents have voted two to one against your conducting experiments in this vicinity." Obviously, a display of defiance would have made things more unpleasant for everybody, but the result would have been the same.

News reports depicted the Bikinians as leaving cheerfully. A Navy press release even described them as "delighted" with their eviction: "Natives are delighted about the atomic bomb, which has already brought them prosperity and a new promising future."[18] The Bikinians were evacuated to Rongerik, a much smaller group of islands to the east of Bikini. They were left with less than two months' supply of food and water, and soon faced considerable hardship. Naval officials had somehow convinced themselves that Rongerik was bigger and richer than Bikini and even that it had coconuts three or four times larger![19] They were quite confident that the former Bikinians would be self-sufficient. Soon, though, the Bikinians were suffering from acute food shortages, and a doctor that visited in July 1947 found that they were seriously malnourished. After another six months they were literally starving and had to be evacuated to a temporary camp on the island of Kwajalein.[20]

To the extent that the planners of Crossroads thought about the Bikinians at all, their removal could only have seemed a regrettable necessity. As we say, the chief concern was not with the well-being of the natives but with avoiding a public relations problem. To that extent they succeeded. There was more outcry about the test animals that were to be exposed to blast and radiation than there was about the removal of the residents of Bikini. Perhaps the most revealing statement of attitudes toward the Marshallese was later expressed by a remark sometimes attributed to Henry Kissinger: "There are only 90,000 people out there. Who gives a damn?"[21] Who indeed?

Despite the meticulous planning, a number of things went badly and dangerously wrong. When you do big, complex, violent things – like the open-air testing of nuclear devices – Murphy's Law inevitably comes into play. There is also the human factor. Even when problems were clearly anticipated, those warnings were sometimes ignored. With Test Able, the unanticipated consequences were merely embarrassing and inconvenient. The worst consequences of Test Baker were anticipated by planners but then ignored by those in charge.

For Test Able, the bomb was to be delivered by a B-29 bomber, like the bombs dropped on Japan. The bomb was a plutonium Fat Man implosion design of approximately twenty kilotons, much like the Nagasaki bomb. The aircraft and crew for the mission were selected on a highly competitive basis. The winning bomber was *Dave's Dream*, piloted by Major Woodrow P. "Woody" Swancutt with Major Harold H. Wood as bombardier. To be awarded the mission, the crew of *Dave's Dream* had to beat even the *Enola Gay* piloted by Colonel Paul W. Tibbets, the plane and the pilot made world-famous by the Hiroshima mission.

Dave's Dream took off from Kwajalein at 5:55 a.m. on July 1. Other aircraft followed, some carrying scientific instruments to record the intensity of the blast, and others carrying VIPs and reporters. At 8:30, as *Dave's Dream* was approaching Bikini, the captains of all the observing ships brought their crews on deck and the reporters on the *Appalachian* relaxed on deck chairs behind rows of typewriters. All observers had been provided with goggles to protect against the literally blinding brilliance of the nuclear explosion. In the target fleet, the old battleship *Nevada* had been selected as the aiming point. The weather was perfect with excellent visibility.

It was late afternoon on the east coast of the United States, and broadcasts were interrupted to bring the bombing of Bikini live to the radio audience. The drama of the moment was heightened as the ticking of a metronome counted off the last minutes. It had been placed on the *Pennsylvania*, one of the target ships, and would tick until silenced by the blast. At a few seconds after 9:00 a.m., the bomb was dropped and a voice over the radio intoned, "Listen, world! This is Crossroads!" The bomb exploded at a height of 518 feet above Bikini Lagoon.[22]

A nuclear explosion is a spectacle without parallel. The first effect noticeable to human beings is the flash of a harsh, unearthly light far brighter and more penetrating than the sun's. Physicist I. I. Rabi, a witness at Trinity, described the light:

Suddenly there was an enormous flash of light, the brightest light I have ever seen or that I think anyone has ever seen. It blasted; it pounced; it bored its way right through you. It was a vision that was seen with more than the eye. It was seen to last forever ... It looked menacing. It seemed to come toward one.[23]

The initial flash may seem to last forever, but in a few seconds the explosion dims to the point where it is bearable by the human eye. The light resolves into a massive fireball, like a second sun, still intensely brilliant. Then it quickly transforms into a great column of fire, thrusting upwards at terrific speed and displaying a spectrum of vivid colors. The iconic mushroom cloud forms and rapidly rises, finally topping off miles into the atmosphere, far higher than any mountain. The devastating shockwave propagates rapidly outwards from the hypocenter. The tail gunner of the *Enola Gay* saw the approaching shockwave from the Hiroshima blast, but had no time to call out a warning before it hit. The Hiroshima survivors closest to the center of destruction often reported a noiseless flash. Those at a greater distance from nuclear blasts describe the sound as a deep, prolonged roar that echoes, seemingly endlessly. For those who witness a nuclear detonation, it is an experience both majestic and eerie. "A foul and awesome display" is how physicist Kenneth Bainbridge described the Trinity event.[24]

The observers of Test Able had a decidedly different reaction. Most of them were much farther away than the witnesses of Trinity had been. The goggles that had been issued were too dark, and many could hardly see the explosion at all. The boom from the blast was not impressive and neither was the initial appearance of the damage done to the target fleet. Everyone had been expecting the apocalypse and instead they got a firecracker. Reporters were underwhelmed, and some were scathing:

"Is that all?" reporters snorted incredulously. "This is a disaster," complained another. "This is Operation Chloroform, the logical sequel to Operations Build-Up and Handout ..." "Blast Force Seems Less than Expected," ran the banner headline in the *New York Times* ... Virtually all the reporters were disappointed. "As a spectacle," wrote one, Able "was, in Broadway parlance, a flop."[25]

Some Congressional observers were equally disappointed. The atomic bomb clearly did not live up to its billing.

Why was there such a difference in the experiences of those at Trinity and the witnesses of Test Able? The Crossroads observers were farther away, and the Trinity test was made more dramatic by being conducted in early morning darkness, while Able was in broad daylight. Subjective factors were probably also at work. Even a nuclear explosion can be overhyped, and people, some of whom should have known better, made wild predictions about the Bikini tests. A Yale University physicist said that it would blow a hole in the ocean floor and that water rushing down the hole would contact molten rock creating a massive steam explosion with mile-high waves. A Johns Hopkins seismologist predicted a major earthquake and tsunamis that would swamp ships. Newspaper headlines also predicted tsunami disasters and even global climate change.[26] When the Able device went off and the world did not end, some people actually felt cheated.

For the military officials conducting the test, there were genuine grounds for disappointment. The bomb badly missed its target. Even with a hand-picked and well-rehearsed crew, the bomb fell a half mile to the west of the *Nevada*, the aiming point. Not only did the bomb miss the target, but it destroyed much of the scientific equipment placed on the surrounding ships to record shock wave velocity and other data. It missed so badly that many of the surviving instruments could not get accurate readings.[27]

Various excuses were offered for why the bomb missed, but none seemed terribly convincing and no conclusive official explanation was given. However, on the morning of the Able test, Paul Tibbets and the bombardiers from the Hiroshima and Nagasaki missions checked the calibration of the bombsight on *Dave's Dream* and reported a significant miscalculation.[28] They ran the numbers themselves and predicted a miss almost exactly like the one that occurred. Tibbets must have felt a degree of vindication after not having been chosen for Able.

The injury to the target fleet might not have seemed impressive at first, but closer inspection showed that the bomb, though badly off target, had nonetheless inflicted very serious damage. Five ships were sunk and others badly damaged. The *Gilliam*, an attack transport 446 feet long, was closest to surface zero and sank in less than a minute. The *Anderson*, a 338-foot destroyer, sank in eight minutes. Another destroyer within a half mile of surface zero sank in eight hours. The Japanese light cruiser *Sakawa* burned fiercely for twenty-four hours and then sank. The *Carlisle*, another attack transport much like the *Gilliam*, sank within forty minutes.[29]

Among nearby ships that did not sink, some were severely damaged. The light carrier *Independence* had part of its 600-foot flight deck blown off and the rest was broken in several places and badly buckled. Damage to the interior was extensive also. The submarine *Skate*, which was on the surface less than a half mile from the surface zero, was a floating wreck.

The *Arkansas*, an old battleship, was within a half mile of the detonation, and the bomb's shockwave did extensive damage even to such a heavily armored ship, damage that would have definitely put it out of action. Shurcliff summed up the damage to the target vessels and projected the damage that such a blast would cause a fleet of such ships:

1. The majority of lighter warships located within a critical radius somewhat less than one-half mile away may be expected to be sunk by an atomic bombing attack ...
2. Heavy warships located within one-half mile may survive, but their superstructures will be badly damaged and ships will be put out of action; extensive repairs at a principal naval base will be required.
3. Ships more than three-fourths of a mile away may suffer damage, but the damage will be relatively light in typical cases.
4. Among the most badly damaged ships, damage to superstructures was very severe; hulls escaped relatively lightly. Damage extends to nearly all kinds of mechanical and electrical equipment.[30]

The test animals placed on the target ships suffered many severe injuries. Pigs, goats, rats, and mice had been placed in various locations to see how the blast would affect living things. Pigs were particularly valuable subjects because their skin and short hair are quite similar to humans'.[31] Public outcry had prevented dogs from being used in the tests. Shurcliff summarizes the results of the Able blast on the test animals:

In all about 35 percent of the animals used in Test A had been killed as of late September, 1946. Ten percent died from air blast, 15 percent from radioactivity, and 10 percent were killed for study. Air blast, as expected, was particularly injurious to the exposed animals. Principal symptoms of air blast were contusions and lung hemorrhages ... Flash burns produced by the thermal radiation did considerable damage to animals situated in a direct line-of-sight from the detonation. Gamma radiation results developed more slowly ... The more heavily-exposed animals exhibited hyper-irritability, muscular weakness, diarrhea, and increased rate of respiration. Some of these were moribund, with exaggeration of symptoms, bloody diarrhea, and inability to stand. These symptoms appeared to have caused the animals no intense pain.[32]

With these lessons learned, preparations got underway for Test Baker.

In Test Baker, the bomb was to be exploded under water, so another Fat Man plutonium device was suspended ninety feet below an amphibious landing craft the *LSM-60*. The target ships were all the surviving ships from the Able test plus seven additional ships, including submerged submarines. Two US capital ships – capital ships being the most important and generally the largest and most heavily armed warships – were placed very near the point of detonation. These ships were the aircraft carrier *Saratoga* and the battleship *Arkansas*. In total there were about forty ships anchored within a mile of the bomb.[33] It was expected that the greatest damage caused by the Baker test would be due to the tremendous shock wave that would be delivered through the water.

On July 25, the world once again listened in by radio as a nuclear bomb was detonated in Bikini Lagoon. Like the Able test, Baker was abundantly documented on film and the effects recorded by numerous scientific instruments. The test was even monitored by television, a real novelty for 1946. British physicist E. W. Titterton counted off the final seconds and at nearly 8:35 a.m., the Baker device was detonated.

The Baker shot more than made up for Able's lack of spectacle. Observers saw two million tons of water erupt with sudden and extreme violence from the surface of the lagoon. The pillar of water instantly transformed into a misty spheroid that dwarfed and engulfed the surrounding warships in the target fleet. The spheroid soon dissolved, revealing a gigantic white column capped with an equally huge, roiling, cauliflower-shaped cloud. This scene is one of the most dramatic and familiar depictions from the era of nuclear testing. The explosion has been shown many times and has, in fact, become stock footage that has run in many films, from *Dr. Strangelove* to *Godzilla 2014*.

The Baker shot caused much more destruction to the target fleet than had Able due to the devastating punch from the water-borne shockwave. Gauges close to blast showed that pressures must have been in excess of 10,000 pounds per square inch, while those one-fourth to one-half mile away still recorded pressures of hundreds or thousands of pounds per square inch.[34] Not even the heaviest steel plate armor of a battleship can withstand such pressures. Cameras located on the Bikini shore showed the shock wave propagating across the surface of the water and jarring the palm trees when it hits land.

The *LSM-60*, the landing craft from which the bomb was suspended, simply disintegrated and only small pieces were ever found. The *Arkansas* sank almost immediately, showing that even the heavily armored hull of a battleship was easily crumpled by the nuclear blast. It was, as Shurcliff noted, the first battleship ever sunk by a bomb that did not strike it directly.[35] The *Saratoga*, anchored only 500 feet from surface zero, sank by the stern seven and a half hours later. This majestic carrier was the veteran of many of the most important campaigns of the Pacific War. Sailors often get sentimental about great ships and the "Sara" was probably the most beloved of all the vessels in the target fleet. It now rests on the bottom of Bikini Lagoon and on a day when the water is calm and clear can still be seen by those flying overhead. The infamous and despised former Japanese battleship *Nagato* sank during the night of July 29/30. Three of the submarines were sunk; the *Pilotfish*, the *Skipjack*, and the *Apogon*. In addition to the ships that were sunk outright, serious damage was done to the battleships *New York* and *Nevada*, the cruiser *Pensacola*, the destroyers *Hughes* and *Mayrant*, as well as various other ships of different types. In case anybody had had any doubts beforehand, the Crossroads tests definitely showed that even the most powerful capital ships could not survive proximity to an atomic explosion.

To the Navy's initial delight, however, most of the ships in the fleet had seemingly suffered little damage. Apparently, fleets could survive atomic attack. Though they had been warned well ahead of time, what the Navy brass failed to realize was the extent to which the surviving target ships would become intensely radioactive and how ineffective decontamination measures would be. When the two-million-ton column of water thrown up by the blast crashed down, it created a huge base surge, as at the bottom of a waterfall. This surge of deadly mist and spray drenched the surviving ships with fission products. Unlike an air burst, in which those products are dispersed by winds over a large area as fallout, in a water burst these materials are largely retained in the surrounding water, turning the water into a witch's brew of radioactivity. A few millionths of a gram of radium ingested by a human being can be lethal. One hour after the Baker shot, the amount of radioactivity in Bikini Lagoon was equal to 5,000 *tons* of radium.[36] Because of the vast scale of the pollution of Bikini Lagoon, Crossroads has been aptly described as "the world's first nuclear disaster."[37]

Dr. Stafford L. Warren, head of the Radiological Safety Section of Crossroads, had explicitly cautioned beforehand that the water burst would make Bikini Lagoon and the target ships dangerously radioactive for an indefinite period. These warnings were ignored. On the afternoon of July 25, the lagoon became so "hot" that the observation fleet had to be moved back. As predicted, the target ships were highly radioactive and dangerous even to approach. Accompanied by Dr. Warren, Admiral Blandy attempted to tour the target fleet on the day after Baker, but as the staccato clicks of the Geiger counter merged into a continuous buzz, they decided to retreat. Since much of the stated purpose of Crossroads was to determine the effects of nuclear explosions on the target ships, that aim was stymied if the ships were too dangerous to inspect. The minutely detailed plans drawn up prior to Crossroads had not projected this eventuality.

Because the radiation danger prevented access to the ships to inspect and evaluate the damage, extensive decontamination efforts were begun. The ships were hosed, scrubbed, scraped, and treated with all manner of cleaners, solvents, and absorbent substances, from hydrochloric acid to ground coffee.[38] Nothing worked. Radiation readings remained excessively high and the crews tasked with the decontamination efforts wore no special gear and exercised no special precautions. Established safety guidelines were largely ignored and some crews worked long hours, ate, and even slept on the contaminated ships. Some sailors absorbed such high doses that they were immediately shipped back to the United States. Warren energetically protested and enforced what regulations he could, but the naval officers responsible for the salvage operations on the target ships responded to his warnings and restrictions with great impatience and with criticism edged with contempt. As they saw it, they had a job to do and Warren was an overly cautious nanny standing in the way of naval business.

Why such defiance of scientific warnings? Were the naval officers living down to the worst stereotypes of the obtuseness of the military mind? Actually, for years into the atomic era both military and civilian officials frequently downplayed or ignored the dangers of radiation. The reasons for what, in hindsight, certainly looks like blatant irresponsibility were various, and bear similarities to the current resistance in many quarters to climate change data. One factor was surely that ionizing radiation posed a new sort of danger that offered no warnings to human senses. Radiation cannot be seen, felt, smelled, or detected by any natural human faculty. It went against common sense that an environment could be deadly when absolutely nothing appeared wrong. Weisgall quotes David Bradley, one of Warren's radiological safety monitors on the frustrations of naval officers in the face of radiation danger:

One afternoon Bradley was assigned to survey the *New York*, whose decks had been sluiced with water, washed with soap, alkali compound, and lye, and then washed again. Radiation levels, though, remained dangerously high. The captain was "completely bewildered" wrote Bradley. "The deck was clean, anybody could see that, clean enough for the Admiral himself to eat breakfast off of. So what was all this goddamn radioactivity?"[39]

The deepest lesson that Crossroads could have taught was that the most insidious and persistent danger of nuclear weapons did not lie in what could be seen – the spectacular blast and heat of the explosion – but in the invisible residue. This lesson was not learned.

So, what *was* learned from Crossroads? Was there any new information that would justify the enormous effort and expense, or was it a showy boondoggle as critics had charged? Did the Navy really learn anything from Crossroads, anything, that is, that could not have been inferred from what was already known about the Trinity, Hiroshima, and Nagasaki blasts? As for defensive measures against nuclear attack, it is hard to see that much was demonstrated by Crossroads other than the truism stated by General Leslie Groves at the time: "At present, the best defense against the atomic bomb is not to be there when it goes off."[40] It was shown that an atomic explosion close to a ship, even a battleship, would sink it, but this had been known all along.

Few changes in ship design resulted from Crossroads data.[41] Nothing was really learned about improving ship armor or strengthening ship construction. Most of the target ships at Bikini escaped the most severe blast effects of the bombs, but were so polluted by the highly radioactive water and mist that their crews would have been killed. No additional armor could protect against radiation. As for tactics, Blandy recommended that ships be spaced more widely apart both when at anchor and when at sea.[42] Again, such a rather obvious point did not seem to require the massive exertions of the Crossroads tests, and certainly does not seem to justify the exposure of people to high levels of radiation.

The Navy did make one big change to adapt itself to the Atomic Age; it became committed to the development of nuclear-powered and nuclear-armed submarines. If the only real defense against nuclear weapons is not to be near their detonations, hiding deep underwater is the most effective way to do that. Nuclear-powered and nuclear-armed submarines became one of the main elements of the strategy of deterrence during the Cold War. Again, though Crossroads may have strengthened the case for the postwar Navy's emphasis on submarine development, it hardly seems to have been a necessary factor.

One thing Crossroads most definitely accomplished was that it provided the locale for the subsequent establishment of the Pacific Proving Grounds. Over the next twelve years, sixty-five other nuclear and thermonuclear tests would blast Bikini and other locations in the Marshall Islands. For the native Marshallese, their travail had just begun.

Admiral Blandy was duly feted upon the completion of Crossroads. An unintentionally amusing photograph shows the admiral slicing a celebratory cake, a true masterpiece of the pastry chef's art. The cake is shaped just like the mushroom cloud of Test Baker. Even more remarkably, a beaming Mrs. Blandy is sporting a hat that itself looks like some sort of atomic explosion.

Crossroads also had one notable cultural impact that is with us still. The most famous and long-lived legacy of the Crossroads tests was a sort of swimwear that exploited another form of dangerous primal energy. This, of course, was the revealing beach attire named by its designer after the Crossroads test site. In 1946, nuclear power was sexy, and the world became aware both of Bikini and of the bikini. It is one of the many ironies of the Atomic Age that an item of tease and titillation would share its name with a place blasted, burned, and poisoned.

NOTES

1 Shurcliff, *Bombs at Bikini*, p. iii.
2 "Operation Castle," Strauss Archives, Box 478, Castle Series III.
3 Freedman, *The Evolution of Nuclear Strategy*, pp. 22–23.
4 General H. Arnold, Chief of Air Staff, quoted in Freedman, *The Evolution of Nuclear Strategy*, p. 22.
5 Freedman, *The Evolution of Nuclear Strategy*, p. 28.
6 Weisgall, *Operation Crossroads*, p. 77.
7 Weisgall, *Operation Crossroads*, p. 87.
8 Weisgall, *Operation Crossroads*, p. 86.
9 Weisgall, *Operation Crossroads*, p. 64.
10 Shurcliff, *Bombs at Bikini*, p. 2.
11 Shurcliff, *Bombs at Bikini*, p. 3.
12 Boyer, *By the Bomb's Early Light*, p. 4.
13 Boyer, *By the Bomb's Early Light*, p. 3.
14 Weisgall, *Operation Crossroads*, p. 90.
15 Weisgall, *Operation Crossroads*, p. 118.
16 Weisgall, *Operation Crossroads*, pp. 104–115.
17 Dibblin, *Day of Two Suns*. p. 21.
18 Dibblin, *Day of Two Suns*, p. 22.
19 Dibblin, *Day of Two Suns*, p. 22.
20 Dibblin, *Day of Two Suns*, p. 22.
21 Dibblin, back cover. This quote is widely attributed to Kissinger, but its specific provenance cannot be identified. Also, if Kissinger did say it, it is not clear whether he was expressing his own view or that of others.
22 Weisgall, *Operation Crossroads*, p. 185.
23 De Groot, *The Bomb*, p. 61.
24 Rhodes, *The Making of the Atomic Bomb*, p. 675.
25 Weisgall, *Operation Crossroads*, p. 187
26 Weisgall, *Operation Crossroads*, 64.
27 Weisgall, *Operation Crossroads*, p. 189.
28 Rhodes, *The Making of the Atomic Bomb*, p. 262.

29   Shurcliff, *Bombs at Bikini*, pp. 130–131.
30   Shurcliff, *Bombs at Bikini*, pp. 137–138.
31   Shurcliff, *Bombs at Bikini*, p. 85.
32   Shurcliff, *Bombs at Bikini*, p. 141.
33   Shurcliff, *Bombs at Bikini*, p. 146.
34   Shurcliff, *Bombs at Bikini*, p. 153.
35   Shurcliff, *Bombs at Bikini*, p. 164.
36   Weisgall, *Operation Crossroads*, p. 227.
37   *The Bomb*, PBS, July 28, 2015.
38   Weisgall, *Operation Crossroads*, p. 227.
39   Weissgall, *Operation Crossroads*, p. 234.
40   Weisgall, *Operation Crossroads*, p. 282.
41   Weisgall, *Operation Crossroads*, p. 281.
42   Weisgall, *Operation Crossroads*, p. 281.

2

The Coming of the "Super"

OPERATIONS SANDSTONE AND GREENHOUSE

The next set of nuclear tests in the Marshall Islands was Operation Sandstone in 1948. These were conducted on Eniwetok Atoll, about 189 miles west of Bikini. Once again, the inhabitants had been evicted (no self-justifying film was made this time). Unlike Crossroads, the Sandstone tests were not a destructive extravaganza, but were scientific experiments intended to test advances in bomb design. Each of the huge, unwieldy, and difficult-to-deliver Fat Man–type bombs was handmade in a scientific laboratory. If atomic bombs were to be stockpiled, they would have to be mass produced, not made one-by-one like a science project. Also, Fat Man was very inefficient and left most of its plutonium unused. Sandstone would test these more efficient and mass-producible designs. The three detonations of Sandstone, codenamed X-Ray, Yoke, and Zebra, tested new bomb cores and initiators and yielded proof of the superiority of the new designs. Sandstone confirmed the superior efficiency of new cores made from a composite of plutonium and uranium 235. The result was the creation of the Mark IV and Mark V bombs, a great advance over the Nagasaki Fat Man and capable of being mass produced and stockpiled. America's nuclear arsenal soon began to grow rapidly.

Another significant difference from Crossroads is that Sandstone was the first set of nuclear tests conducted under civilian, not military, control. The Atomic Energy Act sponsored by Senator Brien McMahon of Connecticut established the Atomic Energy Commission (AEC), which put complete responsibility for nuclear weapons under the control of five civilian commissioners.[1] Under the provisions of this act, only a direct order from the president could authorize the delivery of nuclear weapons to the armed forces. The passage of the McMahon bill and the establishment of the AEC was the culmination of a longstanding debate between scientists and the military over who should control these weapons. Many of the scientists who had worked on the Manhattan Project argued that nuclear weapons should be placed under the control of civilian officials who would be independent of the military. The military naturally assumed that they would have control over the atomic bomb as they did with other weapons. Beginning with the Sandstone tests, the military was relegated to a supporting role and the AEC was in charge.

Greater efficiency in the fission process meant that more powerful explosions could be achieved. Two of the Sandstone detonations, X-Ray and Yoke, were significantly more powerful than the first bombs. X-Ray was thirty-seven kilotons and Yoke was forty-nine, making Yoke over twice as powerful as the bomb dropped on Nagasaki and over three times as powerful as the Hiroshima bomb. Further refinements produced even more powerful fission weapons.

However, there are practical limitations to the explosive force attainable by unboosted fission reactions. In the original gun design of Little Boy, dropped on Hiroshima, uranium 235 was used as the fission fuel. Only about 2 percent of the uranium 235 was consumed in fission reactions before the critical mass of the bomb was blown apart in the explosion; thus, the design was very inefficient. As the amount of fission fuel is increased, such uranium weapons become prohibitively heavy, clumsy, and wasteful. Thus, explosive yields obtainable by the gun design are severely limited by the design itself.

More efficient designs are possible with plutonium. Although plutonium 239 is the desired isotope for fission fuel, plutonium 240 inevitably forms in small amounts during plutonium production in a reactor. The rapid rate of spontaneous fission of plutonium 240 means that neutrons are released too rapidly before the subcritical pieces of plutonium in a gun assembly can assemble to form a complete critical mass. As a result, a low-yield predetonation could occur. In other words, you would get a messy fizzle, not a devastating explosion. This is why the implosion method is used with plutonium.

However, in the implosion process, the subcritical masses of plutonium must be brought together and compressed within a short enough period of time that the number of neutrons emitted by plutonium 240 in that time interval is negligible. This can be achieved by using a shockwave traveling inward toward the center of the bomb. The shockwave will be spherical in shape and concentric around the center of the bomb. In order to set up this shockwave, high explosives must be precisely distributed spherically around the outer portion of the bomb and detonated simultaneously. The explosives must also be of exceptional quality and purity. In principle, there is no inherent limitation in explosive yields that are achievable using the implosion design, but it is much more complicated than the gun method, requiring highly precise construction, engineering, and materials. In practice, the largest fission weapon ever produced yielded a half-megaton.

Thermonuclear weapons, on the other hand, seemed to promise unlimited power in a simpler and easier design. These bombs derive their tremendous energies from fusion reactions, which power the sun and the other stars. However, in the case of the stars, fusion is the result of the immense gravitational collapse of hydrogen gas in the center of the star which then undergoes nuclear fusion. Gravitational collapse is not accessible for the construction of thermonuclear weapons, and they are further limited by technological and practical considerations. Such considerations concern the size, weight, and shape of the bomb, since the weapon must be deliverable to its target. Weapons must fit within aircraft or ballistic missiles, and they must be light enough to be transported. By limiting these factors, the power of thermonuclear weapons will ultimately be limited as well. Really, though, the point is moot since the thermonuclear bombs that are deliverable are of cataclysmic power.

The first thermonuclear experiments were part of Operation Greenhouse, held at Eniwetok in April and May 1951. Greenhouse consisted of four shots: Dog, on April 1; Easy, on April 21; George, on May 9; and Item, on May 25. All the Greenhouse devices were mounted in tall steel towers to simulate the effects of an air burst. The first two shots, Dog and Easy, were tests of fission designs. The Dog test device was a Mark VI bomb of an improved implosion type. It was already being stockpiled in the US armory, and so a test of its capabilities was urgently desired. The Easy device was a major advance in the reduction of the size and weight of implosion bombs. It weighed 2,700 pounds and had a forty-inch diameter, as opposed to the over 10,000-pound and sixty-inch Nagasaki bomb.[2] Naturally, bomb developers wanted leaner, meaner bombs that would be smaller, lighter, and more efficient while delivering a bigger punch.

Dog and Easy were both highly successful, with Dog yielding eighty-one kilotons, nearly four times the yield of the Nagasaki bomb, and Easy yielding forty-seven kilotons, over double the Fat Man's production at a quarter of the weight. The Dog shot produced one of the most iconic images of the testing era. We see a group of goggled VIP observers reclining in Adirondack chairs to view the test. The photographer captures the moment when the flash of the explosion reflected in the observers' goggles and washes them in weird light. They look like moviegoers enjoying a feature.

While the Dog and Easy shots tested refinements in fission bombs, George and Item were the first tests of thermonuclear burning. The technical nature of these designs is discussed in detail in Appendix 1. Briefly, George was an experiment, not a deliverable bomb. It was shaped like a large torus approximately eight feet in diameter and two feet thick with a hole in the axis. The torus was a cylindrical implosion system and the hole contained a small capsule containing cryogenic deuterium and a small amount of tritium as the fusion fuel. When detonated, the fission reaction compressed and heated the deuterium and tritium to temperatures that would initiate the fusion reaction. George's yield was 225 kilotons, the largest explosion to that date and the largest until dwarfed by the Ivy Mike test a year-and-a-half later. The fusion reaction contributed only a small amount to the overall yield.

The Item shot was a test of fusion boosting of the fission reaction. That is, the fusion reaction was used primarily to inject neutrons into an enriched uranium core and thereby increase the efficiency of the fission reaction. The yield of Item was 45.5 kilotons, which was double the yield expected without boosting.

The George and Item shots of Operation Greenhouse showed that fusion reactions could be achieved. However, these were not tests of a "true" thermonuclear design in which the fusion reaction would contribute significantly to achieve spectacular yields, orders of magnitude greater than mere fission bombs. Mere atomic bombs were no longer terrifying enough. Terror had to be taken to an entirely new level.

WHY A SUPER BOMB?

As the decade of the 1940s closed, an animated debate ensued over the development of the fusion or thermonuclear bomb, which we will also call the "Super," the "hydrogen bomb," or the "H-bomb." The theoretical possibility of such weapons had long been known. It had been discussed as early as the summer of 1942 at a secret seminar at Berkeley chaired by Oppenheimer and attended by leading physicists Edward Teller, Hans Bethe, and Robert Serber.[3] The development of the "Super," as

Oppenheimer called it, particularly occupied Edward Teller, who began serious work on the project in 1943. To help he recruited the highly capable Polish mathematician, Stanislaw Ulam, and between the two of them they eventually unlocked the secret of the Super.

Teller was an outstanding physicist but colleagues often regarded him as uncooperative, querulous, and egotistical – egotistical, that is, even by the standards of theoretical physicists, a group where robust egos are the norm. He remains a controversial figure to this day, largely due to his role in the infamous "Oppenheimer Affair." Oppenheimer, the "father of the atomic bomb," lost his security clearance, largely, it seems, due to spite – the ill will of Lewis Strauss, Chair of the AEC. Also, Oppenheimer's left-wing associations in the prewar years, which had not precluded his leading role in the Manhattan Project, became a much bigger issue in the postwar era of feverish anticommunism. After a contentious hearing in 1954, the AEC refused to reinstate Oppenheimer's clearance. Teller's damaging testimony against Oppenheimer at that hearing was – and is – widely regarded as an act of betrayal. Oppenheimer was devastated by the verdict and Teller was ostracized by other physicists.

Historians still often judge Teller harshly. Kai Bird and Martin J. Sherwin, in their biography of Oppenheimer, *American Prometheus*, attribute Teller's testimony to personal animosity and festering resentment against Oppenheimer.[4] They also characterize Teller's later account of events as "disingenuous."[5] Gerard J. DeGroot regards Teller's testimony as "knifing his 'friend' in the back."[6] However, when we recall that Teller was an émigré who had fled both communism and fascism, and who was appalled by both, perhaps our judgment should be less harsh. Whatever animosities and resentments Teller felt toward Oppenheimer, the qualms that he expressed in his testimony may have been sincere and, from his perspective, justified.

Despite Teller's unquestioned ability, the Super resisted him for years. The original idea for a thermonuclear bomb was quite simple: Just attach a fission bomb to a tube of deuterium. Ignite the fission bomb and it will produce the ultra-high temperatures (the "thermo" part of "thermonuclear") needed to ignite a reaction that would fuse the deuterium into helium and convert some mass into enormous quantities of energy. The problem was that nobody could think of a trick to make this "classical" Super design work. Every solution proposed by some of humanity's most ingenious intellects was found to be unworkable. That, basically, is where things were stuck for several years. There must have been times when Teller and other physicists came to doubt Einstein's famous saying,

"Raffiniert ist der Herrgott, aber boshaft ist Er nicht" ("Subtle is The Lord, but He is not malicious"). At times it must have seemed that, on the contrary, nature was intentionally withholding from humanity the secret of the ultimate weapon. Naturally, those who opposed the development of thermonuclear weapons hoped that nature would prohibit such a hellish thing.

Science progresses rapidly but not rapidly enough for policymakers, who must often proceed on assumptions. Assuming that a hydrogen bomb was possible, which it had not been shown not to be, and given the enormous destructive potential of such a weapon, the question was whether to make a commitment to its development. With fusion weapons it would be feasible to talk about explosive yields of megatons, not kilotons; millions of tons of conventional explosive rather than thousands. Whereas Fat Man and Little Boy devastated cities of moderate size, the hydrogen bomb could eradicate any of the largest cities of the world. New York or Moscow could simply be wiped off the map. So, the topic of debate was whether the atomic bomb, with destructive powers unimaginable just a few years before, should be superseded by a weapon more powerful by two or three orders of magnitude.

One of the most important documents relating to the debate about the development of thermonuclear weapons was the report of October 30, 1949, of the General Advisory Committee (GAC) to the AEC. The Committee was chaired by Oppenheimer and consisted of eminent scientists, academics, and engineers who met on October 29 and 30 to discuss questions of defense and security, and, in particular, the hydrogen bomb. The Committee recommended strongly against the development of thermonuclear weapons. First, after noting the steps necessary to achieve such a bomb, they held that an "imaginative and concerted" effort to develop it would likely be successful within five years.[7] They then note that the only limit on the destructive capability of a fusion bomb would be the requirements of delivery, that is, how large a device could be dropped.[8] Consequently, the destructive capacity of the H-bomb would be vastly higher even than the atomic bomb:

It is clear that the use of this weapon would bring about the destruction of innumerable human lives; it is not a weapon that can be used exclusively for the destruction of material installations of military or semi-military purposes. Its use therefore carries much farther than the atomic bomb itself the policy of exterminating civilian populations.[9]

Because the hydrogen bomb would have no inherent limits on its destructive capacity, such a weapon could only be used to devastate vast areas and kill huge numbers of civilians. They conclude: "Therefore, a super bomb might become a weapon of genocide."[10] The Committee also noted that even developing such a potentially genocidal weapon would invite widespread condemnation:

reasonable people the world over would realize that the existence of a weapon of this type whose power of destruction is essentially unlimited represents a threat to the future of the human race which is intolerable. Thus we believe that the psychological effect of the weapon in our hands would be adverse to our interest.[11]

As for the argument that we would have no deterrent if the Soviets had such a weapon and the United States did not, the Committee replied that America's large stock of atomic bombs would be a sufficient deterrent if anything would.[12] That is, the fission weapons already in America's stockpile were of such fearsome destructiveness, that no purpose could be served by a national commitment to achieve the pointless overkill of thermonuclear weapons. They conclude:

In determining not to proceed to develop the super bomb, we see a unique opportunity of providing by example some limitations on the totality of war and thus of limiting the fear and arousing the hopes of mankind.[13]

Two members of the Committee, Enrico Fermi and I. I. Rabi, appended an even more strongly worded statement:

Necessarily such a weapon goes far beyond any military objective and enters the range of very great natural catastrophes. By its very nature it cannot be confined to a military objective but becomes a weapon which in practical effect is almost one of genocide ... It is clear that the use of such a weapon cannot be justified on any ethical ground which gives a human being a certain individuality and dignity even if he happens to be a resident of an enemy country ... The fact that no limits exist to the destructiveness of this weapon makes its very existence and the knowledge of its construction a danger to humanity as a whole. It is necessarily an evil thing regarded in any light.[14]

They end by recommending that the president announce that the United States would not pursue a program to develop the hydrogen bomb and invite other nations to make the same pledge.[15]

The statements of the GAC were eminently reasonable and humane, but they failed to prove the most important point, namely that the hydrogen bomb would cross a moral threshold that had not already been crossed. To distinguish between the atomic bomb and the hydrogen bomb on the grounds that the latter was "genocidal" would have seemed an unfunny joke to the civilians killed at Hiroshima and Nagasaki. How do you draw a line between the killing of hundreds of thousands (the final toll of the atomic bombings of 1945) and the killing of millions?

Would a war fought with enormous stockpiles of atomic bombs have been less destructive than one fought with hydrogen bombs? By 1950, fission bombs had achieved yields of up to a half-megaton, far greater than those of the bombs of 1945. At what yield does a bomb become genocidal? As for deterrence, if one side has a genocidal weapon, could anyone be sure that anything less intimidating would be an effective deterrent? For fission weapons to effectively deter use of thermonuclear weapons, as the GAC had suggested, would it not have to be understood that the fission weapons would be used in a genocidal way?

According to *Race for the Superbomb*:

By 1949 [SAC's chief, General Curtis] LeMay's first war plan was ready. It called for attacks on 70 Soviet cities using 133 atomic bombs during the first few days of war. The concept was dubbed "killing a nation."[16]

Once the idea of killing a nation becomes thinkable, the instrument by which it is done becomes of secondary importance. In fact, the distinction between civilians and combatants had been eroding throughout the twentieth century. From the sinking of the *Lusitania* in 1915 to the fire-bombing of Tokyo thirty years later, the killing of civilians had been justified as a necessary consequence of modern war. Once that justification was accepted, and de facto all warring nations did accept it, principled constraints on carnage became difficult to defend and more difficult to practice.

Once the moral threshold of the mass killing of civilians has been crossed, the only significance of thermonuclear weapons is that they end the hypocrisy, still possible with fission bombs, of claiming that civilian deaths are merely collateral damage. So, a policy of proscribing hydrogen bombs, while stockpiling ever-more-powerful fission bombs, would only be a concession to hypocrisy, not morality.

The arguments of the GAC were also politically naïve. In the tenor of the times, it was simply intolerable for the American public or its leaders to countenance the possibility that the Russians might have a weapon that we lacked. A precisely parallel sentiment was held in the Soviet Union. Thus, the arms race became a process of reciprocal escalation. Weapons advances by one side would provoke advances by the other which would in turn bring further development in the attempt to gain an edge. Since a nuclear war would be over in days or hours, the military forces of both the United States and the Soviet Union had to stay in a state of constant readiness, which meant that a huge and hugely expensive military establishment had to be constantly maintained. Many people at the time could see the madness of the whole process, but they could not think of a feasible alternative to the balance of terror with terror.

Lewis Strauss, one of the commissioners, and future head, of the AEC, wrote a memorandum to President Truman that contradicted the GAC's report on the inadvisability of hydrogen bomb development. Strauss argued that the Russians had the competence to build a thermonuclear weapon and, further, that "A government of atheists is not likely to be dissuaded from producing the weapon on 'moral' grounds."[17] Some of Strauss' arguments are reminiscent of the slogans "Guns don't kill people; people kill people" and "When guns are outlawed, only outlaws will have guns" (this, of course, does not necessarily mean that they are bad arguments):

The danger in the weapon [the hydrogen bomb] does not reside in its physical nature but in human behavior. Its unilateral renunciation by the United States could very easily result in its unilateral possession by the Soviet Government.[18]

Strauss admitted that the hydrogen bomb would have unprecedented destructive potential, but, he argued, so did the atomic bomb when it was developed, and this was not taken as a hindrance. This was a good point, though it did not directly rebut the argument of the GAC that fission weapons were already so destructive that they could serve any practical military purpose, including deterrence. Strauss concluded his letter by arguing that if the president were to renounce development of thermonuclear weapons, then (a) the Soviets would not believe it, (b) it would be tricky if we later changed our minds and decided to pursue such weapons, and (c) that barring universal disarmament, the United States must possess the most powerful weapons it can devise.[19]

Strauss was not the only advocate of the Super. Senator McMahon, the sponsor of the bill establishing the AEC, and Chairman of the Congressional Joint Committee on Atomic Energy, wrote a long letter to President Truman on November 21, 1949, forcefully advocating development. On November 23, the Joint Chiefs of Staff issued a paper that concluded, "possession of a thermonuclear weapon by the USSR without such possession by the United States would be intolerable."[20]

For President Truman, the matter was really quite simple. If the Russians could build a hydrogen bomb, then we needed one. David Lilienthal, head of the AEC, Secretary of State Dean Acheson, and Secretary of Defense Louis Johnson met with Truman on January 31, 1950, to discuss the issue. Lilienthal intended to offer arguments against development of the Super. Jim Baggott records the exchange:

Lilienthal began to put forward the objections. Truman interrupted him. "Can the Russians do it?" he asked. They all nodded. "In that case, we have no choice. We'll go ahead," Truman stated flatly.[21]

Why did Truman proceed with the H-bomb? As historian Barton Bernstein notes, he had no sufficient reason not to:

What would have led Harry Truman in the Cold War, at a time when most Americans wanted more weapons and more powerful weapons, to decide against the H-bomb? It was immoral? He did not view it that way, and that would not have been compelling. It was too expensive? The estimate was 70 to 100 million dollars. At the time the American military budget was probably about 14 billion, so 70 to 100 million is a very small percentage. Was it going to deflect scientists from other activities? That was a danger. That is, it would slow progress on improving atomic weapons. But theoretically, it was possible to add some scientists and some resources and thus you could have an improvement of atomic weapons, a diversified arsenal, and also an H-bomb.[22]

Had Truman opposed the development of the Super, he would have had to face down the military establishment, a very vocal segment of Congress, and an equally vocal large segment of the public. To this day, being perceived as "soft on defense" is political poison for any politician or his party. Later on the evening of the thirty-first, Truman addressed the country by radio and announced that he would direct the AEC to proceed with the development of the H-bomb. The Soviet response was predictable. Lavrentii Beria, head of the Soviet nuclear weapons program, wrote to Stalin advising him to approve the development of hydrogen bomb designs and the production of the necessary materials.

Was an opportunity lost with the decision to develop the H-bomb? Might the atrociously expensive and dangerous arms race have been avoided if the GAC's arguments had prevailed? If the Soviet Union had been approached at the time, might they not have agreed to stop with atomic bombs if the United States did so? As the GAC of the AEC recommended, might not the unilateral announcement that the United States would not pursue thermonuclear weapons serve as an example for others to follow? David Holloway, a leading historian of the Soviet nuclear weapons program, considers these possibilities and remains skeptical:

In his memoirs Sakharov is very skeptical about the possibility that Stalin might have reciprocated American restraint in the development of thermonuclear weapons: "Any U.S. move toward abandoning or suspending work on a thermonuclear weapon would have been perceived as either a cunning, deceitful maneuver, or as evidence of stupidity or weakness." In either case, Stalin's reaction would have been the same. He would have pressed ahead with the hydrogen bomb in order to avoid a possible trap, or to exploit American stupidity. I find it hard to disagree with this judgment. Stalin in the last years of his life was profoundly distrustful of the United States and its intentions. It is hard to imagine that he would have seen American restraint as evidence of good will, or as a sign that agreement was really possible.[23]

Further, it was not only Stalin's paranoia that prevented agreement or cooperation in ending nuclear testing or slowing the arms race:

The proposals from American scientists for mutual restraint and a formal test ban were based on the argument that the hydrogen bomb was qualitatively different from the atomic bomb, that it was a force of genocide, not war. The proposals drew their force from a combination of scientific understanding and moral concern. But there is no evidence on the Soviet side that either the political leaders or the scientists had the same appreciation of what the hydrogen bomb meant.[24]

It appears, then, that the Soviets would have proceeded with the development and testing of thermonuclear weapons whether the United States did so or not. Stalin may have been paranoid, but, to be fair, the Soviet attitude was not much different from Harry Truman's, i.e., if the other side *can* develop thermonuclear weapons, then we have to assume that they *will*, and so we have them too.

In the end, the hydrogen bomb was developed for the same reason as the atomic bomb: (a) nature permitted it, and (b) people were afraid not to build it.

MIKE

After years of frustration in pursuit of the Super, the crucial breakthrough came in early 1951 when Ulam conceived of a way not just to heat the thermonuclear fuel, but to use the blast of the fission bomb to compress it to the high densities needed. Ulam's wife, Françoise, recalled the moment:

Engraved on my memory is the day when I found him at noon staring intensely out of a window in our living room with a very strange expression on his face. He said: "I have found a way to make it work." "What work?" I asked. "The super," he replied. "It's a totally different scheme and it will change history."[25]

Teller, initially skeptical, quickly accepted and then improved upon Ulam's idea by having the radiation (not the blast) from the fission bomb compress, heat, and ignite the thermonuclear fuel. Work then proceeded rapidly. And history was changed.

To test the "true" thermonuclear design, plans were laid for test Ivy Mike; "Ivy" was the name of the test series, and "Mike" was the particular test. The theory of the Super may have sprung from the brains of Teller and Ulam, but the prodigious job of making an actual working model fell upon the engineers and physicists at Los Alamos. First was the question of what fuel to use for the Mike device. Liquid deuterium was ideal from the physicist's perspective since the burning of pure deuterium was relatively simple and straightforward, in particular with respect to the details of the fusion reaction between deuterium nuclei. However, liquid deuterium presented a huge engineering problem: It boils away at nearly 250 degrees centigrade below zero, which is only 23.5 degrees above absolute zero. As historian Richard Rhodes observes, the technology did not yet exist for handling the quantities of material needed while maintaining it at such extremely low temperatures.[26] The decision was to go with the liquid deuterium and solve the engineering problems along the way.

A distraction for the designers was the occasional intrusion of Teller. He had resigned from Los Alamos in a huff in September 1951, furious that Marshall Holloway, not he, had been appointed director of the program to develop thermonuclear weapons.[27] Hating Holloway, Teller was eager to find any flaw in the design and repeatedly claimed that Mike would not work. Despite Teller's carping, work proceeded rapidly and by June 1952, the Los Alamos team had completed the theoretical design of Mike.[28]

Eniwetok Atoll was again chosen as the test site, and the particular location would be the islet of Elugelab at the northern end of the atoll. Like the Crossroads tests, Ivy required extensive and detailed planning and the transfer of massive numbers of people and quantities of material to the remote reaches of the Pacific. Chuck Hansen summarizes the magnitude of such projects:

Large scale nuclear weapons tests far from the continental U.S. assumed all the characteristics of major military war games or invasion exercises; indeed, for most of them the seaborne command post was usually an amphibious force flagship. Hundreds of tons of test devices and experimental and support material, along with thousands of people, had to be shuttled to the distant test site. Test devices and experiments had to be assembled and checked out on site. Movements of sampling, monitoring, and photography flights and seaborne missions had to be rehearsed before each shot date. These activities necessitated the creation, assignment, and training of a major sea and airborne task force, similar in some respects to the U.S. Navy flotillas which fought the war in the Pacific in the mid-1940s.[29]

Fighting a cold war could be almost as big an operation as fighting a hot one.

To house Mike a building like a big black box was erected. Made of corrugated aluminum, it was eighty-eight feet wide, forty-six feet deep, and sixty-one feet high and topped with a 300-foot television and radio control signal tower. The television and radio tower was needed to send signals to and receive them from the firing team that would detonate the device from its control room aboard the *USS Estes*. Instrument readings broadcast by TV from the test site would give the firing party the information it needed to proceed with or halt the countdown.

The particular design of Mike, known as the "Sausage" design, essentially consisted of a cylindrical steel tank containing liquid deuterium, with a fission bomb on one end of it. The tank was nearly seven feet in diameter and over twenty feet tall. The deuterium was kept separate from the fission device so that the fusion reactions could be observed outside of the fission detonation via instrumentation around the tank. The tank containing the deuterium, and helping to preserve its temperature near absolute zero, was a large thermally insulated flask, or "dewar." The Sausage was far too heavy to be a deliverable weapon. When Oppenheimer heard about it, he joked that it could only be delivered by oxcart.[30] Mike was not a bomb but an experiment to determine if fusion reactions could be initiated on a large scale and to study their properties.

A fission device, the primary, would detonate first, releasing vast amounts of thermal radiation in the form of x-rays. As Teller had envisioned, this radiation could then be channeled to a fusion device, or secondary, where the radiation could be focused inward, in the "radiation implosion" process to compress and heat the fuel that would then undergo nuclear fusion. A uranium 238 tamper surrounded the fusion fuel, slowing its expansion during detonation. A lining of lead and polyethylene plastic on the outer surface of the tamper served as the x-ray channel. In the process of channeling x-rays to the secondary, the polyethylene and outer tamper would become vaporized by the incoming x-rays, forming a plasma, a high-temperature ionized state of matter, which would also emit x-rays. These x-rays would then travel inward toward the center of the secondary, exerting pressure, heating and compressing it. In addition, more fission reactions would then occur in the uranium 238 as it was bombarded by high-energy neutrons released from the fusion reactions.

Los Alamos scientists had also placed a narrow column of plutonium with a chamber of tritium gas along the center of the tank within the secondary. Fission reactions occurred within this "fission sparkplug" as it was imploded by the x-rays mentioned before and the tritium enhanced its explosive yield. The sparkplug then exerted outward pressure on the deuterium, so that between this outward pressure, and the inward pressure from the inward traveling x-rays, the deuterium would be heated and compressed even further, leading to the establishment of nuclear fusion. In addition, in a thermonuclear device, neutrons released from fusion reactions will induce more fission reactions, which will in turn fuel more fusion reactions in a feedback loop, significantly contributing to the yield. With this combination of fission and fusion reactions, the result was a device vastly more powerful than a fission bomb.

To supply the large volumes of liquid gasses that would be necessary to keep Mike's deuterium near absolute zero, the cryogenic facilities already present at Eniwetok for the Greenhouse tests had to be completely rebuilt and enlarged. The continuous production of liquid deuterium was necessary for the Mike test. To supply electricity, a 3,000-kilowatt power plant was built in the cryogenics area.[31]

Hundreds of scientific devices were installed at various locations. The most remarkable of these was a 9,000-foot plywood structure that looked like a greatly extended boxcar and was called a Krause-Ogle Box after its inventors. The structure extended in a straight line (even corrected for the curvature of the earth) from the Sausage on Elugelab to the small island Bogon. The box was lined with polyethylene bags filled with helium. The purpose of the structure was to provide an unimpeded channel to conduct gamma rays and neutrons from the explosion to detectors on Bogon. These would record and transmit the readings in the small fraction of a second before the Mike fireball consumed the detection equipment. Such readings would inform scientists of the timing of the fission and fusion reactions.[32]

Components of the Mike device were shipped from the United States on board the *USS Curtiss*, and assembly began in mid-September. There were the expected last-minute glitches, but these were overcome with great ingenuity and strenuous effort. Extensive testing of all equipment and procedures insured that everything was ready. The final assembly was completed at 5:00 p.m. on October 31, and the evacuation of all personnel took place an hour later. All was ready for a blast of unprecedented magnitude to take place the next day.

Once again, an official film was made to record and report the events. Portions of this footage, now grimly amusing, are excerpted in the films *Trinity and Beyond* and *The Atomic Café*. The spokesman, speaking in a fatherly baritone, tells us that we are about to witness a scientific experiment which, if successful, will usher mankind into the thermonuclear age. He pauses to light his pipe, a disarming gesture which, as DeGroot notes, seems intended to reassure the audience of the benign nature of the proceedings.[33] He then calls upon all who wish their country well to hope for the success of the endeavor. At one minute before the blast, a loudspeaker instructs all personnel to put on goggles or to turn away and cover their eyes in anticipation of the blinding flash.

At almost exactly 7:15 a.m. on November 1, 1952, the firing signal was sent from the control room on board the *Estes*. In microseconds, the complex fission and fusion reactions were accomplished, unleashing an explosion of 10.4 megatons, over 500 times as powerful as the device of the Trinity test and 800 times the yield of the bomb that destroyed Hiroshima. Mike's fireball instantly grew to over three-and-a-half miles in diameter, over thirty times the size of Little Boy's fireball. The island of Elugelab was completely vaporized, leaving a crater 164 feet deep and 6,240 feet in diameter.[34] The entire 9,000-foot length of the Krause-Ogle Box was consumed. The temperature on the wings of a B-36 observation plane instantly rose ninety-three degrees, even though the aircraft was fifteen miles from the detonation point and flying at 40,000 feet.[35] Mike was so powerful that it created two entirely new elements, never before seen on earth, einsteinium (element 99) and fermium (element 100).[36] The mushroom cloud grew to a height of over one hundred thousand feet.[37]

The Mike shot made a tremendous impression on eyewitnesses. One of these was Harold Agnew, one of the leading Los Alamos physicists. He had observed the smaller kiloton shots, and said that they paled in comparison to the power of the thermonuclear blast:

One thing that impressed me at the Mike shot, we were on the aircraft tender called the *Curtiss*, and we were about 25 miles away. And when it was detonated it was really hot out there so everybody just had on a pair of shorts. And something I will never forget is the heat. Not the blast. It was a little scary, the cloud – there is an illusion that if something is very high you think it is on top of you. And although they were at least 20 or 25 miles away, I had the feeling that the cloud was on top of me. But the heat just kept coming, just kept coming on and on and on. And it was really scary ... It is really quite a terrifying experience because the heat doesn't go off. Now on kiloton shots it's a flash and it's over, but on those big shots it's really terrifying the heat that comes from those.[38]

The December 1952 issue of *The Bulletin of the Atomic Scientists* reported a number of eyewitness accounts that had been published in various newspapers despite official silence that had been maintained by the AEC:

The first sign of the explosion came to the men aboard ship in the form of a light many times brighter than the sun, followed by a wave of heat across their backs (one observer said that the heat wave that hit his back was "about 180 degrees

F [Fahrenheit]"; another described it as "a momentary touch of a hot iron"). Although the men had their backs turned and their arms across their dark glasses, the blinding light was not kept out. "It would take the light of ten suns to equal the light of the explosion from ten miles," a navigator wrote. Ten seconds after zero the men started to turn around to face the direction of the blast. "I could hardly believe my eyes," one wrote, "A flame about two miles wide was shooting five miles into the air. This lasted for about 7 seconds. Then we saw thousands of tons of earth being thrown straight up into the sky. Then a cloud began to form about twenty seconds after the shot." Several observers described the shape of the "mushroom cloud" as about a mile wide at the bottom and at least thirty miles wide on top ... "You would swear," one sailor wrote, that the whole world was on fire.[39]

The Mike blast had a devastating effect on the plant and animal life of nearby islands. Though fourteen miles from surface zero, the point of the detonation, the trees and brush on one island were burned and wilted in the direction of the blast, and the birds had singed feathers and were sick and reluctant to fly. On another island, there were only stumps of trees, no living animals, and even the fish seemed to be seared on one side, as if they had been dropped into a hot pan. Islands closer to the blast, ones that had previously been thick with trees and birds, were simply stripped of all plant and animal life.[40]

One person very interested in the Mike test found a highly unusual way to observe it. Edward Teller had been invited to Eniwetok to observe the test, but, still on a snit with the Los Alamos people, he refused. Teller waited in the basement of the geology building at the University of California, carefully watching a seismograph. A colleague monitored the radio frequency that carried the firing signal for Mike. They had calculated how long it would take for the seismic wave caused by the blast to travel from Eniwetok to Berkeley. When the firing signal was heard, they knew when to expect the seismic wave. At precisely the predicted time, the seismograph recorded a faint but distinct event, confirming for Teller the birth of his brainchild.

One worry of the planners of the Ivy Mike test was that the Soviets, by analyzing the radioactive debris from Mike, could infer that it had been a two-stage device that had achieved high compression of the fusion fuel.[41] In other words, the test might provide vital information useful to Soviet weapons designers. However, according to historian David Holloway, the effect of Mike on the Soviet thermonuclear project was slight, and they appear to have arrived independently at the idea of a two-stage "true" thermonuclear design.[42] In the early spring of 1954 the two-stage concept clearly emerged in discussions among members of the theoretical division. Like the American physicists, the Russians quickly realized the potential of this design. It was a scenario to be played out again and again: A temporary advantage by one side in the arms race would soon be nullified as the other side raced even harder to catch up.

In the meantime, though the Russians did not yet have a "true" hydrogen bomb, their brilliant young physicist Andrei Sakharov had devised a simple but effective design that layered light elements like deuterium, tritium, and their chemical compounds with heavy elements like uranium 238. These components were layered around a plutonium core like a cake with an icing of high explosive. The device was therefore nicknamed *sloika*, or layer cake. When the cake was detonated, the fission reaction would initiate fusion in the light elements and further fission in the heavy elements, thus significantly increasing the yield.

The Russians tested their layer cake on August 12, 1953, and it yielded 400 kilotons. This was not nearly so vast an explosion as Mike, but the layer cake had one big advantage: It was deliverable. Though no larger than the Fat Man, the layer cake was twenty times more powerful. Four hundred kilotons that could be dropped from a plane were worth a great deal more than ten megatons that would have to be delivered by oxcart. However, the United States was not without a reply. By this time the Mark 18 atomic bomb was in the US arsenal, and it was a deliverable purely fission bomb that yielded 500 kilotons – more than the *sloika*.

It was the Mark 18 bomb that was tested as the second of the Ivy series – Ivy King – fifteen days after Mike. King was dropped from a B-36 bomber at 11:30 a.m. on November 16. The target was the island of Runit, to the southeast of the crater that marked the site of the Mike test – where formerly had stood the island of Elugelab. The damage from King was not as great as that from Mike, but it was bad enough:

Damage from *King* was noted as far north of surface zero as Lojwa, where brush was scorched, and as far south as Jinderol, where brush was burning. Closer ... palms were broken and burned. Much debris from surface objects was on Runit itself with power poles downed and burning and puddles of water standing a quarter mile from the edge of the lagoon. The airblast over the reef of the northern tip of the island had apparently pushed seawater that far onto the island.[43]

When he referred to the Bible in his speech to convince the Bikinians to leave their island, Commodore Wyatt cited the wrong portions of scripture. The Apocalypse of John would have given the Marshallese a better idea of what would be happening to their home.

Clearly, the pressure was on for American scientists to develop a deliverable thermonuclear weapon. Mike had experimentally verified the validity of the Teller-Ulam design, and the next job was to adapt it for military use. This takes us to the next chapter and the story of the largest and most destructive nuclear test every conducted by the United States.

NOTES

1 Cantelon, Hewlett, and Williams (CHW), *The American Atom*, p. 70.
2 "Operation Greenhouse," Nuclear Weapon Archive site.
3 Rhodes, *Dark Sun*, p. 248.
4 Bird and Sherwin, *American Prometheus*, pp. 532–533.
5 Bird and Sherwin, *American Prometheus*, p. 533. For Teller's account see his *Memoirs*, pp. 369–384.
6 DeGroot, *The Bomb*, p. 200.
7 CHW, *The American Atom*, p. 119.
8 CHW, *The American Atom*, p.119.
9 CHW, *The American Atom*, p. 120.
10 CHW, *The American Atom*, p. 121.
11 CHW, *The American Atom*, p. 121.
12 CHW, *The American Atom*, p. 121.
13 CHW, *The American Atom*, p. 122.
14 CHW, *The American Atom*, p. 122.
15 CHW, *The American Atom*, p. 122.
16 "Race for the Superbomb," transcript, *The American Experience*, PBS.
17 CHW, *The American Atom*, p. 123.
18 CHW, *The American Atom*, p. 125
19 CHW, *The American Atom*, pp. 125–126.
20 Holloway, *Stalin and the Bomb*, p. 301.
21 Baggott, *The First War of Physics*, p. 457.
22 Bernstein, "The U.S. Decision to Build the H-bomb," website for "Race for the Superbomb," *The American Experience*, PBS.
23 Holloway, *Stalin and the Bomb*, p. 318.
24 Holloway, *Stalin and the Bomb*, p. 319.
25 "Race for the Superbomb," transcript, *The American Experience*, PBS. Actually, Klaus Fuchs and John von Neumann had first jointly developed the idea of radiation implosion in 1946. However, the idea, though ahead of its time, went nowhere because it was developed in conjunction with the unworkable "classical Super" design. See Rhodes, *Dark Sun*, p. 253. See also Alex Wellerstein "The Spy, the Human Computer, and the H-Bomb," at *Restricted Data: The Nuclear Secrecy* blog.
26 Rhodes, *Dark Sun*, p. 483.
27 Rhodes, *Dark Sun*, p. 479.
28 Hansen, *U.S. Nuclear Weapons*, p. 57.
29 Hansen, *U.S. Nuclear Weapons*, p. 55.

30 "The World's Biggest Bomb," transcript, *Secrets of the Dead*, PBS.
31 Hansen, *U.S. Nuclear Weapons*, p. 55.
32 Rhodes, *Dark Sun*, p. 500.
33 DeGroot, *The Bomb*, p. 178.
34 Hansen, *U.S. Nuclear Weapons*, p. 58.
35 Hansen, *U.S. Nuclear Weapons*, p. 58.
36 Hansen, *U.S. Nuclear Weapons*, p. 60.
37 Rhodes, *Dark Sun*, p. 509.
38 Agnew, "The 'Mike' Test" website for "Race for the Superbomb," *The American Experience*, PBS.
39 "Eyewitness Stories of the Bomb Test," *Bulletin of the Atomic Scientists*, December 1952, p. 300.
40 Hansen, *U.S. Nuclear Weapons*, pp. 59–60.
41 Holloway, *Stalin and the Bomb*, pp. 311–312.
42 Holloway, *Stalin and the Bomb*, p. 313.
43 Hansen, *U.S. Nuclear Weapons*, p. 60.

3

Runaway Bomb

America in 1954. As this is being written, it was merely sixty years ago. Yet even for those Americans who were alive then, it is part of an era that already seems strange and distant. The United States had forty-eight states, and Dwight Eisenhower was the President. Sam Rayburn, a Democrat from solidly Democratic Texas, became Speaker of the House of Representatives. The Interstate highway system did not exist. No artificial satellites orbited the earth. Phones hung on walls and had rotary dials. Jonas Salk was still conducting the field trials of his polio vaccine. Lasers did not exist. Computers were rare and each one filled a large room. The South was still locked up in Jim Crow segregation, though the Supreme Court did rule in that year that the travesty of "separate but equal" public schools was unconstitutional. Businessman Raymond Kroc purchased the franchise rights to a small chain of California hamburger restaurants owned by the McDonald brothers. The New York Giants swept the Cleveland Indians to take the World Series. *On the Waterfront* won the Academy Award for Best Motion Picture, and its star Marlon Brando won the Best Actor award. The most popular song of the year was Kitty Kallen's "Little Things Mean a Lot."

And in that year the United States blasted Bikini Atoll with a total explosive force of nearly fifty megatons. These tests were part of Operation Castle, which was conducted to test designs for the development of deliverable thermonuclear bombs. Seven tests were planned with the code names Bravo, Union, Yankee, Echo, Nectar, Romeo, and Koon. Six tests were carried out, but Echo was canceled. One, of the tests, Koon, was a failure that produced only a fraction of its predicted yield. The rest all yielded over a megaton, and three were even bigger than Ivy Mike.

Even the fizzle, Koon (110 kilotons), had a yield far greater than the bombs used in Crossroads eight years before. Test Baker of Crossroads, which at the time seemed like a demonstration of unlimited power, was a popgun compared to the Castle bombs.

THE BIGGEST BLAST

The first and largest of the series was Castle Bravo, an event that "ran away" from its predicted yield, producing an explosion 150 percent larger than expected. The predicted yield range was four to eight megatons, with a most likely yield of six megatons. In fact, it yielded fifteen megatons.[1] Castle Bravo was, and remains, the largest of any US nuclear test.

The high-yield shots of the Castle tests were moved back to Bikini. Historian Barton C. Hacker explains the reasons for the move:

Enewetak [Eniwetok] was clearly not big enough for all thermonuclear testing. For one thing, the permanent base camp on Enewetak limited test sites to the atoll's northern sector. Residual radioactivity could preclude a rapid sequence of tests with suitable sites so few and close together. Furthermore, high-yield shots might damage the base camp or instruments installed on other islands and impose more delays. Reactivating Bikini, unused since Operation Crossroads in 1946, as part of an expanded proving ground seemed a likely answer to all these constraints.[2]

Notably missing from this discussion was any consideration of the fact that Bikini is nearly 200 miles closer to the inhabited atolls of Rongelap and Utirik, which ultimately received significant fallout from Bravo. Also, by moving the tests back to Bikini, the US government definitively broke its promise to the Bikinians that their exile would only be temporary.

Once again, a joint task force was assembled, Joint Task Force 7, under the command of Major General P. W. Clarkson, and a flotilla was dispatched to the Pacific. Preparations were as massive as for previous operations. A 4,500-foot landing strip was constructed; camps were erected; a causeway and a pier built; and a channel dredged.[3] Barges had to be provided to hold the test devices. As Ivy Mike showed, when you set off a very big bomb on a very small island, the island disappears. The land area of Bikini is only two square miles, spread over twenty-six islands. In order to avoid eliminating an island with each shot, some of them would be detonated from barges anchored in shallow water. Precautions were taken to screen these activities from the prying periscopes of snooping Russian submarines.[4]

Castle Bravo was not to be detonated from a barge, but from a small artificial island built on a reef, 2,950 feet from the southwest tip of Namu (also called "Nam" in some of the literature) Island, which is located on the far northwest of the atoll. The reef was the source of the highly radio-active coral fragments that fell like snow on the *Lucky Dragon* and on the downwind islanders on the day of the Bravo test. Once again, a boxy shot cab was built to house the device. Marine guards were posted with orders to shoot to kill anyone not authorized to approach the device. Some of the guards amused themselves by writing their names on the bomb.[5]

As with Ivy Mike, many scientific instruments were installed to measure the various characteristics and effects of the blast. For weapons development, total energy release or explosive yield and the rate of the release, are of prime importance. One method of measuring yield is to analyze film records of the growth of the fireball, and another is to measure the intensity and duration of the fireball's pulses of thermal and optical radiation. So, cameras and light detectors were placed at various ranges from surface zero. A semicircle of twelve mirror towers was erected next to the shot cab. In the tiny fraction of a second before obliteration, they would reflect early light from the blast to distant ultra-high-speed cameras. Instead of the plywood Krause-Ogle box of Ivy Mike, twelve 7,500-foot pipe arrays led to detectors for measuring the rate of energy release. Careful surveying work was done to make sure that the pipes ran in a straight line-of-sight without diverging more than an inch.[6]

Though weapons development was the main purpose of the Castle tests, there were also a number of effects tests conducted by personnel of the Department of Defense. Thermonuclear weapons were new and the effects of their much greater power could not be reliably extrapolated from the smaller kiloton tests being conducted in Nevada. Effects tests studied both the hostile environment created by the extreme heat, blast, and radiation of thermonuclear devices and the response of various systems, such as military hardware, to such harsh conditions. Rugged gauges had been devised to measure blast and heat and preserve that information. Measurements of radiation, however, required prompt, and potentially dangerous, collection of instruments.[7]

For all of the Pacific tests, radiological safety was a command responsibility, and consequently, the task force took many measures to minimize the radiological dangers of the tests.[8] Meteorologists would carefully monitor the winds before the shots to determine the fallout pattern and direction, and potential dangers to the inhabited atolls. Great caution was to be exercised in the decision to proceed with a test. Over 200 radiation field monitors were trained for the operation. Military aircraft would track the radioactive clouds from the tests to see if they posed danger to the inhabited atolls. Commander Clarkson assured the Navy Commander-in-Chief for the Pacific that task force ships would be made available if evacuations became necessary.

As always when looking back on these tests, it is impossible not to be impressed with the detailed organization and the dedication to the preparation for every contingency. Planners of course realized that megaton tests in the atmosphere posed very significant potential dangers, and they observed precautions that they considered stringent. When the preparations and precautions turned out to be inadequate, as they disastrously did with Castle Bravo, the fault was not that the plans were careless, incompetently considered, or poorly executed. The fault was with fundamental assumptions and priorities underlying the entire testing program.

Like the Manhattan Project, nuclear testing required the organization and funding of a vast amount of topnotch science and world-class engineering. Like the space program of the 1960s, the nuclear testing operations of the 1950s exemplified what we might call the "heroic age" of American science. The United States is – or was – preeminent in the accomplishment of large-scale, expensive, and complicated science and engineering projects. Considered purely as theoretical and technical achievements, the construction and testing of nuclear weapons was remarkable testimony to what a society can do when it has the commitment and the means to pursue such large ambitions.

Ivy Mike was a "wet" bomb. It used liquid deuterium as the fuel, and this made it so heavy that it could not possibly serve as a prototype of a deliverable bomb. The Castle Bravo device, given the nickname "Shrimp," was a dry bomb that used lithium deuteride as fuel. Lithium deuteride is a waxy solid composed of lithium atoms bound to deuterium (hydrogen 2) atoms. The two isotopes lithium 6 and lithium 7 are found in natural lithium with the majority being lithium 7. The lithium used in the Shrimp was enriched to approximately 40 percent lithium 6, whereas natural lithium is only about 7.4 percent lithium 6. Studies of the "cross-section," the probability of neutron capture, of the two isotopes of lithium indicated that lithium 6 would capture neutrons to produce tritium that would then enter the fusion reaction. Lithium 7 would supposedly capture a neutron and transform to beryllium 8 which would decay to two alpha particles seconds later, without any contributions to the fusion reactions. Estimates of Shrimp's yield were based on those studies. Unfortunately, these results were wrong, and the consequences of the error were dramatic.

Shrimp was a Teller-Ulam design with the solid lithium fuel contained within a natural uranium tamper and, like Ivy Mike, containing a plutonium "sparkplug" in the center of the fuel cylinder. Shrimp was about fifteen feet long and four-and-a-half feet wide, weighing nearly twelve tons, lighter, by far, than the sausage design of Ivy Mike due in part to the use of aluminum instead of steel as the external casing. If the Castle devices worked, a deliverable weapon would soon follow.

Shrimp was constructed at Eniwetok and was finished by February 17. It was shipped to Bikini the next day and taken to the shot cab off Namu on the twentieth. Within two days, Shrimp had been installed and the final components and detonators were put in place on the twenty-eighth. The shot was slated for the next day, March 1. Unlike Mike, which was detonated from the control room on board the *Estes*, for Castle Bravo, the firing team was located on land, on the island of Enyu, twenty miles away at the opposite end of the atoll. Except for the firing party, everyone was evacuated and the fleet moved out of the lagoon even before the arming process had been completed.[9]

The major worry for the planners of the Bravo shot was how the radioactive fallout would be distributed and whether any shipping or populated areas would be affected. The indications were that the fallout would drop over empty ocean to the north and northeast of Bikini. Based on this information, extensive searches for shipping were conducted over the area where the fallout was expected. No ships were found in the search area.[10]

According to a 1982 report of the Defense Nuclear Agency by Edwin J. Martin and Richard H. Rowland, the wind speed and direction prior to the shot were meticulously checked.[11] At 11:00 a.m. on the day before the shot, the prediction was that no fallout would occur over populated areas. At the 6:00 p.m. weather briefing, less favorable winds were reported with another weather briefing scheduled for midnight. The midnight report indicated a worsening situation with winds at 20,000 feet blowing east toward the populated island of Rongelap. However, the predicted speed of these winds was low, and the shot was not canceled, dependent upon a final report at 4:30 a.m. When the 4:30 report came in it claimed no significant changes in the winds, and the only change in the plans due to weather was to order some of the smaller and slower ships of the fleet to move farther out.

Shrimp was detonated at 6:45 a.m. on March 1, 1954. Observers onboard the *Curtiss*, at sea twenty-three miles from ground zero, had been instructed to put on dark goggles. Even then, according to the testimony of persons interviewed for the PBS program *The World's Biggest Bomb*, the light from Bravo was so intense that they could see the bones in their arms, silhouetted against the glare.[12] This was the flash that made Ōishi Matashichi jump from his bunk on board the *Lucky Dragon*, seventy-five miles to the east of Bikini. The light was visible for over a minute on Rongerik Atoll, 155 miles east of Bikini. The atmospheric reflection of the blast was seen as far away as Okinawa, 2,600 miles distant – like an explosion in Boston that could be seen in Bogota. The flash could have been seen from Mars had anyone been watching.

It is difficult even to imagine the explosive force of fifteen million tons of TNT. The Bravo explosion was a thousand times as powerful as the Hiroshima bomb that had killed 70,000 people. In less than nine years, human destructive powers had increased by three orders of magnitude, dwarfing the yield of Little Boy, just as Little Boy had outclassed the largest conventional bombs of the Second World War. The blast excavated a crater over a mile in diameter and 240 feet deep. The mushroom cloud rose to a height of over 114,000 feet, which was far up into the stratosphere. Ten minutes after the blast, the mushroom cloud was over seventy miles across and was still rising rapidly.[13]

Why did the bomb "run away" to two and a half times its expected yield? Recall that the lithium in the bomb consisted of two isotopes, lithium 6 and lithium 7. When the primary stage detonated, plutonium fission resulted in the release of neutrons as well as the compression and heating of the lithium deuteride compound to the high temperature and pressure needed to induce nuclear fusion. When a lithium 6 nucleus absorbs a neutron from the primary fission stage the resultant products are an alpha particle and a tritium nucleus, with a release of energy. The tritium nucleus then fuses with the deuterium, to form helium 4 (an alpha particle), with the release of more energy and a neutron. These were the nuclear reactions expected in the Castle Bravo test, it being assumed that lithium 7 would not take part.

What was not taken into consideration was that the lithium 7 nucleus, upon capturing a fast neutron, transforms into an alpha particle, a tritium nucleus, and a neutron. Extra tritium was thus produced, and a larger tritium yield meant a higher number of fusion reactions of the tritium with deuterium. Thus, the higher number of fusion events due to the unexpected reactivity of the lithium 7 resulted in the generation of more energy and a higher number of neutrons released. In turn, the increased release of neutrons also caused more fission reactions in the surrounding uranium tamper than expected, which then led to a further increase in the energy released, and therefore the bomb's yield. In fact, ten megatons of the total fifteen megaton yield of the detonation resulted from fission of the uranium tamper by fast neutrons.[14] In short, extra fusion reactions, due to lithium 7, provoked more fission reactions in the uranium tamper, and these fusion reactions also released more neutrons, which then provoked more fusion reactions ... and so on in a pernicious feedback loop, with each part of this vicious cycle adding its energy to the tremendous total output.

Shrimp was not only an unusually big bomb, it was an unusually "dirty" one, that is, one that produced a great deal of intensely radioactive fallout. The bomb was extra dirty because of the fission reactions in the natural uranium tamper that surrounded the fusion fuel stage. The fission products coated the coral fragments blasted into the atmosphere and so created the "death ash" that rained down on unsuspecting people.

The blast was filmed from many angles and locations. One particularly dramatic sequence looks through a grove of palm trees toward a gigantic pillar of fire that fills the horizon and tints everything with a weird orange glow. The trees emit smoke when the sudden heat sears them. Another shot shows the broad front of the shockwave advancing rapidly over the sea like an accelerated tsunami. When the shock hits the grove of palms, the camera is pelted by debris knocked from the trees. Within a minute the shockwave had stripped nearby islands of their vegetation. Fourteen miles across the lagoon on Eneman Island, buildings were destroyed and an electrical short circuit induced by the blast started a fire that destroyed much scientific equipment.[15] The sailors and marines aboard the *Curtiss* saw the shockwave rushing at them. The *Curtiss* was not a small ship, but the blast rocked it side to side, roughly shaking everyone and tossing about those who had not secured a tight handhold. "I think we're goners!" one marine called out to his buddy, who fully agreed.[16] When they were able to look at the roiling cloud, though it was over twenty miles away, it appeared to loom menacingly right over them.

The raw power of the blast was simply stunning. Bill Bryson records the experience of a soldier who was observing Bravo from a distance:

One soldier, based on the island of Kwajalein, described in a letter home how he thought the blast would blow his barracks away, "All of a sudden the sky lighted up a bright orange and remained that way for what seemed a couple of minutes ... We heard very loud rumblings that sounded like thunder. Then the whole barracks began shaking, as if there had been an earthquake. This was followed by a very high wind." And this was a place nearly two hundred miles from the blast site [actually, more than 200 miles], and goodness knows what the experience was like for those even closer.[17]

Physicist Marshall N. Rosenbluth reported that the growing cloud assumed a sinister aspect:

I think we were about 30 miles away, and it just kept rising and rising. It looked to me what you might imagine a diseased brain or a brain of some madman would look like. You know, the surface with the cortex convolutions, and so on. And it just kept getting bigger and bigger.[18]

Once again, as with Ivy Mike, observers were impressed with how the heat of a thermonuclear bomb just built and built until it became almost unbearable even for observers dozens of miles away. A witness of one of the Russian thermonuclear tests said that it was like putting your head in an open oven.

The most harrowing experiences of the participants in the test were those of the firing team located twenty miles away on Enyu. They were sealed behind blast doors in a reinforced concrete bunker that had been covered with sand. With such protection, and being located twenty miles from the test site, they thought that they would be quite safe during the test. They were wrong. The head of the firing team was Dr. John C. Clark, a physicist and a participant in numerous nuclear tests. He recorded his experiences of the Bravo shot in an article published in *The Saturday Evening Post* in July 1957.

Looking at his control blockhouse on Enyu from a helicopter, it certainly looked sturdy enough to Clark. It had been designed to withstand a five-foot tidal wave and both the overpressure of the blast and the underpressure as the air was violently sucked back afterwards. Procedures to secure the blockhouse were carefully followed. At minus one hour metal plates and gaskets were set over the air-conditioning vents. To provide a door that was watertight and blast proof, a submarine hatch had been installed, and this was carefully sealed. Naturally, they expected to feel some effects of the explosion. A ground shock wave was expected first followed by an air shock wave, but at twenty miles' distance, little damage was expected. However, their expectations were based on a projected yield of six, not fifteen, megatons.[19]

Enclosed in the blockhouse, the firing crew could not see the explosion, but alarming effects were soon felt:

Inside our blockhouse we still had no physical evidence that anything had happened, but we braced ourselves against a possible sharp ground shock. It came – but not as expected. Less than twenty seconds after zero, the entire building started slowly rocking in an indescribable way. I grabbed the side of the control panel for support. Some of the men just sat down on the floor. I had been in earthquakes before, but never anything like this. It lasted only a few seconds but, just as we were breathing easier, another shock hit us with the same undulating motion. Then, a minute later, came the air blast. First the overpressure, then the sucking out by the underpressure. The concrete building creaked but stayed firm.[20]

Another member of the group found the experience of the ground shock equally alarming:

Something was wrong! [Team member] Grier spoke the words first as he reached out to steady himself at the workbench. "Is this building moving, or am I getting dizzy?" he asked. "My God it is. It's moving!" Grier reached for the bench to steady himself as I stood bewildered in the center of the room. The whole building was moving, definitely now, not shaking or shuddering as it would from the [air] shock wave that had not arrived yet, but with a low perceptible rolling motion like a ship's roll; I began to feel a nausea akin to seasickness. I was completely unable to get it through my head that the building was moving. The building is made of concrete, I told myself. The walls are three feet thick. It's anchored like a rock on this island. Besides shock waves can't be here yet. But it *was* moving![21]

The unexpected rolling was only the prelude to the genuinely scary events. Several minutes later Clark and a few others ventured out of the blockhouse to look around:

I went outside, taking along a Geiger counter. The shot cloud had spread out and was pure white. It was an awesome sight. I casually placed the radiation counter on top of a fence outside the door and turned to talk to [team member] Gaelen Felt, who was pointing out that the blast had torn the doors open on his instrument trailers nearby. All of a sudden I noticed that the radiation meter was already reading eight milliroentgen. That meant that we were receiving radiation at the rate of 8/1000 of a roentgen per hour, far less than would be received from an ordinary chest x-ray ... While we watched, the counter went up to twenty milliroentgen, and then to forty. While this was not yet a dangerous amount of radioactivity, there should not have been any radiation at the distance we were from the bomb blast. It could only mean one thing: We were already getting fallout. We could hardly believe it. The wind was supposed to take the fallout in almost an opposite direction. But our Geiger counters were registering radioactivity, and counters are usually accurate.[22]

As the readings continued to rise, Clark ordered everyone back inside, but even inside the blockhouse, radiation rates started to rise.

Clark called for help, but was told that a helicopter rescue would be too dangerous given the rate that the fallout was accumulating. Clark and his team were trapped with no way of knowing how high the radiation would rise in the blockhouse. They took refuge in a small room where the radiation was lowest. They were forced to turn off the air-conditioning to prevent fallout particles from being blown in. Soon, with several men in a small room and no air-conditioning, it began to get quite uncomfortable. Then the generator began to go out and lights faded, leaving only battery-powered equipment workable.

After several hours of discomfort in the dark, they received word that three helicopters had been dispatched to pick them up. To protect themselves from the accumulated radioactive dust while driving the half mile to the landing mats, they wrapped up in bed sheets which they sealed with tape and cut holes for their eyes. Thus, attired like kids trick-or-treating on Halloween, they made their way by jeep to the helicopters. The sheets worked. None of them had received dangerous amounts of radiation. Clark saw a silver lining in the whole nightmarish experience: He said that their experience with the bed sheets had given Civil Defense authorities information about how to protect people in the event of nuclear war.[23]

Contrary to predictions, the fallout hit the *Curtiss* too. Soon radioactive dust was falling over the ship and crew. At least on this occasion, as opposed to what happened at Crossroads, the crew was ordered below decks and hatches were sealed tight. Orders were given to shoot anyone attempting to go out on deck. With poor ventilation, no air-conditioning, and being trapped below decks in a tropical environment, temperatures soon climbed to well above 100 degrees and the stench from so many tightly packed bodies became overpowering. Nuclear testing was not an activity for the sensitive or the squeamish.

RUNAWAY RADIATION

The rain of fallout on Dr. Clark's team and the ships of the task force was a frightening and unexpected event. Two other events became the most infamous and consequential of the effects of Castle Bravo; these were the offsite exposures, the irradiation of the crew of the *Lucky Dragon #5* and of the indigenous Marshallese people. The exposure of these people to dangerous levels of radiation, and the subsequent incidence of radiation sickness among many of them, soon raised a hue and cry in the worldwide press and ballooned into a major international incident. We look at these events in detail in the next chapter.

How did radioactive fallout, which was supposed to fall to the northeast of Bikini, instead go almost due east toward populated islands, and the unlucky Japanese tuna boat? The unexpected amount of fallout to the east of Bikini has often been explained in terms of a wind shift, and the allegedly culpable failure of those conducting the tests to cancel the shot

once that shift was detected. Thus, Jonathan Weisgall explains the fallout
pattern in these terms:

what was described at the time as an "unprecedented" shift in wind direction
sent the fallout eastward over Bikini Island and beyond, covering an area as large
as 7000 square miles. As the bomb cloud rose higher into the upper atmosphere
than had been anticipated, high-altitude winds pulled it to the east rather than the
west. Pellet-sized particles fell to the earth quickly, but the smaller and less visible
ones were carried east by the winds and drifted to earth more slowly. A soft rain
of whitish ash began to fall 50 miles downwind one hour after the blast; several
hours later the ashy rain began to fall 100 miles away. Those sprinkled included
28 American servicemen on Rongerik, the 236 [other sources indicate a total
of 239] inhabitants of Rongelap and Utirik atolls, other Marshallese who were
camping at Ailinginae Atoll, and 23 crewmen of a Japanese fishing vessel, *The
Lucky Dragon*.[24]

Citing the 1982 Defense Nuclear Agency report by Martin and Rowland,
Weisgall questions the judgment of those who proceeded with the test
while knowing that winds at 20,000 feet were blowing due east toward
inhabited islands.[25]

The wind shift theory was also supported by those who sought to
exonerate the ones responsible for the decision to proceed with the test.
According to a press release by Atomic Energy Commission Chairman
Lewis Strauss on March 31, the inhabited atolls were placed in the path
of the fallout by an unexpected wind shift. However, Strauss claimed that
the shift occurred after, not before, the blast.

In January 2013, the Defense Threat Reduction Agency released a special report that addressed the wind shift theory as well as many other
claimed errors and misperceptions about the Bravo test. The report is
titled *Castle Bravo: Fifty Years of Legend and Lore* and was authored
by Thomas Kunkle of the Los Alamos National Laboratory and Byron
Ristvet of the Defense Threat Reduction Agency. As the subtitle indicates,
the authors hold that misinformation and disinformation have accumulated since Bravo, resulting in an unfair depiction of those who conducted
and planned the test.

Kunkle and Ristvet deny that the unexpected fallout was due to a
wind shift, and argue that the highly unfortunate events subsequent to
Bravo could not have been anticipated given what was known at the
time. They also cite the command briefings that reported the weather in
the hours before Bravo:

As was made clear in the command briefings, the winds between 5000 and 15,000
feet were essentially calm, and a 10 kn [knot] speed to the east was assigned as

the most pessimistic situation for shot time. It also was forecast that the winds at these altitudes would reverse within 12 hours and blow to the west, away from the inhabited atolls. Assuming the standard settling rate of 5000 ft/hr. radioactive particles would spend only an hour or two in this wind flow regime. Debris initially at 20,000 ft altitude would thus move at the most only 20 mi east before it would drop into the trade winds and be carried back to the west, away from populated atolls. With this information in mind, the winds from 5000 to 15,000 ft were correctly seen to present no credible threat to the safety of the inhabited atolls.[26]

This is consistent with the Martin and Rowland report, cited previously, that noted the eastward trajectory of the winds, but held that their speed was too slow to allow fallout to reach the inhabited atolls. In fact, say Kunkle and Ristvet, the forecast was quite accurate with real winds differing only slightly from the prediction, and well within the limits of normal forecast error.[27]

The "wind shift" theory assumes that fallout that rained down on the inhabited atolls and the *Lucky Dragon* came from the narrow stem of the mushroom cloud. It was this material that supposedly was transported by the winds toward the east until it fell out over the unsuspecting victims. However, the authors claim that, though the winds at this altitude did initially move in the direction of the inhabited islands, the fallout particles soon fell into the westward-blowing trade winds and were blown back toward Bikini.[28]

According to Kunkle and Ristvet, the actual cause of the fallout seems to have had nothing to do with a wind shift, but was due to the mistaken belief that the stratosphere would trap nearly all of the radioactive debris that made it to that height.[29] The portion of the atmosphere that extends from ground level to about 60,000 feet is known as the troposphere. It is in this layer of the atmosphere that weather occurs. In the troposphere, except under unusual conditions, the temperature decreases with altitude. The air in the troposphere undergoes convection as the sun-heated warm air rises, and denser cold air falls. This convective movement keeps the troposphere in constant and complex motion. Above the troposphere is the stratosphere, and there the relation of height and temperature is reversed. The temperature in the stratosphere increases with height because the ozone in the upper stratosphere absorbs ultraviolet energy from the sun. In the stratosphere, then, any warmer air that tends to rise will be blocked by the warm air above it. Likewise, any cold air that tends to fall will be trapped by dense, cold air below it. The stratosphere therefore lacks convective motion and so tends to be relatively stable when compared to the troposphere. The boundary between the troposphere and the stratosphere is called the tropopause.

The cloud from Bravo punched right through the tropopause and far up into the stratosphere. The bulk of radioactive debris was, in fact, included in the huge "mushroom cap" head of the cloud, which was contained entirely in the stratosphere. Because of the relative stability of the stratosphere, it was widely assumed that radioactive debris in the massive head of the mushroom cloud would remain trapped there for quite some time. When this material did eventually fall out, it would be spread around much of the earth, and so have low concentration. Also, with the passage of time, the radioactivity would "cool" to a much safer level. This assumption was strengthened by the fact that much of the radioactive debris produced by Ivy Mike seemed to have just disappeared, presumably trapped in the stratosphere until it was relatively harmless. With natural disasters, such as the eruption of Krakatoa in 1883, particulate matter blasted into the stratosphere had remained there for months or even years. The assumption was that this would be so with the radioactive debris from Bravo. Unfortunately, say Kunkle and Ristvet, this assumption turned out to be wrong, and very significant amounts of fallout were deposited on unsuspecting human beings.

However, was it the case that there was no information ahead of the Castle test that, with due diligence, might have been recognized as indicating a possible threat to the inhabited islands? Of course, by 1954 the atmospheric testing of nuclear weapons was known to be risky, though there was considerable disagreement about the degree of risk. It was, however, already well known that dangerous amounts of radiation could be transported as far as the distance between Bikini and the inhabited atolls. On May 19, 1953, over nine months before Bravo, the detonation of a thirty-two-kiloton bomb at the Nevada Test Site caused dangerous amounts of fallout to accumulate at St. George, Utah, 135 miles to the east, that is, at about the same relative position as Rongelap is to Bikini. (We will look at the St. George incident in more detail in Chapter 6.)

A paper published in 1997 by Merrill Eisenbud in the *Journal of Health Physics* indicates that by 1954 it was known that significant radioactive fallout could be transported for long distances. In the spring of 1951, two relatively small devices were detonated at the Nevada Test Site as part of Operation Jangle. Eisenbud reports that Salt Lake City, at 640 miles from the test site, received "exceptionally high" levels of fallout.[30] At that time, he and a colleague published their findings about the long-distance transportation of fallout in the widely read journal *Science*, so the information could hardly be considered hidden.

In the run-up to Bravo, Eisenbud reported that he had conferred with meteorologist Lt. Colonel N. M. Lulegian (spelled "Lulejian" in other sources), about the possible dangers posed by a multimegaton blast:

We had several conversations about the possibility of lethal long-range fallout, and in November 1953 he wrote a meteorological analysis in which he confirmed that lethal levels of fallout could occur over an area of 5000 square miles ... a few hours after a 10 megaton thermonuclear explosion ... A copy of his classified report, which essentially confirmed what we believed, was sent to me at the time but a few days later was mysteriously ordered to be returned to the originating office. The report was not declassified for more than forty years.[31]

Kunkle and Ristvet say that the Lulejian report has become an unfortunate part of the "legend" that has grown around the Bravo test.[32] They reply that Lulejian's forecast model had in fact been considered in the planning for Bravo but was rejected on solid scientific grounds. The extrapolations used by Lulejian were based on data from the much smaller Jangle tests in Nevada, data inappropriate for a blast of much larger yield like Bravo. Also, the Lulejian model failed to account for the complexity of the winds aloft at the Pacific Proving Grounds and for the differences between the dry alluvium of the Nevada desert and the wet coral of Bikini. So, the extrapolation analysis recommended by Lulejian had not been summarily dismissed, and the more complex models actually employed did accurately predict the path of the tropospheric fallout. The failure of the models was not with respect to the path of the fallout in the troposphere, but with respect to the fallout expected to be trapped in the stratosphere.[33]

Kunkle and Ristvet may be right that the Task Force radiological safety personnel may have done their jobs conscientiously and with scientific integrity. The planners of Bravo may have taken what appeared to be every reasonable precaution. However, with atmospheric multimegaton nuclear explosions, it is hard even to define "reasonable" precautions. As subsequent events made all too plain, even the best, most conscientiously prepared scientific predictions might fail disastrously due to factors not even considered in the scientific models – like the alleged failure of the expected stratospheric trapping with the Bravo fallout. Further, such models had little of the most relevant data, namely information about previous multimegaton tests in the Pacific. The only instance of a multimegaton test prior to Bravo was Mike, and generalizing from a single case is dicey.

By their very nature, experiments push against the limits of our knowledge. Knowing that, and knowing that the experiment will involve the release of vast and dangerous forces of uncertain magnitude, perhaps a

surfeit of caution was indicated. Perhaps, then, the question the planners
of Bravo should have asked was not where dangerous fallout *would* go,
but where it *could* go, and to have made their plans accordingly. Even if
the extrapolation from the Lulejian report was scientifically unsound, as
Kunkle and Ristvet claim, it would be blithe to assume that a multimegaton blast *could not* project dangerous fallout at least as far as the much
smaller thirty two kiloton device did in the St. George, Utah case. In other
words, in a situation like the Castle Bravo test, where the consequences
of an accident could be so dire, the appropriate precautions should be
based not on the most probable projections but on worst-case scenarios.
This would have been apt since what actually happened was close to the
worst case.

At rock bottom, it is hard to allay the suspicion that the manufacture and testing of thermonuclear weapons was considered to be such an
urgent national priority that it had to proceed even in the face of risks
that were then unknown or even unknowable.

THE POST-BRAVO TESTS

Bravo was only the first of the Castle series of tests. It was the biggest,
but the others were by no means small. The next Castle test, code-
named "Romeo" was detonated at 6:30 a.m. on March 27. The bomb
had been placed on a barge over the crater that had been left by Bravo.
Once again, the yield significantly exceeded projections, producing
an explosion of eleven megatons when only four had been predicted.
Romeo used cheap and readily available unenriched lithium for its lithium deuteride fuel. The inexpensive and plentiful fuel meant that the
device could be made into a practical weapon that could be stockpiled.
The Romeo design was quickly weaponized and made into the Mark
17/24 (the Mark 24 was externally identical to the Mark 17, but used
a different primary), the United States' first deliverable thermonuclear
bomb. The Mark 17/24 was the largest bomb (both in physical dimen-
sions and in yield) ever deployed by the US military. It was twenty-four
feet, eight inches long, 61.4 inches in diameter, and weighed between
41,400 and 42,000 pounds.[34] The bomb was so large that it could only
be delivered by the gigantic B-36 bomber. The yield was also enormous, fifteen to twenty megatons.

The United States now had thermonuclear weapons and the means
to deliver them anywhere. This is the reason that the Castle tests were
performed, to provide that capability. In this sense the tests were highly

successful. The country had committed to developing thermonuclear weapons in 1950, and in only five years, they were acquired. The United States was the first to develop "true" (Teller-Ulam design) thermonuclear weapons, and it is arguable that the technological edge over the Soviet Union was maintained throughout the Cold War. Some historians might see this edge as one crucial factor in ultimate victory of the West in the Cold War. However, even if this is so, the crew of the *Lucky Dragon* and the irradiated Marshall Islanders would remind us of the price that innocent people paid for that victory.

The final sum of the yields of the Castle tests was 48.2 megatons. Yet the Castle series was far from the end of nuclear testing in the Marshall Islands. Following Castle was Operation Redwing, which conducted a series of seventeen tests during May, June, and July of 1956. The Redwing devices ranged from the relatively minuscule *Yuma* that yielded less than a quarter-kiloton, to the massive *Tewa* of five megatons. Once more, the smaller-yield bombs were tested on Eniwetok, and the big ones on Bikini. Following Redwing was Operation Hardtack, an additional thirty-three tests from April through August 1958. Two of these were underwater bursts and two were complete fizzles with yields of zero. Six of the blasts were in excess of a megaton, and the largest, *Poplar*, was 9.3 megatons. With the last of the Hardtack series, the tiny-yield *Fig* (.02 kiloton) on August 18, 1958, the torment of the Marshall Islands at last came to an end. Atmospheric nuclear testing did not end, but it was moved elsewhere.

Counting the underwater shots and the shots with zero yield, a total of sixty-seven nuclear tests were performed in the Marshall Islands. From 1946 to 1958, operations Crossroads, Sandstone, Greenhouse, Ivy, Castle, Redwing, and Hardtack released a total explosive yield of 108 megatons, over 7,000 times the explosive force of the Hiroshima Bomb. There is no question that testing greatly aided the technical development of the American nuclear arsenal. Chuck Hansen notes the advances specifically due to the Castle tests:

Castle achieved a number of scientifically and militarily useful results ... the practicability of using solid-fueled (lithium-6 deuteride and lithium-7 hydride) weapons was amply demonstrated. In addition, *Castle* furnished valuable experimental information that could be used in the design of lighter thermonuclear weapons; gave highly significant effects information on high-yield explosions; provided experimental verification of external fission initiators; and significantly reduced the national requirements for tritium production.[35]

Therefore, much was learned from these tests and, unquestionably, they played a vital part in the US program of weapons development.

However, these advances came at a very considerable human cost. We tell the story of those who paid the price in the next chapter.

NOTES

1   Hansen, *U.S. Nuclear Weapons*, p. 68.
2   Hacker, *Elements of Controversy*, p. 131.
3   Hansen, *U.S. Nuclear Weapons*, p. 62.
4   Hansen, *U.S. Nuclear Weapons*, p.62.
5   "World's Biggest Bomb," transcript, *Secrets of the Dead*, PBS.
6   Martin and Rowland, *Castle Series*, p. 32.
7   Martin and Rowland, *Castle Series*, pp. 35–36.
8   Hacker, *Elements of Controversy*, pp. 135–136.
9   Hansen, *U.S. Nuclear Weapons*, p. 65.
10 Martin and Rowland, *Castle Series*, p. 201.
11 Martin and Rowland, *Castle Series*, pp. 201–202.
12 "World's Biggest Bomb," transcript, *Secrets of the Dead*, PBS.
13 Hansen, *U.S. Nuclear Weapons*, p. 66.
14 Sublette, "Operation Castle." Nuclear Weapon Archive website.
15 Martin and Rowland, *Castle Series*, p. 205.
16 "World's Biggest Bomb," transcript, *Secrets of the Dead*, PBS.
17 Bryson, *The Life and Times of the Thunderbolt Kid*, pp. 123–124.
18 "Race for the Superbomb," transcript, *The American Experience*, PBS.
19 Clark, "We Were Trapped by Radioactive Fallout," Sonicbomb website.
20 Clark, "We Were Trapped by Radioactive Fallout," Sonicbomb website.
21 Hansen, *U.S. Nuclear Weapons*, p.66.
22 Clark, "We Were Trapped by Radioactive Fallout," Sonicbomb website.
23 Clark, "We Were Trapped by Radioactive Fallout," Sonicbomb website.
24 Weisgall, *Operation Crossroads*, p. 303.
25 Weisgall, *Operation Crossroads*, pp. 305–306.
26 Kunkle and Ristvet, *Castle Bravo*, p. 73.
27 Kunkle and Ristvet, *Castle Bravo*, p. 76.
28 Kunkle and Ristvet, *Castle Bravo*, p. 70.
29 Kunkle and Ristvet, *Castle Bravo*, pp. 49–56.
30 Eisenbud, "Monitoring Distant Fallout," p. 22.
31 Eisenbud, "Monitoring Distant Fallout," pp. 22–23.
32 Kunkle and Ristvet, *Castle Bravo*, p. 66.
33 Kunkle and Ristvet, *Castle Bravo*, pp. 66–68.
34 Hansen, *U.S. Nuclear Weapons*, p. 147.
35 Hansen, *U.S. Nuclear Weapons*, p. 68.

4

The Victims of Castle Bravo

Twenty of the nuclear tests in the Marshall Islands produced measurable amounts of fallout.[1] However, by far the greatest damage was done by the first and the biggest of the Castle series, the Bravo shot. Here we look at the two most infamous incidents, the irradiation of the Japanese fishermen and the Marshallese. It was the suffering of these people that made Castle Bravo an international incident, and made nuclear testing a topic of discussion and debate worldwide.

THE *LUCKY DRAGON*

The experiences of the crew of the *Lucky Dragon #5* on the day of the Bravo test have been recounted in the Introduction. Those alarming events were only the beginning of the travails of that unlucky crew. Not only were they each seriously ill, but upon their return to their home port of Yaizu, they were treated as lepers. When the news of their contamination broke in the March 16 newspapers, panic ensued:

The March 16 news stories threw Yaizu into confusion, turned things upside down. The Fisherman's Co-op received a rush of phone calls expressing complaints and worries. The public bath we had gone to said, "Our patrons are staying away." The restaurant we'd eaten at said, "What should we do?" Women of the red light district appealed to doctors, "We slept with the crew on board ship last night. Are we safe?" We crewmembers were quarantined in Yaizu North Hospital, far from town, and all our belongings and clothes were collected and buried on the hospital's grounds.[2]

Worse, the fear was not all blind panic. There was real danger:

The Geiger counter detected radiation one hundred feet from the ship. It detected one hundred milliroentgens on the deck where ropes and glass buoys were heaped up. On the stern deck thirty milliroentgens – far higher than expected. Dr. Shiokawa's pocket dosimeter registered 10 millirems in fifteen minutes. He demanded that the ship be moved at once to a wharf on the opposite side of the fish market, far from other ships and houses; people should be kept away from the ship. Police stood guard.[3]

Crew members themselves exhibited high degrees of contamination. A check of the toilets in their homes found high readings there, indicating that the crew had suffered both external and internal exposure. Their nails and hair had particularly high readings and, since no barber would agree to do it, a nervous city employee had to shave their heads.[4] While Japanese doctors were deeply alarmed, American officials who investigated expressed far less concern. One opined that the fishermen would recover in a few weeks or, at most, in a month. Another dismissed the exposure as not serious and was confident that the crewmembers were getting all the tests they needed.[5] Meanwhile, fear of contaminated fish spread panic far beyond the port of Yaizu. Seventeen tuna from the *Lucky Dragon* had been sent to the market in the city of Osaka, and two of these had already been eaten before public health officials began to check them with Geiger counters. The remaining fish all showed high levels of radioactivity. Inspections on all fish arriving at the Osaka market were begun, but soon other ships began bringing back radioactive fish, and fish shops in Tokyo began to go out of business.[6] Japan seemed headed for a fish-free diet.

Meanwhile the condition of the crew of the *Lucky Dragon* continued to worsen. They were transferred to hospitals in Tokyo; Ōishi spent fourteen months being treated there. Blood samples showed that the white cell and red cell counts of the men began to fall sharply. Platelet counts fell also, meaning that their blood could not coagulate properly, leading to internal bleeding, which caused bloody stools and bleeding from the nose and gums. They also suffered from fever and chronic diarrhea, and were required to remain in bed and take no exercise at all. Some were even fed by the nurses. Because of the very low white cell counts, large doses of antibiotics were administered to stave off infection.

The most seriously afflicted of the crewmen was the radioman Kuboyama Aikichi. Late in August, his condition abruptly worsened and did not respond even to aggressive treatment.[7] He soon became incoherent and disoriented, jerked spasmodically, and was clearly in acute pain.

At times his behavior became so violent that he had to be restrained. On August 30 his condition became critical and he lapsed into a coma. On September 4 he briefly regained consciousness and called out his daughter's name. Unable to fend off opportunistic infections, he contracted pneumonia on September 17 and died on September 23. His final illness and death had been closely followed in Japan and occasioned a national outpouring of grief. An autopsy showed that all of his internal organs had been severely damaged by radiation.[8] Kuboyama's funeral was attended by three thousand people, including officials of the Japanese and US governments.

Although no other member of the crew died in the immediate aftermath of Castle Bravo, each was permanently affected by the exposure to the fallout. On the other hand, some of their problems may have stemmed from their treatment. Liver damage seemed an especially common condition among the other crewmen.[9] In 1995 it was discovered that twelve of the fifteen survivors of the *Lucky Dragon* had hepatitis C, probably acquired from the numerous blood transfusions given in their initial treatment.[10] At the time, some American doctors expressed the thought that Kuboyama's death may have been due to overly aggressive and perhaps inappropriate medical treatment.[11]

Were aspects of the treatment of the *Lucky Dragon* patients overly aggressive or inadvisable? Perhaps; we cannot settle the question here. However, the criticism at that time of the Japanese doctors by American medical personnel could not help but appear to be politically rather than medically motivated, and part of a pattern of denial and dismissal unfortunately displayed by some American officials. The American doctors' analyses, even if medically justified, inevitably seemed to be an effort to shift at least a part of the blame for the victims' suffering away from the radiation exposure and onto the shoulders of Japanese physicians. It is small wonder that tensions increased between American and Japanese doctors, and that, in general, in Japanese eyes American credibility greatly declined. What is absolutely beyond any doubt is that the exceptional suffering of the crew of the *Lucky Dragon* had its origin in their exposure to the radioactive fallout from Castle Bravo and that all they later underwent stemmed from that event.

Comments from highly placed Americans added insult to the crewmen's injuries. On March 17, Congressman W. Sterling Cole (R-NY), chair of the Joint Committee on Atomic Energy, opined that the *Lucky Dragon* intentionally entered the restricted zone on a spy mission.[12] Later, on March 31, Representative Cole repeated his charge that the crew may have been attempting to spy on the atomic test and announced that the Atomic Energy Commission (AEC) would investigate.[13]

The most notorious remarks were made by Lewis Strauss, chair of the AEC, in a statement released to the press on March 31. He began by stating the importance of the tests:

No test is made without a definite purpose and a careful determination that it is directed toward an end of major importance to our military strength and readiness. The result which the scientists at Los Alamos and Livermore had hoped to obtain from these tests were [sic] fully realized. An enormous potential has been added to our military posture by what we have learned.[14]

He also addressed what he regarded as hyperbole concerning the blast:

Now as to this specific test series, the first shot has been described as devastating, out of control and with other exaggerated and mistaken characterizations. I would not wish to minimize it. It was a very large blast in the megaton range. But at no time was the testing out of control. The misapprehension seems to have arisen from two facts; first, that the yield was about double that of the calculated estimate, a margin of error not incompatible with a new weapon ... and second because of the results of the fall-out.[15]

Strauss next commented on the proximity of the *Lucky Dragon* to the explosion:

A Japanese fishing trawler appears to have been missed by the search but based on a statement attributed to her skipper to the effect that he saw the flash of the explosion and heard the concussion six minutes later, it must have been well within the danger area.[16]

He continued:

The 23 crewmembers of the ship, 28 American personnel manning weather stations on the little islands and the 236 natives on these islands were therefore within the area of the fall-out ... The task force commander promptly evacuated all of the people from these islands. They were taken to the Island of Kwajalein and there placed under continuous and competent medical supervision. I visited them last week. Since that time it has been determined that our weather personnel could be returned to duty ... The 236 natives appear to me to be well and happy. Today, a full month after the event, the medical staff at Kwajalein advised us that they anticipated no illness, barring, of course, diseases which might hereafter be contracted. The situation with the 23 Japanese fishermen is less certain, due to the fact that our people have not been permitted by the Japanese authorities to make a proper, clinical examination. It is interesting to note, however, that the reports which have recently come through to us indicate that the blood count of these men is comparable to that of our weather station personnel [which was not judged to be severe – see below].[17]

Elements of Strauss' comments were quickly contradicted by the Japanese Embassy which issued a statement on April 12 indicating that some of Strauss' claims were at odds with the facts as they had ascertained them. First, they challenged the claim that the *Lucky Dragon* had been within the designated danger zone which US government had established around Bikini. The danger zone was a rectangular area 335 miles east-to-west and 150 miles north-to-south that the United States had set up around Eniwetok and Bikini. Mariners were officially warned to stay out of this area. Strauss inferred that since the crew heard the detonation six minutes after the explosion, they must have been within the danger zone. According to the Japanese Embassy, the explosion was heard seven or eight minutes afterwards, which would have placed the ship farther away. Their estimate is that the *Lucky Dragon* was nineteen miles outside the exclusion zone when they saw the flash, and twenty-six miles outside when radioactive ash fell on them.[18]

Why was the exact position of the *Lucky Dragon* an issue? The danger zone had not been established to indicate the limits beyond which dangerous fallout should not be expected. Instead, it had been established as a security measure to designate a region that would be regularly patrolled by task force ships and aircraft, so that any vessels detected could be warned away.[19] In short, the purpose of the zone was not to ensure safety, but to prevent spying on the tests. By indicating that the ship must have been in the excluded zone, was Strauss implying that the *Lucky Dragon* was there to engage in espionage? This seems outrageous, but, in fact, Strauss privately commented to Eisenhower's press secretary that he thought that perhaps the tuna boat was a "Red spy ship."[20] In denying that the ship was within the danger zone, perhaps the Japanese Embassy was attempting to allay any such suspicion.

The Japanese statement also controverted the claim that American doctors had not been given access to the crew:

Dr. John Morton of the Atomic Bomb Casualty Commission examined the Japanese crew members on the 19th of March in Tokyo and on the 20th at Yaizu. Dr. Merrill Eisenbud of the Atomic Energy Commission viewed the affected persons, accompanied by Dr. Morton, on March 25th, in Tokyo, and on the 26th at Yaizu. Their visits included an examination of the injured fisherman both by external observation and by obtaining specimens of their blood and excreta.[21]

Finally, Strauss' implication that the blood counts of the crew were not different from those of the relatively unaffected American weather station personnel is also disputed:

As to the question of the blood counts of the exposed fishermen, information furnished to the American Embassy in Tokyo by the Japanese Government would appear to show that there is little ground to conclude the conditions of the fishermen are not serious, especially when the extraordinary nature of these cases are [sic] taken into consideration.[22]

A declassified memorandum from the American Embassy in Tokyo to the Secretary of State dated March 23 indicates that by that date American doctors had been given only very limited access to the patients and were not allowed to do independent blood counts or urinalysis or to take complete histories. However, a later report from May 5 says that on March 26, American doctors obtained urine from two patients, and on April 1 from five more, but none from the other sixteen. The Japanese Embassy did say that more extensive examinations were not done because of the psychological trauma of the crewmen, and the feeling that, when examined by American doctors, they would be regarded more as experimental subjects than as medical patients.[23]

The American Embassy memorandum dismisses the claim that the men would be treated as "guinea pigs," and attributes this sentiment to sensationalism whipped up by the Japanese press. However, historian Barton C. Hacker, though generally a defender of the actions of American officials and personnel, says that the fears of the fisherman that they would become objects of study by the Americans "may have been closer to the mark than they knew."[24] He quotes the American ambassador John Allison on the possible value of such studies.[25]

What do we make of the immediate responses of American personnel and officials to the events that affected the *Lucky Dragon* and its crew? How did they appear to the Japanese and especially to the victims? Ōishi is not censorious. Rather than point fingers, he lets his story speak for itself. Surely, to most Japanese, the American response appeared cavalier, callous, and unduly suspicious. Strauss' statement, in fact, seems to be a classic instance of bureaucratic obfuscation. Nothing that he said was an outright lie, but the facts were presented to create a misleading impression – the impression that the Castle Bravo test was not as dangerous as it actually was and that it did less damage than it did.

Strauss' characterization of the yield as in the "megaton range" seriously understates the power of the fifteen-megaton blast. Was the test ever "out of control?" When, exactly, is the atmospheric test of a multi-megaton device ever *in* control? What does "control" even mean when it concerns the release of vast energies and huge quantities of radiation? The meaningful question is whether the test significantly exceeded expectations in its yield, destructiveness, and deleterious effects, and it most definitely did. If, on the other hand, those effects were within the expected margin of error, as Strauss indicates, it would seem to imply that the firing crew located in the bunker on Enyu and the sailors, marines, and personnel on the *Curtiss* and other ships were recklessly placed far too close to the blast. In general, when dealing with something as dangerous as a multimegaton explosion, preparations should surely be strongly skewed toward the overly cautious. In fact, as noted previously, the predicted maximum yield for Bravo was eight megatons, and the actual yield nearly doubled that.

Whatever restrictions were placed on American doctors, there seemed to be no basis for the conclusion that the injuries to the crew of the *Lucky Dragon* were light or transitory. Strauss implies that the fishermen were apparently no worse off than the American personnel who had been stationed on Rongerik Atoll to the east of Bikini, and who had also been exposed to fallout. The condition of these twenty-eight servicemen was not deemed serious at the time. However, given the paucity of the information available, as confirmed by the US embassy memorandum cited above, no such comparison was warranted. With respect to the suspicion that the fishermen were spies, which was expressed publicly by Congressman Cole and privately by Strauss, this merely indicates the extent to which the national "red scare" neurosis had gripped even high public officials.

FALLOUT ON THE ISLANDS

Jane Dibblin, in her book *Day of Two Suns*, records the experience of Lemoyo Abo, who was then a fourteen-year-old girl residing on the Island of Rongelap, about 105 miles east of Bikini, on the day of the Bravo test:

I was 14 at the time and my sister was 12. That day our teacher had asked us – my sister and I and my two cousins – to cook rice for the other children. When we saw the bright light and heard a sound – boom – we were really scared. At the time we had no idea what it was. After noon, something powdery fell from the sky. Only later were we told that it was fallout. With Roko and several cousins I went to the end of Rongelap island [sic] to gather some sprouted coconuts. One cousin climbed the tree and got something in her eyes, so we sent another one up. The same thing happened to her. When we went home – ours was the main village on Rongelap – it was raining. We saw something on the leaves, something yellow. Our parents asked us "What's happened to your hair?" It looked like we had rubbed soap powder in it. That night we couldn't sleep our skin itched so much. On our feet were burns, as if from hot water. Our hair fell out. We would look at each other and laugh – you're bald, you look like an old man. But really we were frightened and sad.[26]

John Anjain was an adult who was serving as a magistrate on Rongelap at the time, and this is what he witnessed:

On the morning of the "bomb" I was awake and drinking coffee. I thought I saw what appeared to be the sunrise, but it was in the west. It was truly beautiful with many colors – red, green, and yellow – and I was surprised. A little while later the sun rose in the east. Then some time later something like smoke filled the entire sky and shortly after that a strong and warm wind – as in a typhoon – swept across Rongelap. Then all of the people heard the sound of the explosion. Some people began to cry with fright. Several hours later the powder began to fall on Rongelap. We saw four planes fly overhead, and we thought perhaps the planes had dropped this powder, which covered our island and stuck to our bodies.[27]

The powder, of course, was the same as that that had fallen on the *Lucky Dragon*. It was the highly radioactive residue of the coral that had been blasted into the atmosphere by Castle Bravo.

Anthropologist Holly C. Barker in *Bravo for the Marshallese* records the testimony of Aruko Bobo:

I was living with my parents and some other family members on the islet across the reef from the main island [of Rongelap] ... On that March morning my father woke me while it was still pitch dark to cross the reef with some of my friends to the main island to buy some coffee, flour, and sugar ... Well, we were in the middle of the reef when the whole of the western sky lit up. It seemed like it was afternoon, not early morning. The color went from bright white to deep red and then to a mixture of both with some yellow. We jumped behind big rocks on the reef. We were too afraid to decide whether to run back to the small island or to run across the reef to the main island. It was Hiroshi [a boy in the group] who finally pushed us to run to the main island. Just as we reached the last sandbank, the air around us was split open by an awful noise. I cannot describe what it was like. It felt like the air was alive. We ran the last bit to the island ... That afternoon, I found my hair was covered with a white powder-like substance. It had no smell and no taste when I tried tasting it. Nearly all of the people on Rongelap became violently ill. Most had painful headaches and extreme nausea and diarrhea. By the time of our evacuation ... all the parts of my body that had been exposed that morning blistered and my hair began to fall out in clumps.[28]

Jack Niedenthal's oral history of the people of Bikini, *For the Good of Mankind*, also recounts the events of that day on Rongelap:

three or four hours after the blast the ... white, snow-like ash began to fall from the sky on the 64 people who were living there and also onto the 18 people residing on Ailinginae Atoll [Other sources indicate that Ailinginae was uninhabited and that the eighteen people there at the time of Bravo were from Rongelap and were there on a fishing trip] ... The Rongelapese, not understanding what was happening, watched as two suns rose that morning, observed with amazement as the radioactive dust soon formed a layer on their island two inches deep turning the drinking water to a brackish yellow. Children played in the fallout; their mothers watching in horror as night came and they began to show all the physical signs of exposure. The people experienced severe vomiting and diarrhea, their hair began to fall out, the island fell into a state of terrified panic. The people had received no explanations or warnings whatsoever from the United States government.[29]

One thing that these testimonies make clear is that the Bravo shot took the Marshallese completely by surprise, and it was a terrifying event. They had been given no warning or any information about possible dangers and no advice to prepare for evacuation. A short time later when the first symptoms of radiation sickness began to appear, the islanders had no understanding of the nature or cause of the illness. Their experience was much like that of Europeans of the fourteenth century when they encountered the bubonic plague. It was a terrifying and mysterious malady of unknown cause and with no known cure or treatment.

On March 3, the sixty-four Rongelapese, plus eighteen from Ailinginae, were evacuated to Kwajalein. They suffered itching and burning of the skin and eyes, weakness, fatigue, nausea, hair loss, skin lesions, beta burns (from exposure to beta radiation), and hematological changes.[30] Onboard ship, the decontamination process was distressing and humiliating. Without being told why, people of both sexes and of all ages and relations were required to strip naked and be hosed down by ship's crew. It was strongly against Marshallese custom for women to be seen naked by male relatives.[31]

By early April the white blood cell and platelet counts of the evacuees began to increase, and the acute phase of radiation poisoning appeared to be passing. But damage had been done, damage that would cause various problems sometimes years later. Even Kunkle and Ristvet, though they are largely motivated to correct what they see as hyperbole concerning the culpability of the personnel conducting the Bravo test, admit that it is "beyond doubt" that the Rongelapese, especially the children, suffered medically from their fallout exposure.[32]

Utirik Atoll is much further east of Bikini than Rongelap, and it received a significantly lower, but still dangerous, amount of fallout. Its 157 inhabitants were evacuated on March 4. The Utirik residents were allowed to go home in just three months, though they still had many quite understandable misgivings. They were supplied with food and drinking water and told not to eat or drink from the island.[33] When the supplied food and water ran out, naturally, local sources were used again. Even after suffering from the initial exposure, and after years of eating radioactively tainted food following their return to Utirik, these persons were examined by American medical personnel only once every three years.[34] These facts raise obvious questions: Why were the islands deemed fit for human habitation if no local food or water was to be consumed? Why was it considered sufficient for the inhabitants to have such limited medical monitoring?

The inhabitants of Rongelap had to wait three years before being allowed to go home. Finally, in 1957 they were permitted to return and were told that they could eat anything except the coconut crab. However, they found that all of their traditional foods had changed. One traditional food is the arrowroot, which is a starch similar to tapioca that is obtained from the rhizomes of a local plant. After exposure to the fallout, the arrowroot died or shrank in size, and burned the mouth when consumed.[35] Other foods had changed color, which no doubt made them appear unappetizing and possibly dangerous. When American medical personnel visited in 1961, they told the Rongelapese that the arrowroot had caused the mouth burns because it had been improperly prepared.[36] As Dibblin notes, this is an odd claim since arrowroot is a traditional food of the Marshallese.[37]

In fact, it was only much later revealed that areas of the Rongelap Atoll continued to be as radioactive as Bikini, where no resettlement had been allowed:

It wasn't until 1982 ... that the US Department of Energy released a study, conducted in 1978, which numbered the different islands of Rongelap according to a scale whereby one was the least amount of radioactivity and four was the highest. It showed that certain inhabited parts of Rongelap were still as "hot" as Bikini, on which it was still considered too dangerous to live. Islands on the north of the atoll used by the Rongelapese to gather food – coconut, pandanus, breadfruit, fish, birds, and fresh water in dry times – were numbered four.[38]

After their initial exposure to radiation after Bravo, medical authorities had said that Rongelap's inhabitants should have no further exposure to radiation for at least twelve years.[39] Yet after returning home they continued for many years to live in an environment with significant residual radiation. In the 1970s, the inhabitants of Rongelap became convinced that it was still unhealthy to live there. In 1985, with the help of the organization Greenpeace, they left Rongelap again, and have not returned.

According to Dibblin, in the years following their return to their native islands, the islanders suffered an unusually large number of miscarriages and births of children with severe defects. Some women gave birth to unformed fetuses that were not recognizably human, which midwives referred to as "jellyfish babies."[40] Dibblin states that, "The testimonies of women who gave birth to an unformed fetus or who had suffered repeated miscarriages are too numerous to include them all here."[41] Holly Barker also records testimonies of women who reported severe birth defects.[42] This testimony is from inhabitants of the islands of Ailuk and Likiep, not just the Rongelap and Utirik, the atolls normally considered most severely affected. What about medical statistics to back up these testimonies? These are harder to come by. As Dibblin notes, Marshallese culture is not traditionally literate, and does not compile statistics or conduct studies.

The Brookhaven National Laboratory conducted yearly examinations of the Rongelapese. They divided them into two groups, those who had been present on Rongelap at the time of the fallout and those who had been away from the atoll. The former were classified as the "exposed" group and the latter as "unexposed" (though, as Dibblin notes, the "unexposed" group was exposed to lingering radiation in the soil and food; see Appendix 2).[43] The Brookhaven publication *Medical Survey of Rongelap People Seven Years after Exposure to Fallout* has this to say about the fertility of the Rongelapese:

It was difficult to evaluate the effects on fertility. However, a review of the birth rate of the exposed group over the past 6 years seems to indicate no noticeable effect of their exposure on fertility. The 24 births represent a rate of 48 per 1000 population, compared with 37.3 for the Marshall Islands (1957). The 20 births over a 3-year period for the comparison ["unexposed"] population represent a rate of 62 per 1000 population. A somewhat greater incidence of *miscarriages* and *stillbirths* has been noted in the exposed women, but because of the paucity of vital statistics in the Marshallese and the small number of people involved, the data are not amenable to statistical analysis.[44]

There *appears* to be a discrepancy between the testimonies "too numerous to be included" referred to by Dibblin and the reports of the Brookhaven doctors. However the apparent discrepancy could be due to the fact that Dibblin conducted her interviews in 1986, over thirty years after Bravo, and talked to women not only from Rongelap, but from Utirik and other islands. The above quote from the Brookhaven report was taken from a report just on women from Rongelap, and covered only the period up to seven years after the event. Yet Rongelap was, by far, the atoll that suffered the most severe exposure to fallout, and the expectation would be that problems with fertility would definitely show up in this group if anywhere. An earlier report on the Rongelapese from 1959, noted that in the previous year there had been three miscarriages among women of the exposed population and that each of these had previously had a miscarriage.[45] Out of a population of nineteen women of child-bearing age this sounds like a lot, but as the previous quote noted, doing meaningful statistical analyses with such small numbers is not possible. If the sample size is too small, reliable statistics are hard to obtain.

At any rate, says Dibblin, none of these reports mentions the "jel-lyfish babies" born to the women exposed to Bravo fallout. Dibblin thinks that it is possible that with no interpreter and no female doc-tor with whom to discuss gynecological problems, the Brookhaven doctors may not have been informed about these.[46] Also, Dibblin and Barker report testimonies of birth defects from atolls not covered by the Brookhaven studies. Though strong statistical confirmation of the claims of stillbirths and miscarriages is difficult to obtain from the Brookhaven reports, we cannot dismiss the numerous testimonies cited by Dibblin and Barker of the experiences of the mothers and midwives. As Barker records:

Birth is a very public experience for Marshallese women. Female relatives and care providers come in and out of the birthing area, and frequently the commu-nity will gather nearby to see the baby or hear news after the Baby is born.[47]

Miscarriages and birth defects would therefore have a number of wit-nesses. It seems possible, then, even plausible, that the examinations by the Brookhaven doctors, though thorough, might have underreported some of the medical problems of those exposed to the fallout.

Other health problems, including thyroid tumors, showed up in later years. Dibblin reports:

Years after Bravo was detonated, children and adults began developing thy-roid problems – benign and malignant tumors and under-active thyroids – on Rongelap, Utirik, and other islands in the north of the Marshalls. Indeed, most of those who were children at the time of Bravo have since developed thyroid tumors. Reduced thyroid function can lead to stunted growth in chil-dren and lethargy and depression in adults. Alek Biliet, for example, was exposed when he was six weeks old. His growth stopped suddenly when he was nine, and he is still only 4 ft 7 ins tall. Jilej Antak stopped growing when he was 3 ft 7 ins.[48]

She concludes, "The Rongelapese have suffered damage to their thyroids because of the large quantities of radioactive iodine (iodine 131) pro-duced by Bravo."[49]

Testimony before the US Senate Committee on Energy and Natural Resources in 2005 reinforces these claims:

Cancers, hypothyroidism and thyroid nodules are clearly linked to ionizing radiation exposure. The 2004 NCI [National Cancer Institute] report estimates 530 excess cancers from the USNWTP [US Nuclear Weapons Testing Program] in the RMI [Republic of the Marshall Islands]. Half of the 530 excess cancers have yet to manifest themselves in the Marshall Islands population because of the length of time (latency) it takes for a cancer to manifest itself following the deleterious effects of ionizing radiation.[50]

Kunkle and Ristvet, on the other hand, argue that the general Marshallese population did not suffer thyroid abnormalities due to the Castle tests. They do affirm, however, that the inhabitants of Rongelap were adversely affected, "In contrast to the situation prevailing in the general Marshallese population, the elevated prevalence of palpable thyroid nodules at Rongelap clearly indicates medical harm from the BRAVO fallout contamination."[51]

So, all sides agree that at least some of the Marshallese, particularly the inhabitants of Rongelap and Utirik, experienced significant exposure to fallout from Castle Bravo, and that they consequently suffered serious medical effects from that exposure. The details, however, remain controversial to this day. Exactly how much fallout was deposited by Bravo and the other Castle tests? What was the external and internal exposure to skin and major organs? What adverse long-term effects followed from this exposure? Specifically, how much did exposure to the fallout increase the danger of cancer? How widespread were the adverse health effects of Bravo and the other tests? Were just a few atolls impacted, or many more? Testimony such as that reported by Dibblin and Barker is important and disturbing, but without the supporting hard data there is a danger that such testimony will be dismissed as anecdotal.

As stated in the Introduction, in this work we cannot satisfactorily address all of the complex claims and counterclaims that still roil about the incidents in the Marshall Islands in 1954. There are many issues and their answers will often involve many scientific and medical details. However, to indicate answers to some of the questions, answers that are as accurate and precise as possible, we turn to the authoritative article "Radiation Doses in the Marshall Islands Associated with Exposure to Radioactive Fallout from Bikini and Enewetak Nuclear Weapons Test: Summary," authored by Steven L. Simon and co-authors. This article was published along with supporting articles in a special issue of the journal *Health*

Physics.[52] These authors report the results of an extensive study of the highly exposed Marshallese from the Rongelap, Utirik, and Ailinginae atolls conducted by the Division of Cancer Epidemiology and Genetics of the National Cancer Institute. This study draws upon data going back to tests and measurements taken right after Bravo. The following several paragraphs summarize the major conclusions and findings.

The nuclear tests in the Marshall Islands created sixty-three different radionuclides, radioactive isotopes, which, with plutonium 239 and plutonium 240 were deposited in detectable quantities.[53] A map and table accompanying the article follows the deposition of one radionuclide, cesium 137, over the Marshalls. The density of the deposition increases from south to north, with Rongelap and Utirik receiving the most of any inhabited atolls. The northern part of Rongelap received even more than the southern part. Naturally, the radiation doses and the cancer risks of the inhabitants correlated with the greater deposition.[54].

The crucial question is the actual dosage absorbed by the inhabitants of the affected islands. There were three sources of exposure:

(1) external irradiation from fallout deposited on the ground; (2) internal irradiation from acute radionuclide intakes immediately or soon after deposition of fallout from each test; and (3) internal irradiation from chronic intakes of radionuclides resulting from the continuous presence of long-lived radionuclides in the environment.[55]

In other words, there were both "acute" and "chronic" exposures, that is, exposure from fallout deposited immediately after Bravo, and long-term irradiation that occurred after the inhabitants had returned to their islands.

External irradiation was due to gamma rays absorbed from outside the body while internal irradiation occurred when radioactive material was ingested in food and water. Internal radiation absorbed doses were estimated with respect to four specific organs or tissues: the thyroid gland, the red bone marrow (RBM), the stomach wall and the colon wall. The focus was on these tissues because they were expected to produce the most cancers for these reasons:

• The thyroid gland, far more than any other organ, concentrates radio-iodine (radioactive isotopes of iodine), which is amply produced by detonations of nuclear weapons.
• Irradiation of the blood-forming cells of the RBM was caused mainly by external exposure to gamma-emitting radionuclides but also by internal

exposure to radiostrontiums (radioactive isotopes of strontium), and would be expected to have increased the risk of leukemia which has shown an especially strong relationship with radiation exposure in many epidemiologic studies ...

- The colon and stomach walls can be highly exposed after ingestion of fallout because many of the radionuclides produced by nuclear fission are highly insoluble, even in the gastrointestinal tract, thereby irradiating the stomach and colon as they pass through.[56]

By comparing the best estimates of the radiation doses of three different groups of representative adults, it can be seen how much more affected were the residents of Rongelap, than those living on the southern atoll Majuro or the middle-latitude atoll Kwajalein. The best estimates of cumulative internal and external dose in milligrays (see Appendix 2 for explanation) for Majuro residents (south), Kwajalein residents (mid-latitude) and Rongelap community (northern) is as follows[57]:

	Majuro	Kwajalein	Rongelap
Total internal thyroid	23	67	7,600
Total internal RBM	1.1	2.0	42
Total internal stomach wall	1.1	2.4	540
Total internal colon	5.4	14	2,800
External dose	9.8	22	1,600

Behind these dry statistics we see shocking evidence of how doses increased from Majuro, the farthest from Castle Bravo, to Rongelap, the closest.

Most relevant for us are the health effects, particularly cancers attributable to radiation exposure. The authors list the Lifetime Attributable Fraction, that is, the projected percentage of total lifetime cancers attributable to radiation exposure for leukemia, thyroid, stomach, colon, and all other solid cancers for inhabitants of different geographical groups. In each case, the projected percentage of cancers attributable to radiation exposure increases in correlation with increased exposure, with, by far, the highest percentages among the Rongelapese with respect to each kind of cancer. Yet even among the inhabitants of the southern and mid-latitude atolls some percentage of their expected cancers is attributable to radiation exposure.[58]

Of particular note is the projected effect of these doses on thyroid cancers. Simon and his colleagues calculate that 12 percent of projected thyroid cancers are attributable to radiation exposures for inhabitants of the southern atolls; 25 percent for inhabitants of the mid-latitude atolls; 71 percent for the Utirik community; and 95 percent for the Rongelap and Ailinginae communities. For the entire Marshall Islands, 21 percent of thyroid cancers of those exposed to radiation from the tests are attributable to such exposure. There is, then, no question that Castle Bravo, and to a lesser extent other tests, caused serious and long-term harm to the health and well-being of all these people, and not just the residents of the atolls most severely affected. Even inhabitants of the southern and mid-latitude islands suffered cancer-inducing radiation exposure.[59]

QUESTIONS ABOUT THE EVACUATIONS

The rain of fallout on the inhabited atolls east of Bikini was genuinely unanticipated. Planners trusted their meteorologists to give them accurate information about the expected direction of the fallout. Merrill Eisenbud reports that General P. W. Clarkson, Commander of Task Force Seven, was advised to prepare plans for evacuation of the natives, but replied that the devices would not be fired unless they were sure that the tests would be safe.[60] In fact, there were plans for evacuation, but they do not appear to have been designed for maximum speed or efficiency. For instance, there were no ships specifically dedicated for the evacuation of natives.[61] Rather, task force warships had to be diverted from their regular patrols and sent to conduct the rescues, a process that took several extra hours when time was of the essence.

The order to evacuate Rongelap and Ailinginae was given at 1:40 p.m. on March 2, when reports were received confirming dangerous radiation levels on both islands.[62] In other words, evacuation *began* only when the radiation levels were already dangerous, and had been so for some time. Why, then, were the people on Rongelap and Utirik not evacuated sooner? Within hours of the blast it was known that heavy fallout had reached the firing team's headquarters on Enyu and the deck of the *Curtiss*. This already showed that the fallout was not following the predicted pattern. By the morning of March 2, it was known that dangerous levels of fallout had reached Rongerik Atoll, east of Rongelap and farther from the Bravo blast and evacuation of the twenty-eight weather station personnel was begun.[63] Why were the Rongelap islanders not evacuated until March 3?

Dibblin notes that earlier evacuation would have permitted quicker decontamination and would have mitigated some of the effects of the radiation exposure. She asks why evacuation was not begun as soon as it was known that the inhabited islands were in the path of the fallout and makes a serious charge:

Not far from Rongelap, U.S. Navy ships were monitoring the intensity of the radiation. They were not instructed to rescue the Rongelap people; indeed the task force command ordered them to sail away from the area. It was two days before the Navy arrived to pick up the Rongelap islanders ... two days in which they breathed, slept, and ate the fallout.[64]

Clearly, quick action is required when people are being exposed to radiation. Why the apparent delay in evacuating the Islanders? The answer, as reported by Kunkle and Ristvet, seems to be a complicated mixture of snafus, miscommunication, conflicting information, and misjudgment rather than any callousness or unconcern on the part of the task force.[65] They do apparently agree that the task force command should have inferred the need for the evacuation sooner; they indicate that by 9:00 p.m. on March 1 the available information justified such a decision.[66] They suggest, though, that there was still uncertainty about the urgency of the need to evacuate.[67]

However, given the potentially dire effects of radiation exposure, the very uncertainty of the information makes it hard to justify any delay or any lack of urgency. When it is a matter of human beings potentially exposed to dangerous levels of radioactive fallout, prompt action is warranted, even action that in other circumstances would seem precipitate. Some situations demand a surfeit of caution. Again we have to ask why action was not based on worst-case projections. As soon as Dr. John C. Clark, head of the Bravo firing team, concluded that they were getting fallout, he sealed himself and his men in their bunker and sought immediate evacuation. When fallout began to rain down on the *Curtiss*, the sailors and marines onboard were immediately sequestered below decks. It is legitimate to ask whether equally expeditious action could have been taken to evacuate the Marshallese.

Professor Kim Skoog of the University of Guam reinforces these points:

If safety precautions were made to protect the people in the light of the anticipated "worst-case scenarios" predicted by some scientists over the years, then a great deal of the collateral damage that has so adversely affected so many people's lives could have been avoided or at least greatly minimized. Instead, the U.S. policy-making efforts followed a "learn as we go along" attitude, taking moderate precautions that countered only what was collectively recognized as indisputable dangers that would be inflicted on the inhabitants of the two islands used in the bombing if they were not moved far enough from the test sites.[68]

The upshot is that the Commander and personnel of the task force acted conscientiously, if sometimes too slowly, within the context of established procedures. Likewise, those personnel specifically charged with maintaining radiological safety apparently took their jobs seriously and discharged their duties competently. The disaster of Bravo was not due to the failures of the onsite people to perform diligently and competently within the confines of the established precautions. The problem was that those precautions seem to have been designed more to react to problems as they arose rather than to take aggressive measures to make sure the problems did not occur.

Practically speaking, what more effective precautions could have been taken? Obviously, the tests could have been canceled. However, the thermonuclear tests were regarded as a geopolitical necessity, a matter of survival, in fact, not just for the nation but perhaps for humanity. The testing of thermonuclear weapons would go forward.

A second option would have been to relocate the tests to an even more remote and uninhabited locale. In fact, this was done with the removal of testing to Johnston Island in 1958. Certainly, the tests, including the multimegaton tests, could have all been held at Eniwetok, which was nearly 200 miles west of Bikini, and so that much farther from the populated Islands of Rongelap and Utirik. Of course, there would have been inconveniences, as we have noted, but these would have been found manageable had the people at the top made the safety of the indigenous population a higher priority.

Could the Castle tests have been moved underground, thus preventing fallout? But the science of underground testing was still at a very rudimentary stage even two years later, and when you are in an arms race you cannot afford delay.[69] Given the perceived urgency of the situation, and the need to develop thermonuclear weapons as rapidly as possible, at that time atmospheric testing was the only feasible option. Further, with the acceptance of the theory of stratospheric trapping, the planners believed that with careful meteorological protocols, the distribution of fallout could be controlled.

At the very least, the inhabitants of the populated atolls could have been told ahead of time to prepare for a possible evacuation that could occur at any time, day or night. Everyone could have been warned that they might see a brilliant flash and hear a stupendous noise at which point they should go indoors and await either the all-clear or notice to begin evacuation. Ships specifically designated for the evacuations could have stood by ready to act. Evacuations could have been ordered as soon as it was clear (late on March 1) that fallout was occurring in the direction of the inhabited atolls. These precautions would not have prevented all exposure, but it certainly could have been minimized.

Another victim of Bravo was not a person but an idea – the idea that such events can be controlled. On the contrary, in unleashing the primal power of the atom on the surface of the earth, we have created something that is too strong for us, something which, despite assiduous preparations, we cannot control. It is another episode of the ancient Promethean story, the mythos put into classic modern form by Mary Shelly's *Frankenstein*. In Shelly's tale, the fear of death motivates a scientist to discover how dead flesh can be reanimated, and so a creature is made that eventually destroys its creator.

Fear also was the driver in the development of nuclear weapons, first the fear of Nazi Germany, and then the fear of Soviet Russia. Some fears are rational and some are not, but in either case fear is such an urgently and powerfully compelling emotion that the fearful are driven to do whatever they think will relieve it. The problem is that fear interferes with the ability to think clearly, yet clear thinking is the one thing most needed in a fearful situation. When intractable fear is combined with vast powers of destruction and an illusion of control, bad things can happen.

NOTES

1 Simon et al., "Radiation Doses and Cancer Risks ..." p. 5.
2 Ōishi, *The Day the Sun Rose in the West*, pp. 25, 27.
3 Ōishi, *The Day the Sun Rose in the West*, p. 27.
4 Ōishi, *The Day the Sun Rose in the West*, pp. 27–28.
5 Ōishi, *The Day the Sun Rose in the West*, pp. 27–28.
6 Ōishi, *The Day the Sun Rose in the West*, p. 37.
7 Ōishi, *The Day the Sun Rose in the West*, p. 43.
8 Ōishi, *The Day the Sun Rose in the West*, p. 46.
9 Ōishi, *The Day the Sun Rose in the West*, p. 76.
10 Ōishi, *The Day the Sun Rose in the West*, p. 78.
11 Kunkle and Ristvet, *Castle Bravo*, p. 129.
12 Ōishi, *The Day the Sun Rose in the West*, p. 27.
13 Ōishi, *The Day the Sun Rose in the West*, p. 35.
14 "Race for the Superbomb" website, "Lewis Strauss's Complete Statement ..."
15 "Race for the Superbomb" website, "Lewis Strauss's Complete Statement ..."
16 "Race for the Superbomb" website, "Lewis Strauss's Complete Statement ..."
17 "Race for the Superbomb" website, "Lewis Strauss's Complete Statement ..."
18 "Race for the Superbomb" website, "Lewis Strauss's Complete Statement ..."
19 Kunkle and Ristvet, *Castle Bravo*, p. 88.
20 Rhodes, *Dark Sun*, p. 542.

21   "Race for the Superbomb" website, "Lewis Strauss's Complete Statement ..."
22   "Race for the Superbomb" website, "Lewis Strauss's Complete Statement ..."
23   The Nuclear Vault website.
24   Hacker, *Elements of Controversy*, p. 151.
25   Hacker, *Elements of Controversy*, p. 151.
26   Dibblin, *Day of Two Suns*, pp. 24–25.
27   Dibblin, *Day of Two Suns*, p. 25.
28   Barker, *Bravo for the Marshallese*, p. 51.
29   Niedenthal, *For the Good of all Mankind*, p. 6.
30   Kunkle and Ristvet, *Castle Bravo*, p. 119; Dibblin, *Day of Two Suns*, p. 26.
31   Barker, *Bravo for the Marshallese*, p. 53.
32   Kunkle and Ristvet, *Castle Bravo*, p. 120.
33   Dibblin, *Day of Two Suns*, p. 30.
34   Dibblin, *Day of Two Suns*, p. 31.
35   Dibblin, *Day of Two Suns*, pp. 30–33.
36   Conard et al., "Medical Survey of Rongelap People Seven Years after Exposure," p. 7.
37   Dibblin, *Day of Two Suns*, p. 30.
38   Dibblin, *Day of Two Suns*, p. 34.
39   Barker, *Bravo for the Marshallese*, p. 65.
40   Dibblin, *Day of Two Suns*, pp. 36, 37.
41   Dibblin, *Day of Two Suns*, p. 37.
42   Barker, *Bravo for the Marshallese*, pp. 53–55.
43   Dibblin, *Day of Two Suns*, p. 31.
44   Conard et al., "Medical Survey of Rongelap People Seven Years after Exposure," p. 3; emphasis in original.
45   Conard et al., "Medical Survey of Rongelap People Four Years after Exposure," p. 9.
46   Dibblin, *Day of Two Suns*, p. 40.
47   Barker, *Bravo for the Marshallese*, p. 106.
48   Dibblin, *Day of Two Suns*, p. 43.
49   Dibblin, *Day of Two Suns*, p. 45.
50   Palafox, "Testimony before the U.S. Senate Committee on Energy and Natural Resources," p. 2.
51   Kunkle and Ristvet, *Castle Bravo*, pp. 149–152.
52   Simon et al., "Radiation Doses and Cancer Risks," pp. 1–38 (page references here are from the article as made available online by NIH Public Access).
53   Simon, et al. "Radiation Doses and Cancer Risks," pp.1, 27–28.
54   Simon et al., "Radiation Doses and Cancer Risks," p. 8.
55   Simon et al., "Radiation Doses and Cancer Risks," pp. 8–9.
56   Simon et al., "Radiation Doses and Cancer Risks," p. 6.
57   Modified from table 6, Simon et al., "Radiation Doses and Cancer Risks," p. 31.
58   Simon et al., "Radiation Doses and Cancer Risks," p. 38.
59   Simon *et al.*, "Radiation Doses and Cancer Risks," p. 38.
60   Eisenbud, "Monitoring Distant Fallout," p. 24.
61   Kunkle and Ristvet, *Castle Bravo*, p. 114.

62 Kunkle and Ristvet, *Castle Bravo*, p. 114.
63 Kunkle and Ristvet, *Castle Bravo*, p. 114.
64 Dibblin, *Day of Two Suns*, p. 26.
65 Kunkle and Ristvet, *Castle Bravo*, pp. 107–115.
66 Kunkle and Ristvet, *Castle Bravo*, p. 111.
67 Kunkle and Ristvet, *Castle Bravo*, p. 111.
68 Skoog, "U.S. Nuclear Testing on the Marshall Islands," p. 74.
69 Brownlee, Robert R. "Learning to Contain Underground Nuclear Explosions."

5

Monsters and Movements

The Cultural "Fallout" of Nuclear Testing

In the 1950s, American moviegoers consumed a steady diet of films featuring marauding aliens, mutants, and monsters. In features such as *Them*; *The Amazing Colossal Man*; *The Incredible Shrinking Man*; *Godzilla*; *The Blob*; *Beast from 20,000 Fathoms*; *The Giant Behemoth*; and *It Came from Beneath the Sea*, movie studios conjured an endless variety of beasts, bugs, and blobs to titillate and horrify drive-in movie patrons. These films, often produced on a shoestring budget, frequently had special effects that would appear comical in comparison to today's CGI effects. Some were terrible films, instantly forgettable. Others, such as *Them*, had intelligent scripts, a good cast, and were effectively frightening.

A prominent theme of these films is that the monster is an unintended effect of nuclear weapons testing. Often, also, the creature itself is radioactive. In *Them*, filmed in 1954, lingering radiation from the 1945 Trinity test has produced a horde of monstrous killer ants in the New Mexico desert. The monster in *Beast from 20,000 Fathoms* (1953) is a giant dinosaur that has been in suspended animation in the arctic for 100 million years until awakened by a nuclear test. Both the uncontrolled growth of the colossal man and the opposite problem of the shrinking one were due to exposure to radiation from nuclear tests. Godzilla, the most famous of the fifties movie monsters, not only is aroused by nuclear testing, but is himself intensely radioactive and can project nuclear fire from his throat. So pervasive was the nuclear theme in the science fiction films of the era that it was obvious to any reflective moviegoer that the cinematic monsters were visible representations of a deeper fear. The hydrogen bomb was the real monster loose in the world.

In this chapter we look at some of the cultural "fallout" from Castle Bravo and atmospheric nuclear testing in general. Why is this important? Why is it an integral part of the story? An event like Bravo is significant not just because of its scientific results or its physical effects, but because it helps to define an era. Some events seem to focus the fears of an age, and, as such, they sear themselves into the collective consciousness and change how people see and think. The nuclear tests of the 1950s were such events, and Bravo was the biggest and scariest of them. Americans wanted to believe the official line that constant preparation and vigilance would keep them safe, and so they supported films like *Strategic Air Command* (1955) that inculcated that message. However, they also flocked to the lower-budget science fiction films with the assorted nasty Atomic Age creatures. Clearly, despite official reassurances, they feared that nuclear testing would spawn something monstrous.

Perhaps the most profound lesson of the nuclear tests in the Marshall Islands is that isolation is an illusion and that the modern world is deeply connected at many different levels. The Marshalls were chosen as the site of the Pacific Proving Ground because of their remoteness. The hope was to limit the physical effects of the tests to a particular area and, by means of military security and an exclusion zone, also to restrict public awareness of the tests. Antitesting activism was already becoming troublesome, and the AEC, ever sensitive to public relations issues, wanted to control the flow of information about the tests. Remoteness served that aim.

However, by the 1950s, no place on earth was truly remote. Efforts at both sorts of control failed. The Pacific tests, and Castle Bravo in particular, had unexpected effects that propagated through the natural and cultural worlds. Who would have expected that radioactive isotopes from the tests would show up in the milk of dairy cows in the Midwest?[1] Who would have thought that the tests would strike a chord in the popular imagination and inspire moviemakers to terrify drive-in moviegoers? Who would have expected the tests to motivate a world-famous philosopher to devote the remainder of his life to antinuclear activism? In a world that is intricately connected, both ecologically and electronically, the idea that big, dangerous things can be controlled and isolated is an illusion.

The cultural consequences of nuclear testing are therefore essential to the story. Popular culture often reflects the anxieties and obsessions of an age with great vividness, as historian Paul Boyer documented in his remarkable study *By the Bomb's Early Light*. Boyer examined multifarious sources, from serious books and intellectual essays to cartoons and song lyrics. He showed in great detail how deeply the bomb had penetrated into every niche of public consciousness. This chapter does the same sort of thing, though, of course, on a much smaller scale.

If we want to know how people felt in the era of nuclear testing, it is highly instructive to look at the movies they watched. We begin by looking at two films, one American, and one Japanese. Both films were released in the immediate aftermath of Castle Bravo and the irradiation of the *Lucky Dragon*. The films are *Strategic Air Command*, mentioned above, and *Gojira* (1954), the original Japanese film released in America as *Godzilla*. The original Japanese version became widely available only in recent years, and was recognized by critics as far superior to the highly altered version made available to American audiences.

Why focus on these two films? Because they show that by 1955 thinking about nuclear weapons was hardening into the dualism of abolition vs. deterrence. In the years immediately following Hiroshima, the shock of the bomb had provoked several imaginative schemes for dealing with the nuclear threat.[2] A movement for one-world government had gotten a remarkable amount of traction, even with the general public. Atomic scientists campaigned for the international control of nuclear weapons. In those early days, there was still hope that an arms race might be avoided. By 1950 the Cold War and the arms race were in full swing and those earlier schemes had come to seem hopelessly idealistic. As Boyer notes, the national mood shifted from obsessive worry about the horrors of the bomb to an uneasy acceptance of the arms race and the goal of maintaining superiority over the Soviets.[3] However, anxieties increased dramatically once again with the Bikini tests of 1954.[4]

The international opposition that arose after Bravo took the form of antitesting and nuclear disarmament movements. Ban-the-bomb protests and marches became a fixture of the age and calls to end testing became prominent in the media. In response, Cold Warriors doubled down and insisted that deterrence, which required bomb development and hence testing, was the only means of preventing nuclear war, short of abject surrender to the Soviets. These two films vividly portray these clashing positions. The view expressed in *Gojira*, a view strongly motivated by the Castle Bravo test, was that nuclear weapons are intrinsically and irremediably evil; they are genocidal devices and nothing could justify their continued existence. The abolition of nuclear weapons is the *only* rational and moral goal. The message of *Strategic Air Command* was that nuclear weapons were an unavoidable fact of twentieth-century life and that, since there were no practical means for their elimination, the only feasible course was to deter their use by constant military preparedness.

The news about the Bravo test and its unfortunate consequences got the attention of politically active intellectuals. One of the best known of these was the philosopher Bertrand Russell, whose energy and eloquence, undimmed by his eighty-plus years, put him at the center of the burgeoning antinuclear movement. In addition to numerous writings, he helped found the Campaign for Nuclear Disarmament (CND), perhaps the foremost of the activist organizations. The CND staged marches, mass rallies, and protests that brought much media attention to the antinuclear movement. Russell was himself in the front lines of the protests, committing acts of civil disobedience when he was nearly ninety.

The antinuclear movement was not the only sort of activism prompted by the nuclear tests. A recent article from the *Bulletin of the Atomic Scientists* argues that the rise of the modern environmental movement was linked to Castle Bravo.[5] We will trace some of these movements that grew in reaction to nuclear testing, focusing mainly on Russell, the most famous and most eloquent of the antinuclear activists.

Unquestionably, the most dangerous aspect of atmospheric nuclear testing was that it was part of the accelerating arms race between the United States and the Soviet Union. The nuclear tests were scientific experiments, but they were also more than that. Testing was a public demonstration to the Soviets that America was committed – and in no half-hearted way – to the maintenance of technological superiority in the development of nuclear weapons and their means of delivery. Persistence in testing, even in the face of growing international opposition, would certainly send a message of American resolve.

However, it is one thing to send a message and quite another to control how it is received. Far from being intimidated by American success in developing thermonuclear weapons, the Russians forged rapidly ahead to develop their own, exploding their first "true" thermonuclear bomb in 1955. This test bore disturbing similarities to Castle Bravo.

TWO FILMS

In 1955 Hollywood had no bigger star than James Maitland (Jimmy) Stewart. Just the previous year he had played opposite Grace Kelly in Alfred Hitchcock's classic *Rear Window* and his films of that year were the highest grossing of any actor's. *Strategic Air Command* was one of several films Stewart made with leading director Anthony Mann.

Stewart's co-star was June Allyson, whom he had worked with before in the films *The Glenn Miller Story* and *The Stratton Story*. Allyson's wholesome image and Stewart's familiar drawl gave their characters a comfortable and likable presence that more exotic and glamorous actors could not achieve. The supporting cast was strong, with Frank Lovejoy as a cigar-chomping, hard-nosed simulacrum of General Curtis Le May, the actual commander of SAC. Accompanied by an appropriately soaring musical score by Victor Young, the movie was filmed in a widescreen "Vista-Vision" format that made the flying scenes even more spectacular. *Strategic Air Command* was released on March 25, 1955, slightly more than a year after Castle Bravo.

In the movie Stewart plays the part of Robert "Dutch" Holland, a professional baseball player who is also an officer in the Air Force Reserve. He is recalled to active duty and is assigned to fly the Air Force's strategic bomber, the B-36 "Peacemaker." Dutch's wife Sally, played by Allyson, is forced to cope with the disruptions of life due to Dutch's unpredictable absences when his aircraft is put on alert and he has to be away on patrols for days on end. On a flight to Greenland, an engine catches fire and then the entire left wing and Dutch is forced to crash land, injuring his arm. Despite his injury, he decides to remain in the Air Force even after his twenty-one-month period of active duty has expired, much to Sally's chagrin. He is next assigned to fly the new bomber, the B-47 Stratojet. However, while attempting to land in worsening weather, he finds his injury does not permit him to operate some of the controls, requiring him to depend on his co-pilot. With the injury, Dutch's days in the Air Force are over, and, unfortunately, so is his career as a baseball player. However, as the film ends he looks forward to a possible new career as a team manager.

Actually, the real star of the film is the B-36 bomber. There are many dazzling flying scenes, and the B-36 was a very impressive aircraft. Mainly, it was enormous, with a wingspan of 230 feet, a length of 169 feet, one inch, and four bomb bays that could accommodate a maximum payload of up to 86,000 pounds.[6] As mentioned in the last chapter, the B-36 was the only American bomber that could accommodate the twenty-one-ton Mark 17/24, the first operational hydrogen bomb. In addition to its stupendous size, the B-36 was also unusual in that it was a hybrid that was both propeller and jet powered. The six huge piston engines generated 3,800 horsepower each, and the twin turbojets were housed in pods, one pod on each wing. With all ten engines running full-blast, the B-36 could attain a maximum speed of 411 mph. That speed would have been most impressive in the Second World War, but by the mid-1950s, in an era of jet fighters, this was far too slow. The plane would have been easy meat for the Russian MiG fighters. Still, with its great range of 6,795 miles and its huge payload, it had to serve as the United States' main strategic bomber until the B-52 Stratofortress could be introduced.

Strategic Air Command was made with the full cooperation of the Air Force, and it is easy to see why. The movie is a frank glorification of SAC and its people and planes. There is no hint of irony or the gallows humor of Stanley Kubrick's *Doctor Strangelove* released nine years later in 1964. The message of the film is clear, and is stated explicitly and repeatedly to make sure that it is not missed: In the nuclear age, to maintain peace, a state of constant combat readiness must be maintained, as if on a wartime footing. The only way to prevent a nuclear attack is to always be prepared to launch one. In the film on several occasions a character will complain that too many sacrifices are being demanded given that it is peacetime. The answer is always tantamount to "We are not really at peace; wartime readiness must be maintained." The message is unequivocal that careers and family life may have to be disrupted, and even personal injury suffered, to serve the higher purpose of maintaining a credible deterrent.

The movie also employs subtler means of getting its message across. There are many scenes of bombers flying into glorious sunsets, over snow-capped mountains, or through ethereal wisps of cloud. The bombers themselves are portrayed as icons of strength and beauty. Interestingly, the hydrogen bomb is never named and is mentioned only obliquely. At one point in a briefing reference is made to a "new weapon" with more destructive capability than the entire fleet of B-29's deployed in the Pacific Theater in the Second World War.

The dangers of radioactivity or fallout are not mentioned. One character says that, just as in the Second World War, it is all about getting a bomb on a target. The implication seems to be that nuclear weapons differ from the conventional weapons of previous wars only by being bigger. There is no indication that nuclear war would be a cataclysm far greater than any war fought with conventional weapons, or that the lingering effects of radiation would be felt for generations. Nevertheless, the assumption throughout the film was that America faced a danger of such magnitude that the nuclear deterrent had to be kept in a state of constant readiness, primed for use at any moment.

The film therefore seems to be somewhat at odds with itself. It wants to frighten moviegoers but not too much. Actually, such mixed messages were common at the time. For instance, the Civil Defense authorities wanted you to be frightened enough to build a fallout shelter but not so frightened that you saw no point in taking precautions, so nuclear war was depicted as scary but survivable. Moderate fear can be a stimulus to action, but excessive fear can lead to despair, and the film was meant to promote vigilance, not apathy.

In short, the theme of *Strategic Air Command* is that in the nuclear age preparedness is the essential means of preventing nuclear attack and that personal sacrifice on the part of ordinary citizens may be required. Nevertheless, those who fly in the bombers are brave men involved in a great adventure, and their faithful, self-sacrificing wives are brave women. After viewing *Strategic Air Command*, it is easier to understand the attitudes behind the remarks that AEC chairman Lewis Strauss made after Castle Bravo. The development of thermonuclear weapons and the means to deliver them anywhere at any time was a goal of overriding urgency, a priority that demanded considerable sacrifice from the American people. Americans understandably felt that, having helped deliver the world from monstrous evil in the Second World War, they now deserved the prosperity that was the reward of their sacrifice. News that more sacrifices might be required was unwelcome. However, if Americans were to be asked to endure more pain and inconvenience, then surely the incidental suffering of a few non-Americans who happened to be in harm's way, while regrettable, was a risk that had to be run. Survival was the imperative that trumped every other concern.

Strategic Air Command and *Gojira* are very different films that presented two very different perspectives on the new reality that nuclear weapons had imposed on the world. The American perspective – at least the officially approved one – was that nuclear weapons, and, concomitantly, their development and testing, are unavoidable evils. No practical plan had ever been offered for the mutual elimination of nuclear weapons, and unilateral disarmament was out of the question. Apparently, there was nothing for it but for Americans to grit their teeth, endure the anxiety and sacrifice demanded by the Cold War, and hope that someday, before Armageddon, an alternative would arise. In the meantime, incidents like the *Lucky Dragon* and the irradiation of the Marshallese were most unfortunate events and to be prevented whenever possible. However, if, despite precautions, such events did occasionally occur, nuclear testing and the arms race had to continue.

There is nothing in *Gojira* that directly contradicts the above arguments. The film does demand that we see the human face and the appalling reality of mass destruction. It is far too easy for those who wield great power to obscure the face of raw suffering with a mass of generalities and abstractions. *Gojira* confronts us with the monstrous reality made visible.

Godzilla has long been one of the icons of pop culture. Many American children grew up watching scenes of rubbery monsters fighting slapstick battles in a miniaturized Japanese landscape. The human characters in these movies had corny lines comically delivered in highly accented and badly dubbed English. Given the kitschy associations of Godzilla, it is hard to realize that the original Japanese film, *Gojira*, was a well-crafted piece of cinema, perhaps not a great film but certainly a good and important one. The original version was not readily available in the United States until 2004, fifty years after its release in Japan. The film that was originally shown to American audiences as *Godzilla* (1956) was a highly adulterated version. Scenes with American actor Raymond Burr – which were unconnected with the original plot or characters – were spliced into the Japanese film, producing a clumsy pastiche that greatly diminished the quality of the original.

Gojira was released in Japan on November 3, 1954, almost exactly eight months after the irradiation of the *Lucky Dragon*.[7] The opening scene of the movie is an unmistakable reference to the fate of the *Lucky Dragon* and its crew. Somewhere in the Pacific, a small freighter is placidly going about its business when suddenly the sea boils white-hot. The crew rushes to see what is happening and is struck by a blinding flash of light. The ship then bursts into flame. The connection between the theme of *Gojira* and the events of the nuclear age was made explicit by the film's producer, Tomoyuki Tanaka, "The theme of the film, from the beginning, was the terror of the Bomb. Mankind had created the Bomb, and now nature was going to take revenge on Mankind."[8]

According to Steve Ryfle, whose informative essay "Godzilla's Footprint" is included with the Classic Media release of the Japanese original, it was during the time of the media hubbub about the *Lucky Dragon* that Tanaka, an employee of the Toho Motion Picture Company, got the idea of making Japan's first movie featuring a giant monster.[9] Tanaka approached his boss Iwao Mori with the idea of a movie about a monster that wreaks havoc after having been awakened by a nuclear test. This had been the theme of *Beast from 20,000 Fathoms*, which had made a lot of money for Warner Brothers the previous year.

Chosen to direct the film was Ishiro Honda, a student and friend of famed director Akira Kurosawa. Honda had seen the devastation of Hiroshima firsthand, and the images of mass destruction in the film were taken from his wartime experience.[10] Honda decided that Godzilla should be a visual representation of the terror and mystery of nuclear weapons:

for Honda, Godzilla was not a metaphor for the bomb, but a physical manifestation of it … After the war, all of Japan, as well as Tokyo, was left in ashes. The atomic bomb had emerged and had completely destroyed Hiroshima. If Godzilla had been a dinosaur or some other animal, he would have been killed by just one cannonball. But if he were equal to an atomic bomb, we would not know what to do. So I took the characteristics of an atomic bomb and applied them to Godzilla.[11]

In the 1950s, state-of-the art special effects were created by the laborious process of stop-motion animation, as perfected by masters like Ray Harryhausen and Willis O'Brien. Such animation is achieved with scale models that are painstakingly posed and moved just slightly from one frame to the next, as with regular pen-and-ink animation. The result, if done skillfully, is a very natural and lifelike movement when the film is shown at the usual rate of twenty-four frames per second. Classic monsters such as King Kong, the Ymir from *20 Million Miles to Earth*, and the rampaging Rhedosaurus from *Beast from 20,000 Fathoms* were top-notch stop-motion creatures.

Godzilla could not be a stop-motion monster. The stop-motion process is very slow, and Eiji Tsuburaya, special effects designer for *Gojira*, was given only three months to complete filming.[12] Consequently, the creature would have to be played by a stuntman in a monster suit. First, though, what would Godzilla look like? The name "Gojira" comes from the Japanese words for gorilla and whale, so the initial concept was some sort of whale/gorilla hybrid. Most fortunately, Tanaka decided that Godzilla would instead be a dinosaur-like creature. Though he could not use the preferred stop-motion method, the classic beast Tsuburaya created was an impressively monstrous entity that combined the anatomical features of various dinosaurs and depicted them on a much larger scale.

Of course, Godzilla is imagined as far larger than any actual flesh-and-blood creature could be. The largest actual land-dwelling animals, the sauropod dinosaurs such as *Brachiosaurus* and *Diplodocus*, were stupendous, but only a fraction of Godzilla's mass. Any actual creature of that size would be crushed under its own weight as soon as it tried to set foot on land. Further, Godzilla is impervious to conventional weapons of any magnitude, absorbing blows that would sink a battleship. Again, though, Godzilla is not conceived as a biological entity, but as the visual manifestation of a nuclear weapon. To do justice to such a concept, the monster had to be enormous and unstoppable.

The climax of *Gojira* is a thirteen-minute nocturnal assault on Tokyo that leaves much of the city a flaming ruin. Neither shellfire nor high-tension electrical wires can stop the rampaging beast. Like a nuclear weapon that destroys with both blast and heat, Godzilla tears down buildings with his immense strength and incinerates the rest with flaming breath that melts steel. The scene is riveting and horrifying, with panicked crowds struggling to escape and authorities watching helplessly as the city is destroyed. Finally, jet squadrons appear and unleash a furious rocket attack, and Godzilla retreats to the depths of Tokyo Bay. Once the monster is gone, we see the horrific destruction of life and property he has caused. These scenes are clearly reminiscent of the damage caused to Japan in the Second World War, particularly the devastation of Hiroshima and Nagasaki.

Godzilla is finally killed by a Japanese scientist who has devised his own weapon of mass destruction, a device that can destroy all of the oxygen in water, which has the effect of skeletonizing any animal in the vicinity. At first, he is reluctant to use it, since he considers the device too horrible to employ in any circumstance. At last he agrees and, after eliminating all information about his weapon, he descends into Tokyo Bay and faces Godzilla. He detonates his device, destroying Godzilla, himself, and the secret of his weapon. The film therefore ends with the message that the only hope is the eradication of all doomsday weapons.

Gojira, therefore, was not just kitsch, but was a serious and effective antiwar movie. What makes it effective? Movie monsters, frightening as they are, are often less frightening than the things they symbolize. Consider the scene from the 1977 movie *Alien* in which John Hurt's character is killed when a loathsome creature bursts from his chest. Some reviewers suggested that this scene was so horrifying because it was symbolic of our fear of cancer; a cancerous tumor is a sort of devouring parasite. As disturbing as the scene was, it was not as disturbing as cancer itself, a topic that most people prefer not to think about at all.

Likewise, to confront the actual nature of nuclear weapons and their effects is too gruesome for most people. The recollections of Hiroshima survivors are difficult to read, as are accounts of the birth of "jellyfish babies" among the Marshallese women exposed to radiation. When reality is too terrifying, the human tendency is to try to ignore it and push it aside, in order not to think of it at all, or to obscure it behind a mass of abstractions. By symbolizing the intolerably real horrors of nuclear weapons with a scary but make-believe monster, *Gojira* permits us to experience that which we would rather not confront and to understand its truly monstrous nature.

The makers of *Strategic Air Command* could have responded that their movie is an antiwar film also. The point of the film was that the best way to avoid war is to make a potential aggressor realize that an attack will guarantee his own destruction. So, two polarized positions, deterrence and abolition, had become entrenched and they would clash again and again throughout the Cold War.

BERTRAND RUSSELL VERSUS THE BOMB

Bertrand Arthur William, the third Earl Russell (1872–1970), was one of the leading mathematicians, logicians, and philosophers of the twentieth century. Early in that century he coauthored *Principia Mathematica* with Alfred North Whitehead. This renowned three-volume work of dense mathematical argument represented a herculean ten-year effort by the authors. Its aim is nothing less than to establish the logical foundations of mathematics. In seventy books and innumerable articles and essays written over a long lifetime, Russell addressed an astonishing variety of subjects. In addition to mathematical logic, he made important and original contributions to the philosophy of logic, the philosophy of language, epistemology, metaphysics, and the philosophy of mind. He is regarded as one of the founders of the analytic tradition of philosophy. His more popular writings addressed ethics, politics, and religion, and were written in a clear, vigorous, and witty style.

Russell never shied from public controversy and became one of the most famous social critics of his time. During the First World War his pacifism and his trenchant criticisms of the government led to a term of imprisonment. His critique of conventional religion and morality exposed him to animosity and occasional calumny. Such was the animus against him that in 1940, when he was perhaps the world's most eminent philosopher, he was denied an appointment at the City College of New York. The mother of a college-aged student brought a lawsuit against Russell's appointment, which a biased judge supported, ruling that employing Russell would establish a "chair of indecency." Russell, by the way, had the last laugh when the title page of his next book, *An Inquiry into Meaning and Truth*, listed his many degrees, honors, academic appointments, and awards and concluded with "Judicially pronounced unworthy to be Professor of Philosophy at the City College of New York."[13]

In the late 1950s, when Russell was well over eighty years old, he did not rest on his laurels. Motivated largely by Castle Bravo and the other nuclear tests, he took on the mission of saving the world from nuclear war. He had not always been opposed to nuclear weapons or even their use. In the period of 1945–1949 when the United States possessed a monopoly on the atomic bomb, he advocated curbing Soviet aggression with the threat of the bomb. He admitted that the Russians might respond to such a threat by the Western powers by calling their bluff, and so the bomb might have to be used.[14] However, with the beginning of the arms race, and the prospect of a global nuclear war, he returned to a more pacifist position. In 1957, with noted scholars, writers, and churchmen, he helped found the CND, which became the largest and most influential of the antinuclear organizations.

The CND is still a very active organization. Kate Hudson, General Secretary of the CND as of 2014, recently wrote "An Open Letter to President Loeak of the Marshall Islands." This letter indicates the significance of the events there for the antinuclear movement:

> The test on Bikini Atoll, in your country, in March 1954 [i.e., Castle Bravo] with its terrible radiation impact on the people of Rongelap, moved countless people around the world to action. The tragic consequences for the *Lucky Dragon*, caught in the impact, stirred a whole generation of activists to oppose nuclear weapons. The experience of your country and of your people is at the very heart of our movement.[15]

Of course, Castle Bravo was not the only cause of the antinuclear movement, but the events of March 1954 and the concomitant publicity brought the issue of nuclear testing before the international community in a vivid and disturbing way. Operation Crossroads had been a public spectacle, and atomic bombs blowing up some old ships did not seem particularly threatening. Operations Sandstone and Greenhouse had been kept so secret that little was known about them. Ivy Mike was too big to be kept a secret, but everything seemed to be under control. Castle Bravo vividly demonstrated the illusory nature of that control. Something vastly more powerful and sinister than a mere atomic bomb had been unleashed. Increasingly, many thoughtful people began to think of nuclear weapons not as the ultimate defense against an enemy, but as the enemy itself.

Biographer Ronald Clark notes that the Russian development of nuclear weapons, particularly nuclear missiles sited in central Europe, convinced Russell that the Soviets could not be defeated without the destruction of Britain as well. In particular, the US development of the H-bomb motivated him to spend the rest of his life in trying to prevent nuclear war:

the Russians began to deploy nuclear-tipped missiles targeted on Western Europe and both America and the Soviet Union kept almost level-pegging in their attempts to perfect a transportable hydrogen bomb. *American success in this enterprise in the spring of 1954* [i.e., Operation Castle] *was probably the decisive factor in determining how Russell would spend the rest of his life.*[16]

Interestingly, in April 1954, just one month after Bravo, Russell's judgment on nuclear testing was somewhat reserved. An interviewer from the newspaper *The News Chronicle* asked him whether some "disastrous miscalculation may occur in the H-bomb tests?" His mild response contrasted with some of the more strident rhetoric following Bravo:

Though, obviously, there will come a time when these experiments are too dangerous, I don't think we have reached that point yet. If there were a hydrogen bomb war it is quite clear that practically everybody in London would perish. A shower of hydrogen bombs would almost certainly sterilize large agricultural areas, and the resulting famine would be fearful. But we are talking of the current tests in peacetime. I do not expect disaster from them. I think those who have been showered with radio-active ash, whose fishing catches have been damaged or destroyed, undoubtedly have every right to complain. But I do not see a rain of radioactive ash comparable with the phenomena we saw after the explosion of the Krakatoa volcano in 1883 (which I remember well).[17]

When asked whether he saw any merit in stopping the tests he replied:

None whatever unless we have found a way of causing the Russian experiments to be stopped, too. In my opinion there is only one way. It is to convince the Russians beyond doubt that they can win no victory: They cannot ever communize the world with the hydrogen bomb … I would hasten the process. I would invite all the leaders of the world, and particularly the Russians, to see the results of the American tests. It ought to be made as plain as it can be made.[18]

In Russell's view, the tests might have a useful function. Their terrifying consequences might intimidate the Russians into cooperation. Later developments would show how wrong this assumption was.

By the end of 1954, the tenor of Russell's public comments had changed considerably. In "Man's Peril," a famous BBC address broadcast December 23, he eloquently and passionately urged recognition of the dangers of thermonuclear war and called upon all people, in the name of their shared humanity, to seek to avert that disaster. He noted that the hydrogen bomb places new demands on us, demands that previous generations had not faced. We can no longer ask how to win a war, since a war with thermonuclear weapons would destroy both sides – as well as neutrals. We must instead ask how to avoid war:

We have to learn to think in a new way. We have to learn not to ask what steps can be taken to give military victory to whatever group we prefer, for there no longer are such steps. The question we have to ask ourselves is: What steps can be taken to avert a military contest of which the issue must be disastrous to all sides?[19]

The first step is to realize that warfare with thermonuclear weapons would be vastly more destructive than any previously waged, and even much more destructive than warfare with atomic bombs. He illustrates the dangers with allusions to Castle Bravo and to *The Lucky Dragon*:

But we now know, especially since the Bikini test, that hydrogen bombs can gradually spread destruction over a much wider area than had been supposed … Such a bomb, if exploded near the ground or under water, sends radio-active particles into the upper air. They sink gradually and reach the earth in the form of a deadly dust or rain. It was this dust that infected the Japanese fishermen and their catch of fish although they were outside what American experts believed to be the danger zone. No one knows how widely such radio-active particles might be diffused, but the best authorities are unanimous in saying that a war with hydrogen bombs is quite likely to put an end to the human race.[20]

Of course, Russell realizes that there are severe political obstacles in the way of peace. If only one side unilaterally renounces war, it would be at the mercy of the other side. Each side must state that certain provocations will not be borne.[21] The burden therefore falls on neutral countries to approach the nuclear powers and urge them to come to an understanding – for the sake of human survival. Russell admits that his feelings are not neutral; he would not want to see a submission by the West.[22] However, the stark new reality imposed by the hydrogen bomb is that the aims of neither side can be promoted by nuclear war.

Nineteenth-century theoretician of war Carl von Clausewitz famously said "war is politics by other means." As Clark notes, Russell's point is that thermonuclear weapons refute Clausewitz's aphorism.[23] Throughout history, nations have resorted to war when their ambitions could not be achieved by peaceful means. However in a thermonuclear age, political aims cannot be achieved by war because there can be no winner or loser, only mutually devastating destruction. Russell says that both sides must fully realize this truth.

Despite all the frailties of the human race, Russell holds that achievements in art, science, literature, and religion have made our species worthy of preservation, and he asks a series of profound and disquieting questions:

Is all this to end in trivial horror because so few are able to think of man rather than of this or that group of men? Is our race so destitute of wisdom, so incapable of impartial love, so blind even to the simplest dictates of self-preservation that the last proof of its silly cleverness is to be the extermination of all life on our planet?[24]

He closes with a splendid peroration that places a stark and simple choice before the listener, a choice that comes down to putting your humanity ahead of every parochial concern:

There lies before us, if we choose, continual progress in happiness, knowledge, and wisdom. Shall we, instead, choose death, because we cannot forget our quarrels? I appeal as a human being to other human beings: remember your humanity, and forget all the rest. If you can do so, the way lies open to a new Paradise; if you cannot, nothing lies before you but universal death.[25]

"Man's Peril" was a resounding success, a "wake up" call not only for officials and scientists, but for ordinary people around the world. Supportive letters poured in and Russell was aware that this was a moment to be seized. With an energy and dedication that would have been astonishing in a much younger person, he began a career of activism that was to last until his death and would draw international attention to the antinuclear movement.

Russell contacted Albert Einstein, who was in his final year of life, and asked for his support in publishing a joint Russell–Einstein Manifesto concerning nuclear war. Einstein gladly agreed, and his support of the document was his last public act. The Manifesto was a redraft of "Man's Peril"; additionally, it invited scientists from both Communist and non-Communist countries to meet and to call upon their governments to recognize that national or ideological aims could no longer be promoted by war. Russell collected a number of signatures of prominent scientists, including many Nobel Prize winners, but the total number of signers was fewer than he had hoped.[26] One problem, a problem that was to dog the antinuclear movement through its history, was that skeptics tended to regard antinuclear activists as witting or unwitting dupes of communists. Russell strove again and again to portray his message as ideologically neutral and directed toward the preservation of humanity, not the promotion of any doctrine. Still, the suspicion could never be wholly allayed.

The two organizations most closely associated with Russell's activism are the Pugwash Conferences and the CND. Pugwash is a small village in Nova Scotia, and the home of Cyrus Eaton, a wealthy industrialist of liberal views who often sponsored informal gatherings of statesmen, scientists, and intellectuals to discuss world problems. Eaton invited Russell to organize a conference where scientists from East and West could meet and confer on the problems of the nuclear age. In July 1957 an international group of twenty-two scientists met at the first Pugwash Conference. The statement they issued gained support in both Communist and non-Communist countries.[27] Russell carefully avoided any association with groups identified as pro-Communist, and continued to maintain a position of neutrality. His stance paid off, and suspicions about Pugwash declined. In consequence, the participants in later conferences were more numerous and more prestigious, as scientists with official links to government began to feel comfortable about attending.[28] Ultimately, the Pugwash Conferences became one of the most respected forums for discussion of issues concerning nuclear war and weapons.

CND was always more confrontational and controversial. As we have seen in the interview quoted above, as of April 1954, one month after Bravo, Russell's views on nuclear testing were supportive of the tests, and certainly did not favor a unilateral cessation. According to Clark, the Bikini tests brought Russell around to another view:

he eventually came round to the orthodox protest view, influenced largely, he said, by the after-effects of the Bikini Atoll tests of 1954 which showed the dangers from fall-out to be greater than estimated.[29]

By the "orthodox protest view," Clark means the view of the active protestors of the day that condemned all nuclear testing. Apparently, with further reflection on the consequences of Bravo, and perhaps the accumulating evidence of its dire effects, Russell became more alarmed at the dangers of the tests.

Another frightening development was the launch of the Russian satellite Sputnik in October 1957, which was propelled into space by a rocket of such power that it was clear that Russia could develop intercontinental ballistic missiles (ICBMs). ICBMs launched from the United States or Russia could reach their targets in minutes, and no adequate defense was possible. With the development of ICBMs, the threat of a devastating first strike, one that would largely knock out the retaliatory capability of the other side, became a very real threat. If one side could deliver a crushing blow and receive acceptable damage in return, then the motivation to carry out such a first strike was apparent. These fears were further destabilizing, and propelled an even more frenetic arms race as each side rushed to develop a credible retaliatory capability that could not be disabled by a first strike. The prospect of hydrogen bombs on ICBMs made the world a far scarier place than it had been a few years before, when the threat was fission bombs delivered by bombers.

Late in 1957 several distinguished men, the journalist Kingsley Martin, editor of the left-leaning political journal *The New Statesman*, novelist J. B. Priestley, and Lewis John Collins, the Canon of St. Paul's Cathedral, began to organize the CND. They then approached Russell:

> they needed someone who could be a rallying-point and a symbol. Who better than Russell, with his televisually perfect mane of white hair, his stern principles and lucid prose, the philosopher who with his "Man's Peril" seemed genuinely to have awakened in many countries at least a tentative realization of what nuclear war would mean? So Russell, now in his eighty-sixth year, entered the world of protest meetings and sit-downs on wet pavements that could look ridiculous or heroic according to point of view, and of vilification by much of the press.[30]

Indeed, unlike Pugwash, the CND was not a forum for discussion, but a protest organization that emphasized demonstrations and civil disobedience. Eventually, in 1961, forty-three years after his imprisonment in the First World War, and at nearly ninety years old, Russell was charged with inciting the public to civil disobedience, as was his wife Edith Finch.[31] Both were convicted, a verdict that delighted Russell, and each was given a two-month sentence. The sentence was commuted to a week, and they were allowed to serve the term in prison hospitals.

The story of Russell's relationship, and eventual break, with CND, and his later activism, are interesting stories, but have been told in great detail elsewhere.[32] The point here is that when you set off big bombs, you never really know what you are going to get. One of the things you might get is a highly publicized movement by famous intellectuals and activists opposing everything that you are doing. One of the many ironies associated with Castle Bravo is that it became a potent stimulus to the antinuclear movement.

We see, then, that the explosion of a thermonuclear device on a remote Pacific Atoll can have many unpredictable effects. In addition to the localized physical effects of the blast and radiation, there were distant impacts on what moviegoers watched and what philosophers thought. Not only was Castle Bravo a stimulus to antinuclear activism, author William Souder says that it prompted the modern environmental movement. The book often credited with the beginning of that movement, Rachel Carson's *Silent Spring*, drew a parallel between radiation and pesticides:

One of Carson's challenges in writing *Silent Spring* was how to convince her readers of the then-novel idea that an unseen chemical contaminant that might be anywhere (or everywhere) might cause unanticipated collateral damage to ecosystems. She solved this problem by perceiving a parallel between pesticides and radiation. Invisible, ubiquitous, and accumulating in the tissues of living things over time, pesticides and radioactive fallout from nuclear testing were, Carson argued, the twin existential problems of the modern age.[33]

In 1962 nuclear testing was so widespread that there was a nuclear explosion somewhere in the world every few days on average. Fission products began to show up in the milk of cows in the American heartland.[34] People were genuinely scared, and understandably so.

Things eventually got better, with the signing of the test ban treaty between the United States, the United Kingdom, and the Soviet Union on August 5, 1963. This treaty banned nuclear tests in the atmosphere, in outer space, and under water. Underground tests were permitted to continue, but a further treaty of 1974 limited underground tests to yields of 150 kilotons. However, before the treaties made things better, they had to get a lot worse. They began to get worse in November 1955.

THE RUSSIAN "CASTLE BRAVO"

In less than two years after Castle Bravo, Soviet scientists had developed a "true" two-stage device and were ready to test it. On November 22, 1955, officials, military men, and scientists gathered at a remote site in Kazakhstan to witness the test. To minimize fallout, the bomb was delivered by bomber and detonated as an airburst. The Tu-16 bomber was painted white to reflect the heat of the blast. The bomb was designed to yield three megatons, but for the test the yield was reduced to about half that. The effects of that reduced yield were tremendous, even when viewed from seventy kilometers' distance, as Sakharov recalled:

I saw a blinding yellow-white sphere swiftly expand, turn orange in a fraction of a second, then turn bright red and touch the horizon, flattening out at its base. Soon everything was obscured by rising dust which formed an enormous, swirling gray-blue cloud, its surface streaked with fiery crimson flashes. Between the cloud and the swirling dust grew a mushroom stem ... Shock waves criss-crossed the sky, emitting sporadic milky-white cones and adding to the mushroom image. I felt heat like that from an open furnace on my face – and this was in freezing weather tens of miles from ground zero. The whole magical spectacle unfolded in complete silence. Several minutes passed, and then all of a sudden the shock wave was coming at us, approaching swiftly, flattening the feather-grass.[35]

The test was spectacular, but it was also deadly. A temperature inversion caused the shock wave to be much more powerful than calculated. A young soldier in a trench dozens of kilometers from ground zero was killed when his trench fell in. In a village outside of the test area a bitterly ironic turn of events killed a two-year-old girl. The people of the village had gathered in a bomb shelter. When they saw the flash of the explosion, they all rushed outside, leaving the girl in the shelter. When the boosted shock wave hit, those who had rushed from the shelter were not injured, but the shelter collapsed on the girl.

Like Castle Bravo, the Russian test had unintended and tragic consequences. Apparently, the Russians were no better than the Americans at anticipating or controlling the consequences of thermonuclear detonations. No site, whether in the tropical Pacific or the frozen steppes of Kazakhstan, is so remote that the effects of thermonuclear tests can all be foreseen and controlled.

CONCLUSION: THE LEGACY OF CASTLE BRAVO

In this chapter and the last we have looked at the Castle Bravo event and its effects. We have seen that the following were immediate or indirect effects:

1. With the information from Castle Bravo and subsequent tests of the Castle series, the United States was soon able to produce a deliverable thermonuclear weapon.
2. The *Lucky Dragon #5* was dusted with highly radioactive fallout, causing the crew of twenty-three to suffer acute radiation sickness. One crewmember later died and the others were variously affected.
3. Radioactive fish were marketed in Japan, leading to widespread anxiety and significant harm to the fishing industry.
4. Due to the last two consequences, an uproar ensued in the Japanese press and led to a strong popular reaction and worsening of relations between the United States and Japan.
5. Inhabited atolls of the Marshall Islands were also exposed to fallout, resulting in significant and longstanding harm to the indigenous population, particularly to the inhabitants of Rongelap and Utirik atolls. These persons were displaced from their homes, at first temporarily, but eventually permanently for some. Exposure to radiation caused both acute and chronic health problems for many people.

6. In the United States, popular entertainment tapped the deep reservoir of anxiety about nuclear testing as science fiction movies gave visibly monstrous shape to those fears. Other films, like *Strategic Air Command*, countered by portraying the atomic warriors as heroic, and the nuclear deterrent as the best guarantor of peace. Meanwhile, in Japan, the particular horror inspired by Castle Bravo and subsequent events led to the creation of the iconic nuclear monster *Gojira* (Godzilla) that was the visible manifestation of the terror of nuclear weapons.

7. The worldwide reporting on Castle Bravo and subsequent events prompted a strong antinuclear reaction. In particular, philosopher Bertrand Russell and other public intellectuals became sufficiently alarmed that they committed themselves to activism against nuclear weapons. CND, the most prominent of the activist organizations, was particularly motivated by Castle Bravo and the subsequent harm done to the *Lucky Dragon* crew and the people of the Marshall Islands.

Of these seven categories of effects, only the first had been anticipated by those who planned and conducted the tests. The drive-in movies had it right: Exploding multimegaton bombs in the earth's atmosphere is indeed like unleashing a large and dangerous animal. Once released, it cannot be caged again. It will go where it will and where and when it will come to rest, no one can say.

NOTES

1 Souder, "The Link between Castle Bravo and Modern Environmentalism," p. 2.
2 See Boyer, *By the Bomb's Early Light*.
3 Boyer, *By the Bomb's Early Light*, p. 352.
4 Boyer, *By the Bomb's Early Light*, p. 352.
5 Souder, "The Link between Castle Bravo and Modern Environmentalism."
6 "The B-36," Military History website.
7 Ryfle, "Godzilla's Footprint," p. 1.
8 Ryfle, "Godzilla's Footprint," p. 2.
9 Ryfle, "Godzilla's Footprint," p. 2.
10 Ryfle, "Godzilla's Footprint," p. 3.
11 Ryfle, "Godzilla's Footprint," p.3.
12 Ryfle, "Godzilla's Footprint," p. 4.
13 Clark, *Bertrand Russell and His World*, p. 88.
14 Clark, *The Life of Bertrand Russell*.
15 Hudson, "An Open Letter to President Loeak," CND website.

16 Clark, *Bertrand Russell and His World*, p. 98; emphasis added.
17 Russell, *Autobiography*, pp. 554–555.
18 Russell, *Autobiography*, p. 555.
19 Russell, "Man's Peril," *The Basic Writings of Bertrand Russell*, p. 729.
20 Russell, "Man's Peril," *The Basic Writings of Bertrand Russell*, pp. 729–730.
21 Russell, "Man's Peril," *The Basic Writings of Bertrand Russell*, p. 731.
22 Russell, "Man's Peril," *The Basic Writings of Bertrand Russell*, p. 731.
23 Clark, *The Life of Bertrand Russell*, p. 535.
24 Russell, "Man's Peril," *The Basic Writings of Bertrand Russell*, p. 732.
25 Russell, "Man's Peril," *The Basic Writings of Bertrand Russell*, p. 732.
26 Clark, *The Life of Bertrand Russell*, p. 541.
27 Clark, *The Life of Bertrand Russell*, p. 545.
28 Clark, *The Life of Bertrand Russell*, p. 545.
29 Clark, *The Life of Bertrand Russell*, p. 555.
30 Clark, *Bertrand Russell and His World*, p. 102.
31 Clark, *Bertrand Russell and His World*, p. 109. Another source (private communication) indicates that the charge against Russell was actually "breach of peace."
32 See Clark, *The Life of Bertrand Russell*.
33 Souder, "The Link between Castle Bravo and Modern Environmentalism," p. 2.
34 Souder, "The Link between Castle Bravo and Modern Environmentalism," p. 2.
35 Holloway, *Stalin and the Bomb*, p. 315.

6

Bikini Postmortem, Part I

Public Perceptions and Official Obsessions

WHAT IS HISTORICAL UNDERSTANDING?

We have seen that the nuclear tests in the Marshall Islands were crucial to the development of the nuclear arsenal of the United States. Insofar as the development of thermonuclear weapons was an urgent national priority at that time, these tests effectively served that aim. However, we have also seen that these tests had deleterious and even tragic consequences. Innocent people were irradiated, causing long-term, severe health problems. Others were displaced from their ancestral homes, which were subsequently rendered uninhabitable. The former inhabitants of Bikini and Rongelap (now chiefly their descendants) have not yet returned to those islands, even though it will soon be sixty years since the tests ended.

In a broader context, these tests were part of the expensive and dangerous arms race between the United States and the Soviet Union. Measures that were seen as defensive by one side were perceived as offensive by the other, so that any development by one side had to be matched by the other, which had to be matched in turn. In this context, nuclear tests by the "others" were seen as provocative and yours were seen as necessary. Far from discouraging the Soviets, as Bertrand Russell, among others, had hoped, the US nuclear tests, if anything, only prompted them to work harder and faster at developing and testing their own bombs and delivery systems.

In the previous chapters we have told this story. In this chapter we seek a deeper historical understanding of those events in terms of what was believed, hoped, and feared at the time. Understanding the past is always tricky, and not always because of a paucity of data. In fact, when dealing with recent history, as we are doing here, there is often a superabundance of relevant material so that the historian's job is not to track down vague clues or locate rare documents but to sort through a tsunami of disparate sources and try to distinguish signal from noise. This is especially difficult when the topic involves controversy since controversy always increases the noise-to-signal ratio. The nuclear tests in the Marshall Islands were controversial then and remain so today.

However, dealing with the degradation or distortion of information is not the only or even necessarily the biggest impediment to historical understanding. An ever-present danger is the ease with which we slide into making ahistorical judgments. British historian Herbert Butterfield coined the term "Whig History" to describe the sort of partisan account that elevates the heroes of your own party (the Whigs, in Butterfield's example) while automatically disparaging those of other parties.[1] The well-known saying about the winners writing the history books is a comment on such ideological distortion.

We often misjudge history by forgetting that things familiar to us could not have been known then, or were understood very differently. For instance, we cringe when reading accounts of past medical practice, appalled by the lack of even the most elementary principles of antisepsis. We have to remind ourselves that two centuries ago people lacked even the rudimentary knowledge of the nature of infection that we take for granted today. Health professionals were not cruel or negligent when they failed to wash their hands before treating patients. They simply could not know what we now take for granted. Similarly, an ethical imperative that seems basic to us might not have seemed so even to an enlightened individual of the past, and instead of rushing to condemn, a historian must endeavor to understand this difference. In understanding the past we neither condone nor condemn, but endeavor to approach it on its own terms. Thus, an action that seems irrational or patently wrong to us might not have seemed so to reasonable persons of good will at that time and a historian must attempt to recapture *their* understanding.

In the present context, that means that we have to resolve to understand nuclear testing in the terms in which it was understood by those who authorized and supported that policy. When we consider a policy that required the displacement of indigenous people from their homeland, portions of which were then poisoned and rendered uninhabitable, such a policy, viewed from sixty years' distance, appears insupportable, even appalling and outrageous. Yet at the time the policy was vigorously defended by persons who viewed the tests as a moral imperative and who, at least by the standards of that day, could not be regarded as particularly callous or insensitive.

But was not a grave injustice done to the crew of the *Lucky Dragon*, to the Marshallese people, and to the American service personnel who were exposed to dangerous levels of radiation? Are these not points of absolute moral clarity that emerge from the complexities of this story? Yes, undoubtedly they are. However, in speaking this way we cannot be speaking as historians. We might be speaking as philosophers, or as activists, or advocates, or merely as empathetic fellow human beings, but we cannot be speaking as historians. The historian is not called upon to sermonize or moralize. All that the historian *qua* historian can do is to account for what happened and why it happened in the most objective terms possible and to present diverse perspectives without grinding an ax for any of them. What we *can* do is to make sure that neglected or dissenting voices are heard, and that the "other" side's story is told. In this case, we can ensure that the victims of the tests are heard as plainly as those who planned and carried them out. We do this in our Epilogue.

In this chapter, therefore, we will attempt to understand the nuclear tests in the Marshall Islands as they were seen by the highest American policymakers. What emerges is not a straightforward narrative with a simple or obvious lesson. Historical events often resist categorization in familiar or comfortable ways. When we make the earnest effort to understand these events in the terms that they were understood by the people who lived them, then we will see that no simplistic good guy/bad guy scenario fits the facts.

The real lessons of the history of nuclear testing in the Marshall Islands are deeper and more troubling. We will see that the suffering of the Marshallese people was due to a characteristic failure of the powerful when dealing with the powerless, namely, the failure to see that a great differential in power inevitably produces a vast and unbridgeable difference in perspective. For the powerful, when faced with a terrifying situation that seemed to present few alternatives, the irradiation of remote, tiny atolls and the injury and dislocation of a couple of hundred people were just regrettable incidents. For those people, it was the destruction of their world.

THE TENOR OF THE TIMES

To explain Castle Bravo and its aftermath, we have to understand both the general and the specific. That is, we have to ask what were the reigning assumptions and pervasive attitudes of that time and place. However, we also have to look at events as they were shaped by the beliefs, attitudes, and actions of individuals, or, in this case, of a particularly important individual.

First, then, what was the tenor of the times, that is, what were the prevailing fears, attitudes, and perceptions? The *zeitgeist* of the mid-1950s seems strange, distant, and hard to comprehend now, but we cannot understand the actions and decisions made then without a grasp of that milieu. In any era, people respond to the world, not as it is, but as their collective beliefs represent it. So to understand what people did, we have to have some insight into how they conceived their world.

Further, we must ask how the top policymakers understood the world situation and the testing program. To understand the behavior of any complex organization, one must start at the top. The highest government official was, of course, President Dwight Eisenhower. We will focus on Lewis L. Strauss, Chairman of the AEC at the time of Castle Bravo, and thus the highest official charged with the formulation and defense of US nuclear policy.

In the Western world of the 1950s, and particularly in the United States, the prevailing, and even obsessive, object of fear was the Soviet Union. The early years of the Cold War were times of increasing anxiety about communism and its dangers, real or imagined. Beginning with Winston Churchill's famous "iron curtain" speech delivered at Fulton, Missouri in 1946, fear of Soviet domination and expansion figured increasingly in policy decisions and held an ever-stronger grip on the public imagination. Eventually, the fear of communism came to resemble a countrywide psychosis as anti-Communist activists envisaged a conspiracy of diabolical nature and unlimited extent, with tendrils creeping into every aspect of American life. In their minds, the invisibility of the menace only proved its insidiousness. FBI Director J. Edgar Hoover expressed it best in the title of his popular book on Communist subversion: *Masters of Deceit.*

Zeal to foil communism led state and federal lawmakers into the depths of extremism and downright lunacy, as Bill Bryson records in his memoir, *The Life and Times of the Thunderbolt Kid*:

At the peak of the Red Scare, thirty two of the forty eight states had loyalty oaths of one kind or another. In New York ... it was necessary to swear a loyalty oath to gain a fishing permit. In Indiana, loyalty oaths were administered to professional wrestlers. The Communist Control Act of 1954 made it a federal offense to communicate any Communist thoughts by any means including semaphore. In Connecticut, it became illegal to criticize the government, or to speak ill of the army or the American flag. In Texas you could be sent to prison for twenty years for being a Communist. In Birmingham, Alabama it was illegal merely to be seen conversing with a Communist.[2]

Senator Joseph McCarthy of Wisconsin, supreme anti-Communist – and an editorial cartoonist's dream with his black brows and shadowy cheeks – supplied the iconic image of the era as he postured before TV cameras, brandishing his list of supposed Communist agents.

When people go to extremes, future generations tend to view all that they did through the lens of that extremism. It is all too easy to dismiss the era of nuclear arms development and testing as an excrescence of anti-Communist hysteria. The problem with such a facile analysis is that it obscures two serious questions that need unbiased answers: (1) Was the fear of Soviet expansionism a rational attitude, i.e., a reasonable response at that time? (2) Did nuclear policy have to take Russian nuclear capabilities and intentions into consideration? The answer to each question is unequivocally "yes."

The alliance between the United States and the USSR during the Second World War was not a marriage of convenience but a pact of dire necessity. Adolf Hitler was like a rabid dog loose on the streets of the world. He had to be stopped, and only the combined resources of the United States, the Soviet Union, and the British Empire could do it. The alliance between America and Britain was fractious enough, even though both were Western democracies with a shared history and a common language. Stalin's Russia was the very model of a totalitarian state; it was the template for the nightmarish "Oceania" of George Orwell's *1984* and the target of his satirical fable *Animal Farm*. Stalinist society took on the personal characteristics of its ruler – xenophobia, paranoia, rigidity, secrecy, a mania for control, and an utter ruthlessness that would not hesitate to crush millions on a suspicion or in pursuit of ideological ends. "A single death is a tragedy; a million deaths is a statistic" is a saying probably misattributed to Stalin.[3] However, in practice, Stalin generated such "statistics" many times over.

Even while allied from 1941 to 1945, the United States and the Soviet Union regarded each other with deep suspicion. The United States attempted to keep the development of the atomic bomb a secret from the Russians until after the Trinity test. The Soviets, on the other hand, undertook major espionage operations against the United States during the war and, in fact, achieved three separate penetrations of security at Los Alamos.[4] It took little prescience to see that the coalition formed to defeat Hitler would dissolve as soon as that goal was accomplished.

Under Stalin, Soviet citizens lived lives of constant fear, as documented in Orlando Figes' *The Whisperers*. During the Great Terror of the 1930s a stray word could send you to be starved and worked to death in a labor camp:

Talking could be dangerous at the best of Soviet times, but during the Great Terror a few careless words were all it took for someone to vanish for ever [sic]. Informers were everywhere. "Today a man talks freely only with his wife – at night with the blankets pulled over his head," the writer Isaak Babel once remarked ... The Great Terror effectively silenced the Soviet people.[5]

There is no question that to be a citizen of the Soviet Union under Stalin was to be in a dire circumstance, much like being a North Korean today. This was especially so for a creative artist such as the composer Dmitri Shostakovich. Stalin's obsessive control extended even to the visual and musical arts. As Shostakovich discovered, when his opera *Lady Macbeth of Mtsensk* was officially censured, even offending Stalin's musical taste could be dangerous.

But the Soviet Union's internal repression, however deplorable, did not directly affect the United States, so what made it necessary to regard the Soviets as a threat and base policy upon that perception? For one thing, by the fall of 1949 all doubts were erased concerning the reality of an arms race between the United States and the USSR. On August 29, 1949, in the steppes of Kazakhstan in the USSR at 7:00 a.m. Soviet scientists detonated Joe-1, the first Russian nuclear device. With a yield of twenty kilotons, Joe-1 was virtually identical in design and power to the American Fat Man bomb of 1945. Because the test had been conducted in conditions of secrecy in remote Kazakhstan, the West did not begin to learn about the test until September 3, when radioactive fallout was collected by an American weather reconnaissance aircraft flying east of the Kamchatka Peninsula. By mid-September American scientists had pinpointed the time of the test to within an hour of its actual occurrence.[6]

The fact of Soviet nuclear capability ended the comfortable complacency many had adopted about the American nuclear monopoly. As Gerard DeGroot notes, many Americans "whistled in the dark," reassuring themselves that Russians lacked American knowhow and industrial capability, and assuming that it would be many years before the Soviets would have a bomb.[7] There is a hilarious scene in Stanley Kubrick's film *Dr. Strangelove* where the boorish general played by George C. Scott dismisses the Russians as ignorant "peons," incapable of understanding advanced technology. As with many funny scenes in movies, when played out in real life, the scenario was not so amusing.

In reality, the Soviet Union had a number of world-class physicists, such as Igor Kurchatov, Iulii Khariton, Iakov Zel'dovich, Peter Kapitsa, and Andrei Sakharov, who were quite as able as their counterparts in the West. These physicists were also patriots who saw their work on nuclear weapons as necessary for the survival of their country. The USSR also had enormous industrial capacity, as demonstrated in the Second World War when, in the face of the German invasion, all heavy industry was packed up and moved east of the Urals. By 1943, munitions were being produced on an overwhelming scale. Finally, the Soviets gained some advantage through espionage, though just how much is highly debatable. Physicist Klaus Fuchs, who had worked on the Manhattan Project, provided a detailed description of the plutonium bomb to the Soviets, as well as other information. The most reliable estimates seem to be that espionage took one to two years' work off the time it would have taken the Soviets to develop the bomb.[8]

Most importantly, Stalin was absolutely determined to have the bomb. In the aftermath of Hiroshima, in hopes of averting an arms race, various proposals to establish international control over nuclear weapons were considered. All such proposals were doomed, as Jeremy Bernstein notes:

> In retrospect it is clear that the Russians would not have accepted any proposal for internationalizing nuclear energy after the bombing of Hiroshima. Stalin was determined that the Soviet Union would have an atomic bomb at any cost. Even Russians like Andrei Sakharov, who later turned against the Soviet nuclear weapons program, felt it was necessary for the survival of the Soviet Union.[9]

David Holloway's thorough study, *Stalin and the Bomb*, also makes it clear that by the end of the Second World War Stalin's mind was made up:

> Stalin had already decided, by the time of the formal Japanese surrender on September 2, to organize a high-priority atomic project. There is no evidence of any discussion in the political leadership – at this time or later – about the wisdom of this decision. It was assumed that if the United States had the atomic bomb, the Soviet Union needed to have it too. But building the bomb was ... an expensive undertaking. This was especially so for a country whose economy was in ruins after a bitter and destructive war. Yet Stalin did not stint the project.[10]

As for the hydrogen bomb, Holloway reports that, probably in response to intelligence about American research, Soviet scientists began working on the hydrogen bomb in 1946.[11] Even if at some point the door might have been open for averting the arms race, by 1949 that door was firmly closed.

Because of the enormous losses suffered by the Soviet Union in the Second World War, Stalin felt that a considerable expansion of its territory and sphere of influence was justified, as leading Cold War historian John Lewis Gaddis explains:

Wartime expenditures in blood and treasure, Stalin believed, should largely determine who got what after the war: The Soviet Union would therefore get a lot. Not only would it regain the territories it had lost to the Germans during World War Two; it would also retain the territories it had taken as a result of the opportunistic but short-sighted "non-aggression" pact Stalin had concluded with Hitler in August, 1939 – portions of Finland, Poland, and Romania, all of the Baltic States. It would require that states beyond these expanded borders remain within Moscow's sphere of influence. It would seek territorial concessions at the expense of Iran and Turkey (including control of the Turkish Straits), as well as naval bases in the Mediterranean. Finally, it would punish a defeated and devastated Germany through military occupation, property expropriations, reparations payments, and ideological transformation.[12]

Stalin then proceeded to try to make good on these expansionist aims, and was taken aback when the United States and Britain balked at his demands.[13]

Stalin's boldest move was the blockade of Berlin, which began in 1948. His motives were not clear but his intention to starve Berliners was. The blockade backfired as the allies improvised the famous Berlin airlift to supply the city. As Gaddis notes, the result was to make Stalin look both brutal and incompetent and to achieve a major public relations victory for the West.[14] Competent or not, the blockade conveyed a message of aggression and ruthlessness, and that message was duly received.

In short, then, by the fall of 1949, when the debate over the hydrogen bomb was peaking, three things were clear about the Soviet Union: (1) it was a brutally repressive totalitarian society; (2) it could produce nuclear weapons; and (3) it had expansionist aims and was willing to use ruthless means to pursue them. So, Soviet behavior, aims, and capabilities had to be considered when formulating US nuclear policy. There used to be a poster with the saying "Just because you are paranoid does not mean people are not out to get you." Likewise, we might say that just because the fear of communism had reached a point of paranoid excess in US society does not mean that the Soviet Union posed no threat.

Looking back at Cold War fears today, we can afford to be more restrained in our judgments. We can take the view expressed in the above quote by John Gaddis that Soviet expansionism was an understandable, if deplorable, reaction to the exceptional suffering and sacrifice of the Soviet people in the Second World War. Soviet leaders did not aim at world domination, but they were determined to make sure that the territories on their Western borders were in the hands of militarily and ideologically reliable client states. Never again would Russia suffer a *Barbarossa*, the surprise German offensive that had cost them so dearly in 1941. Further, in the 1950s, nobody in the West could see the clay feet of the Soviet colossus or know that it would topple in another generation.

Physicist Herbert York explains how the threat of international communism appeared even to intelligent and reflective persons at the time:

You have to recall that in 1948 was the Berlin blockade, in 1948 was the coup in Czechoslovakia, and the expansion that these things represented seemed quite real. And then there was the fall of China ... to the Communists, the creation of the Sino-Soviet bloc, the Korean War in the early fifties. So, looking back in the late fifties, what we saw was a lot of successes or what seemed to be successes on the part of the Russians, including territorial expansion. That was the high-water mark but we didn't know it at the time.[15]

People in the mid-1950s were afraid. Some of their fears were rational, and some were not, but fear – fear of communism and fear of nuclear war – was pervasive and powerful. Fear is the intolerable emotion. When people are mortally afraid they will seek any means of relief. Also, fear increases by orders of magnitude the human capacity for rationalization. Risks that otherwise would seem reckless in the extreme, like the possibility of exposing innocent human beings to dangerous quantities of ionizing radiation, will suddenly seem eminently reasonable and tolerable. Americans were quite willing to detonate nuclear weapons, including some very radioactively dirty ones, at the Nevada Proving Grounds, where the sprouting mushroom clouds were easily visible from Las Vegas. Few would spare a thought for risks, considered slight in any case, for a few hundred inhabitants of distant atolls.

CHAIRMAN STRAUSS: INSIDE THE MIND OF A COLD WARRIOR

When complex organizations cause disasters, whether it is a massive oil spill in the Gulf of Mexico, the release of deadly toxic fumes in Bhopal, India, or the irradiation of inhabitants of the Marshall Islands, you have to look at the actions, beliefs, and attitudes of the people at the top of those organizations. Did the top decision-makers and policy-shapers display sufficient concern for potential dangers, or did they foster a "corporate culture" that discounted safety considerations in favor of other goals? Could a fundamentally different approach have led to the establishment of more adequate precautions?

To answer these questions others must be asked: Was the safety of the Marshallese a priority for those at the highest levels of responsibility for the nuclear testing policies of the United States? Was there any genuine concern ahead of time that something bad might happen, something very much like what actually did happen? Even after Castle Bravo made the risks apparent, was any serious consideration given to the possibility that the other tests might be dangerous? Is there any evidence that the deleterious consequences of the Bravo test were downplayed, distorted, or covered up?

To address these questions we have to examine the attitudes, beliefs, and decisions of nuclear policy makers at the highest level of the American Government. During the time of the Operation Castle tests, the chairman of the Atomic Energy Commission was Lewis L. Strauss. Strauss was therefore the highest official charged with the direction and administration of US nuclear policy. His advice was sought and respected by President Eisenhower, and he was a very energetic articulator and defender of the Administration's pro-testing nuclear policies.

By examining Strauss' published memoirs, *Men and Decisions* (1962), and the voluminous archival material deposited at the Herbert Hoover Presidential Library, we can get a clear picture of the beliefs, reasoning, and attitudes that shaped the decision to pursue the tests, and to continue atmospheric testing even after the events of Castle Bravo and after the international outcry had become strident. In the PBS program *The Bomb* that aired on July 28, 2015, some of the commentators expressed harshly negative views of Strauss. One called him a "horrible, horrible" person. Another described him as "evil." It is certainly true that Strauss was not a genial man. By all accounts, he was thin-skinned and a tenacious holder of grudges. A man of ironclad conviction, it was said that he viewed those who disagreed with him as either fools or traitors.[16] As noted in Chapter 2, many historians regard Strauss' successful campaign to remove J. Robert Oppenheimer's security clearance as a vendetta motivated by personal spite. The facts seem to back up that claim.[17]

In all fairness, though, Strauss was clearly a man deeply devoted to public service and one who assiduously supported the interests of his country, and the world, as he perceived them. Further, some of his concerns were unquestionably legitimate and the country benefited by following some of his recommendations. For instance, as a statement by members of the Congressional Joint Task Force on Nuclear energy, dated January 27, 1953, makes clear, Strauss was an early and ardent proponent of the development of techniques for the long-range detection of nuclear explosions.[18] It was by such means that the first Soviet nuclear test was detected in 1949.

Actually, Strauss' commitment to nuclear policy was based on something even deeper and more urgent than patriotism. As he saw it, he was, literally, helping to save the world. In his view, a view widely shared at the time (recall *Strategic Air Command*), only American nuclear deterrence could prevent the ultimate disaster of a nuclear war or the nightmare of a world under Soviet hegemony. If Strauss and others seemed dismissive of the rights and well-being of the victims of Castle Bravo, we have to interpret those failings in the light of the exigencies of a situation that seemed to threaten the whole world. Again, we do not have to condone their attitudes, but we must understand them in the terms of how things appeared to people like Lewis Strauss.

Strauss viewed the Soviet Union with profound suspicion, which was a common Cold War sentiment, and not a groundless one. However, having had a very successful career as a Wall Street financier, he no doubt felt a visceral antipathy toward the Soviet system and Communist ideology. In a speech before the Virginia State Chamber of Commerce on April 14, 1950, Strauss rejects as a "most dangerous" fallacy the idea that disarmament could proceed on the basis of mutual trust and respect for obligations spelled out by treaties and pacts.[19] After all, no nation that rejects religion, and consequently the moral law, can be trusted to respect covenants:

no nation can be assumed to be governed by moral standards to which we subscribe if it is a nation that, as a matter of public doctrine, rejects religion, denies the authority of moral law, and had a record of action in treating solemn covenants as matters of temporary expediency.[20]

An atheist state is inherently untrustworthy; having rejected the putative religious foundation of morality and integrity, it will ruthlessly seek only its own advantage, and will regard treaties as opportunities to cheat. Such an implacable and amoral enemy can be expected to respect only force, and its aggression can be restrained only by the threat of its own destruction.

Of course, Soviet authorities precisely reciprocated these attitudes. As they saw it, a state run by and for capitalists was inherently duplicitous and imperialistic, and the Soviet Union could only be safe if it opposed strength with strength. They therefore forged ahead with their own programs of testing and stockpiling.

In general, Strauss' rhetoric is not out of line for the time and was even moderate in tone compared to some of the red-baiting philippics of the day. Even the condemnation of the Soviets as godless was a common theme. As noted in an earlier chapter, it is easy today to criticize the apparent demonization and stereotyping of the Soviets by American politicians and officials. However, the Soviets all too often lived down to the stereotype.

Where exactly did Strauss stand on the program of nuclear testing? He elaborates and defends his views in his memoirs *Men and Decisions*. His comments recorded in archival documents underscore the genuineness and depth of his convictions about the value and necessity of testing. In sum, Strauss held that, in the absence of any genuinely effective means of inspection and control, there was no alternative to the active development and testing of nuclear weapons by the United States. His reasoning for this conclusion may be represented as follows:

a. Unilateral disarmament by the United States is out of the question.
b. In the absence of a reliable program of inspection, and adequate safeguards against cheating, mutual disarmament is impossible with an enemy as untrustworthy as the Soviet Union.
c. Therefore, since disarmament is impossible, the only alternative is deterrence.
d. Deterrence is possible only if the United States actively develops and improves its nuclear weapons systems.
e. The development and improvement of nuclear weapons systems require an aggressive program of testing.
f. Therefore, testing should continue.

While expressing personal respect for pacifists, Strauss simply notes that a pacifist government could not survive.[21] Others, while not strict pacifists, argue that nuclear weapons belong to a different category than conventional ones, and should be eliminated. Strauss replies, first, that conventional weapons can be and have been used for mass destruction, as with the firebombing of Tokyo in 1945.[22] Further, if, in principle, it is acceptable to use the threat of force to deter aggression, then there is no consistent argument against using nuclear weapons for deterrence.[23] In fact, though the development of powerful conventional weapons did not deter full-scale conflict between the major powers, nuclear weapons seemed to have done so.[24] Strauss would have had no objection to Russell's argument that no victory is possible in a nuclear war since both sides would be devastated. It is precisely the awesome destruction that would be inflicted on an aggressor nation that makes nuclear weapons an effective deterrent.

In other words, Strauss defends the doctrine that later came to be known by the acronym MAD – mutual assured destruction. If both sides will be destroyed in a nuclear war, then neither side will initiate one. Of course, the ironic aptness of the acronym MAD has been pointed out many times. Richard Rhodes likens the situation of the United States and the USSR to two men standing in a pool of gasoline each with a box of matches and saying to each other "Don't do that or I will kill us both."[25] Given that each side had thermonuclear weapons, and given the level of enmity and distrust between them, then, as mad as MAD was, it is not clear that there was any feasible alternative. Perhaps the only *sane* use for a thermonuclear bomb is to deter somebody else from using one. In fact, as we will see in the next chapter, in the mid-1950s, top nuclear policymakers held a more bellicose view than Strauss with his emphasis on deterrence. For many top military and civilian planners, the use of nuclear weapons in warfare remained quite thinkable. Compared to these theorists, Strauss' view was more moderate and less aggressive.

A draft of a letter from Strauss to David Lawrence, editorial writer for *U.S. News and World Report*, succinctly and uncompromisingly summarizes Strauss' position on testing:

On my return from Europe this morning the first thing I want to do is to thank you for your editorial of April 23rd. This fantastic nonsense about ceasing tests (that is tantamount to saying ceasing the development) of our nuclear weapons plays into the hands of the Soviets. We must either have assured disarmament or our armament must continue to be second best to that of no other nation – there is no middle ground.[26]

Strauss devotes most of his argument to defending the necessity of testing and addressing the concerns of critics. First, Strauss argues that weapons systems have to be tested because of the insufficiency and inaccuracy of theoretical calculations:

The difference between theoretical calculations, on the one hand, and the phenomena actually experienced in a nuclear explosion, on the other, may be so great that without an experiment it is impossible to be certain of the result. Before the Alamogordo [Trinity] test, some of the scientists who worked on the bomb had a pool on the yield (explosive force) of the weapon, and, except for one or two wild guesses, most were far from the mark. The first thermonuclear test at Eniwetok in the Castle series [Castle Bravo] was substantially more powerful than estimated. Changes in design may be promising on paper but may not work at all at the proving ground. Effects also develop from tests and lead to new information and new ideas of value not only for military use but for civil defense and peaceful application as well.[27]

The allusion by Strauss in the above quote to the Bravo test appears to present the "runaway" nature of the explosion as a reason *for* testing. We learn from mistakes, even multimegaton mistakes. Even the fallout produced by the thermonuclear tests provided valuable knowledge. Learning the radiological effects of thermonuclear weapons was therefore an *additional* justification for testing – along with the benefits for technical developments. Strauss quotes approvingly from a 1955 AEC report on the effects of high-yield nuclear explosions:

If we had not conducted the full-scale thermonuclear tests in question, we would have been in ignorance of the effects of radioactive fall-out and, therefore, we would have been much more vulnerable to the dangers of fall-out in the event an enemy should resort to radiological warfare against us ... until the possibility of an atomic attack is eliminated by a *workable international plan for general disarmament*, the study and evaluation of the effects of weapons which might be used against us and the improvement of our means of self-defense are a paramount duty of our government.[28]

Needless to say, the crew of the *Lucky Dragon* and the islanders irradiated by Castle Bravo were probably not happy to have played the role of accidental and unwilling test subjects.

Strauss did recognize that objections to nuclear testing focused on the dangers of fallout and he addressed that concern repeatedly and at length. While not oblivious to the danger, he argues that it is minimal and that some degree of risk is justifiable in order to serve the larger goal of deterrence. He summarizes much of his case in a 1957 letter addressed to Mr. A. J. Muste but marked as unsent:

The possible risks from continued weapons testing have been carefully considered by competent scientists, both within and outside the Atomic Energy Commission, by independent scientific organizations in the United States such as the National Academy of Sciences, and by authoritative groups abroad such as the British Medical Research Council. In essence they conclude that the risks from the current rate of nuclear testing are small, exceedingly small in fact when compared to other risks that we routinely and readily accept every day ... I believe the conclusion we must reach after balancing all factors is this – we have the choice of running a very small risk from testing or a risk of catastrophe which might result from a surrender of our leadership in nuclear armament. That leadership, we believe, has been the deterrent to aggression since 1945. The cause for most serious concern is not the effect of radiation resulting from the tests to keep our weapons posture strong, but rather the effect of the devastation that would result from the massive use of nuclear weapons in warfare.[29]

Strauss was especially at pains to rebut the charges of prominent scientific critics such as Nobel Prize–winning chemist Linus Pauling. He notes that Pauling, as a chemist, was not an expert on nuclear weapons.[30] He cites Pauling's warning that the tests were dangerously increasing the levels of radioactive carbon 14 in the atmosphere. He then quotes a group of Columbia University geologists who contradicted Pauling's claim and said that the actual increase in atmospheric carbon 14 was much lower than Pauling had claimed. They also asserted that the increase in exposure to radioactivity for an individual would be less than that received by wearing a luminous-dial watch for two hours a year.[31] On several different occasions Strauss cites the 1957 report of the National Academy of Sciences titled "The Biological Effects of Atomic Radiation." The report notes that with the exception of some accidents affecting "small numbers" of people, the biological effects of the testing of nuclear weapons was "essentially negligible."[32]

Were the effects negligible? Were they reasonably thought to be at that time? We now know much more about the long-term effects of exposure to radiation than was known at the time, however, even then some authoritative voices argued that the effects were not negligible. In 1957 Andrei Sakharov published two papers disputing the reassurances about the safety of nuclear tests. Sakharov calculated that even the detonation of a relatively "clean" one-megaton bomb would produce enough carbon 14 to cause 6,600 deaths over the next 8,000 years.[33] Strauss had cited development of "clean" bombs as another reason for continued testing.[34] Of course, these potential effects would have to be multiplied many times given the large number of tests, the fact that many were radioactively "dirty," and the fact that many were larger than one megaton. Sakharov argued that the fact that some of these deaths would occur in the relatively distant future does not absolve us from responsibility. Strauss never mentions Sakharov's arguments. If he was aware of them, then perhaps he dismissed them as Communist propaganda, or perhaps he regarded the calculated deaths per megaton as negligible.

So was Strauss what today we would call a "spin doctor," someone who cleverly distorts and conceals scientific information to promote a political or ideological agenda? Such a judgment seems harsh. It seems fair to say that in the mid- to late 1950s scientific opinion really was divided about the global effects of nuclear tests and whether or not they were "negligible." Strauss could have conceded that the scientific evidence about the long-term and global effects of testing, such as those mentioned by Sakharov, were in dispute. However, he could have argued that in this case a doubt has to be weighed against what he regarded as a certainty – that testing was needed for the United States to retain a credible deterrent against Soviet aggression.

Less understandable is Strauss' failure to mention certain other consequences of testing. He fails to note that events such as the irradiation of the Japanese fishermen and the Marshallese were just the tip of a very large iceberg. The relatively small numbers of people accidentally irradiated in the Pacific were greatly exceeded by those both accidentally and intentionally exposed in the United States. While the tests in the Pacific were being conducted, many more tests were being carried out in Nevada, and these resulted in the direct and indirect exposure of many thousands of military personnel and civilians to significant doses of radiation. Strauss failed to mention that *people* were being tested and not just technology. As DeGroot notes, some of the Nevada tests were specifically intended to assess the physical and psychological effects of nuclear explosions on soldiers. Around ninety thousand soldiers were involved in these exercises.[35]

Films such as *The Atomic Café* and *Trinity and Beyond* contain archival footage of US soldiers advancing directly toward ground zero just after the detonation of an atomic bomb. The gigantic mushroom cloud, still roiling and resounding, towers just ahead. They are wearing no protective equipment at all, not even gas masks to prevent the inhalation of radioactive dust. It hardly needs saying that the Soviets performed the same sorts of exercises. While the accidental irradiation of the Japanese fishermen and the islanders made international headlines, the *intentional* exposure of American servicemen was ignored both by the press and by officials such as Strauss. Further, civilians were accidentally exposed to high levels of fallout – high even by AEC standards – not only on Rongelap and Utirik, but in places like St. George, Utah.

On May 19, 1953 at Yucca Flat in the Nevada Test Site, a thirty-two-kiloton bomb was detonated. Though the yield was, by that time, relatively modest, the bomb produced a vast amount of radioactive fallout, leading it to be nicknamed "Dirty Harry." Winds carried a large plume of fallout 135 miles east to St. George. The AEC had set up detectors in St. George, but had no plan to warn the population. When high levels of radiation were detected in the town – 6,000 milliroentgens – it took an hour for any warning to be broadcast. People who had been outside began to complain of headache, fever, thirst, nausea, diarrhea, vomiting, and other unpleasant symptoms. The AEC set up roadblocks in an attempt to intercept cars heading out of town to hose them down. Meanwhile, the AEC was assuring local media that the radiation had not reached dangerous levels. Years later, it was found that children under fourteen exposed to the fallout died of leukemia at 2.4 times the rate of people of that age who lived in the same area before the fallout and since.[36]

The irradiation of St. George was just one incident. Millions of "downwinders," residents of communities potentially in the path of fallout, were in the states of Nevada, Utah, Colorado, Arizona, and New Mexico. Global effects of fallout from nuclear testing may have been in dispute in the mid-fifties, but no one could dispute that there were deleterious local effects, where "local" is taken quite loosely.

In a memorandum to Eisenhower written on May 25, 1953, Strauss advises against a seventy-five-kiloton test in Nevada (orders of magnitude smaller than the multimegaton Castle devices). He recognizes that the Nevada test site would be more convenient but advises against tests of that size in the United States:

There is no question of the greater convenience of the Nevada testing ground, but I have the feeling that a 75 kiloton bomb is uncomfortably near or beyond the limit of the size that should be tested on the continent and I recommend against it at this time.[37]

But why would he want to go to the delay and expense of having the seventy-five-kiloton test in the Marshall Islands rather than in Nevada? Here is what he says in the same memo:

The test will be an air drop in Nevada and the estimated yield will be more than the equivalent of 75,000 tons of TNT which is half-again as large as any weapon that has ever been tested within the United States. As a member of the Commission, I was dubious of the tests of atomic weapons in the Unites States because of unfavorable public reaction. This has now materialized as evidenced by a large number of protests. The recent radio-active fall out on a small town in Utah [St. George] and the generally growing reaction in the surrounding areas leads me to question the wisdom of conducting this test as planned.[38]

In a follow-up memorandum written the next day, Strauss withdraws his objection to the seventy-five-kiloton test. He notes that the protests were mostly due to the occurrence of fallout, and he has been assured that the seventy-five-kiloton bomb will be air-dropped and detonated at an altitude sufficient to prevent most fallout.[39]

Conspicuously missing from these memoranda is any mention of concern for the well-being or safety of "downwinders." In other words, the sort of fallout that really worried Strauss appeared to be the fallout of negative public opinion, not the radioactive kind. Tests of large bombs could not be conducted in Nevada because of public relations problems, which, supposedly, would not be a factor in the Marshall Islands. It is hard to deny that for Strauss and like-minded officials, one of the greatest advantages of conducting the megaton tests in the Marshalls was that the PR problems seemed to be minimal there. How ironic, then, that it was the Castle Bravo test at Bikini that generated by far the most protest and negative publicity.

Given the insouciance (if that is the right word) shown by military and civilian officials concerning the radiation generated by the Nevada tests and the possible deleterious effect on American soldiers and civilians, it seems likely that they were even less concerned about the impact of testing on the Marshallese. Recall that, as shown by films like *Strategic Air Command*, the tenor of the times was that the United States was already at war and in war sacrifices have to be made and risks have to be run. Over four hundred thousand American soldiers and civilians had been killed in the Second World War, and untold millions in the Soviet Union. Given the recent memory of those sacrifices, and the prevailing Cold War anxieties, the exposure of an indefinite number to some indeterminate degree of danger from radiation was an acceptable risk for many on both sides. The Soviets, by the way, never hesitated to test even thermonuclear weapons in their own territory and large areas were rendered grossly polluted by radiation.

Strauss' main public statement about the Marshallese victims of Castle Bravo was contained in his press release of March 31, 1954, quoted in Chapter 3. There he recounted visiting the islanders and describing them as "well and happy." He goes into a bit more detail in *Men and Decisions*:

Before the end of 1954, we had conducted medical follow-ups on the Marshallese natives. They had continued in excellent health, their blood counts were approximately normal, and a few skin lesions had healed. A check made three years later (1957) indicated that no deaths had occurred among the Rongelap people except for one stillbirth resulting from an infection and a forty-six year old man whose death was attributed to hypertension. Neither was in any way related to radiation effects. The persons who were originally exposed on the island of Uterik, were examined and found to be in good health, with no illnesses or clinical conditions that could be related to radiation effects.[40]

Of course, such rosy reassurances were premature. Many of the harmful effects of exposure to radiation show up in the form of cancers decades after the exposure. We saw in a previous chapter that Steven Simon and his colleagues have demonstrated excess cases of thyroid cancer, attributable to exposure to radiation from nuclear tests, among the inhabitants of a number of the islands, and not just Rongelap and Utirik.[41]

Ōishi Matashichi details the health problems that he and other members of the *Lucky Dragon* crew suffered in subsequent years.[42] Strauss and other defenders of the testing program appear to have rushed to judgment in their assessment of the effects on the Marshallese, motivated, no doubt, by their desire to rebut what they saw as hyperbolic and alarmist claims by antitesters. Common sense, if nothing else, would seem to dictate some hesitancy about drawing conclusions about the well-being of those irradiated. Unfortunately, the exigencies of polemic often eclipse common sense.

Actually, Strauss received some information before his public statement of March 31 that did raise doubts about long-term medical complications. In Strauss' archival materials on the Castle tests is a brief report on the condition of the islanders as of March 20, 1954, nearly three weeks after Bravo.[43] This report, with extensive handwritten annotations by Strauss, warns that blood tests show unequivocal radiation injury. The prognosis is given as "fair," unless epidemic disease is introduced. Future miscarriages, abortions, and stillbirths are possible. Longevity cannot be studied because of lack of precise birth records. Late effects such as leukemia are said to be "unlikely" at the dosage level, but "absence of vital statistics makes any reasonable study impossible." Perhaps this information, of which Strauss was clearly aware, should have given him pause before declaring the Marshallese to be "well and happy."

It is hard to escape the impression that for Strauss and others at the highest levels, the well-being of the Marshall islanders was not a priority ahead of time, and the main problem that the Marshallese presented post-Bravo was with respect to public relations. There is no indication that Strauss felt any particular disdain for the Marshallese or even wrote them off as "simple" natives. It was not, then, that Strauss looked down on the Marshallese; he just looked through them. His interests were not contrary to theirs; those interests were incommensurable. Strauss' aim was to save America, and, indeed, the world from both nuclear war and Soviet domination. The Marshallese just wanted to live as they and their ancestors had lived for many generations. When you are fighting a war, even a Cold War, and the stakes of that war are so high, then the irradiation of a few hundred – or a few hundred thousand, for that matter – will be seen as collateral damage. When you are saving the world, some eggs might get broken.

At the beginning of this section we asked these questions:

Was the safety of the Marshallese a priority for those at the highest levels of responsibility for the nuclear testing policies of the United States? Was there any genuine concern ahead of time that something bad might happen, something very much like what actually did happen? Even after Castle Bravo made the risks apparent, was any serious consideration given to the possibility that the other tests might be dangerous? Is there any evidence that the deleterious consequences of the Bravo test were downplayed, distorted, or covered up?

Judging by the published memoirs and Strauss' archival materials, we have to say that the safety of the Marshallese was not a high priority for the makers of American nuclear policy. The success of the tests was the priority and the well-being of the indigenous people was a secondary concern, and only became urgent when their exposure to radiation became a public relations problem.

Our conclusion is not inconsistent with the thesis defended by Barton C. Hacker in *Elements of Controversy*, his thorough history of the radiological safety record of the nuclear tests:

The thesis this book argues is straightforward and relatively simple. Those responsible for radiation safety in nuclear weapons testing under the auspices of the Atomic Energy Commission were competent, diligent, and cautious. They understood the hazards and took every precaution within their power to avoid injuring either test participants or bystanders. Testing, of course, meant taking risks, and *safety could never be the highest priority*. Those in charge sometimes made mistakes, but for the most part they managed to ensure that neither test participants nor bystanders suffered any apparent damage from fallout.[44]

That is, those on site who were tasked with the responsibility of ensuring radiological safety carried out their duties conscientiously and capably as those duties were understood within the confines of established policies and priorities.

The problem, as Hacker notes, is that when you are testing multimegaton thermonuclear bombs, safety *cannot* be your highest priority, and those at the highest levels like Strauss were determined that the tests would proceed. Strauss and other officials surely just assumed that the safety measures enacted by the task force were adequate. Such comfortable complacency was no doubt easy to rationalize. However when you are dealing with the danger of the exposure of innocent people to intensely radioactive fallout, procedures that ensure safety "for the most part" are just not good enough.

Some changes in testing procedures were made after the Bravo events. For instance, stringent new standards were required for the preshot weather forecasts.[45] However, at this stage, these changes seem a bit like the proverbial closing of the barn door after the horses are gone. Further, the tests in the Marshalls did continue, with many in the multimegaton range, until 1958.

As for official information about the victims of Bravo, there was no cover-up of the incidents. How could there be, with the story flooding the international press? The medical information about the victims in Strauss' public statement does not seem to have been intentionally distorted, though when observers are strongly motivated, they can see even radiation poisoning through rose-colored glasses. The suffering of the victims was definitely downplayed. As we say, the main problem posed to American officials by the fate of the *Lucky Dragon* crew and the inhabitants of Rongelap and Utirik was managing public opinion. This led to pronouncements that were far more anodyne and optimistic than the facts justified.

Perhaps the fairest assessment of the treatment of the Marshallese people by the US government is given by Kim Skoog, Professor of Philosophy at the University of Guam:

It is difficult to make a single characterization of the U.S. government's care in safeguarding the well-being of the people of the Marshall Islands during and after the time it carried out these tests. Often in conducting research there are a lot of uncertainties and unexpected results. If one examines the complex history that surrounds these nuclear tests and the years of litigation, scientific studies, and assorted efforts to clean up the affected areas and relocation of peoples, one will see that much of the efforts by the U.S. government were *reactive* rather than *proactive*, in the minimum, one could make a case for fault with regard to this general attitude, given the high stakes brought on by these extremely powerful and dangerous nuclear explosions.[46]

The salient and undeniable fact is that the precautions established for Castle Bravo proved grossly insufficient. Had the well-being of the Marshallese been a greater priority for men like Strauss, and had a more proactive policy originated from the top, then perhaps a more adequate set of precautions would have been in place by the time of Bravo. The established precautions might have been based on an awareness of what could happen rather than projections of what would happen. In any organization that conducts potentially dangerous or destructive activities, such as deep water drilling for oil, manufacturing pesticides, or testing nuclear bombs, the people at the top are the ones who set the priorities. They are the ones who determine how much emphasis is to be given to safety vis-à-vis other goals. Even if, as Hacker notes, safety cannot be the highest priority, then neither need it be relegated to an afterthought.

Still, our judgment of Strauss should not be as censorious as some of those condemnations quoted earlier. Looking back from sixty years' distance it may be hard for us to realize just how scared people were at the time – and not without reason. Thermonuclear war would have been a calamity that would have made the Black Death look pale. Was Lewis Strauss frightened? He would have been a fool not to be, and he was no fool. If there is a straw that you can clutch that might save you from calamity, then you will grasp that straw, and thereby you also accept all the consequences of doing so. Fear is one of the most powerful emotions, and hope is one of the most seductive. In this case the hope, amounting to a delusion, was that the testers were in control of forces that defied control.

In the end, the Marshallese faced what the weak have always faced when the strong decide what they must do. In his *History of the Peloponnesian War*, Thucydides recounts the speech of the mighty Athenians to the inhabitants of the small island of Melos: "the strong do what they can and the weak suffer what they must." This was the way of the world in the fifth century BCE and in 1954, and it remains so today.

NOTES

1 Butterfield, *The Whig Interpretation of History.*
2 Bryson, *The Life and Times of the Thunderbolt Kid*, p. 129.
3 WikiQuotes, "Stalin."
4 Gaddis, *The Cold War: A New History*, p. 25.
5 Figes, *The Whisperers*, p. 251.
6 Baggott, *The First War of Physics*, p. 451.
7 DeGroot, *The Bomb*, pp. 133–134.
8 Holloway, *Stalin and the Bomb*, p. 222.
9 Bernstein, *Oppenheimer*, p. 103.
10 Holloway, *Stalin and the Bomb*, pp. 131–132.
11 Holloway, *Stalin and the Bomb*, pp. 295–296.
12 Gaddis, *The Cold War: A New History*, p. 11.
13 Gaddis, *The Cold War: A New History*, p. 28.
14 Gaddis, *The Cold War: A New History*, p. 34.
15 Quoted in Nelson, *Radiance*, p. 236.
16 Bird and Sherwin, *American Prometheus*, p. 362.
17 Bird and Sherwin, *American Prometheus*, pp. 401–402.
18 Joint Committee on Atomic Energy, January 27, 1953, Strauss Archives, Box 534, Tests and Testing, 1947–1954.
19 Address before Virginia State Chamber of Commerce, April 14, 1950, Box 534, Tests and Testing, 1947–1954, p. 2.
20 Address before Virginia State Chamber of Commerce, April 14, 1950, Box 534, Tests and Testing, 1947–1954, p. 2.
21 Strauss, *Men and Decisions*, p. 406.
22 Strauss, *Men and Decisions*, p. 406.
23 Strauss, *Men and Decisions*, p. 406.

24 Strauss, *Men and Decisions*, p. 406.
25 Rhodes, transcript of *Race for the Superbomb*.
26 Strauss, draft of letter to David Lawrence, Strauss Archives, Box 534, Tests and Testing, 1955–1957.
27 Strauss, *Men and Decisions*, p. 407.
28 Strauss, *Men and Decisions*, p. 412; emphasis in original.
29 Letter to A. J. Muste, Strauss Archives, Box 534, Tests and Testing, 1955–1957.
30 Strauss, *Men and Decisions*, p. 413.
31 Strauss, *Men and Decisions*, pp. 413–414.
32 Strauss, *Men and Decisions*, p. 415.
33 DeGroot, *The Bomb*, p. 246.
34 Strauss, *Men and Decisions*, p. 419.
35 DeGroot, *The Bomb*, p. 239.
36 Washington Nuclear Museum website, "Radioactive Fallout to St. George, UT."
37 Memorandum, May 25, 1953, Strauss Archives, Box 534, Tests and Testing, 1947–1954.
38 Memorandum, May 25, 1953, Strauss Archives, Box 534, Tests and Testing, 1947–1954.
39 Memorandum, May 26, 1953, Strauss Archives, Box 534, Tests and Testing, 1947–1954.
40 Strauss, *Men and Decisions*, pp. 412–413.
41 Simon et al., "Radiation Doses and Cancer Risks."
42 Ōishi, *The Day the Sun Rose in the West*.
43 "Notes about Natives," undated, Strauss Archives, Box 428, Castle Series I.
44 Hacker, *Elements of Controversy*, p. 9; emphasis added.
45 Hansen, *U.S. Nuclear Weapons*, p. 66.
46 Skoog, "U.S. Nuclear Testing in the Marshall Islands, p. 73; emphasis in original.

7

Bikini Postmortem, Part II

Nuclear Policy and Nuclear Tests

As stated in the Introduction, the purpose of this book is twofold: First, to tell the story of the Marshall Islands tests and, in particular, the effects of these tests on the victims. Second, we aim to understand the context, and especially why a program of atmospheric testing of nuclear and thermonuclear weapons was considered necessary, despite the risks that were knowable ahead of time and which became all too apparent with Castle Bravo. In the previous chapter we examined the *zeitgeist*, the character of the times and the reigning fears and perceptions that motivated the arms race and therefore the tests essential to weapons development. We also looked at the character and convictions of Lewis L. Strauss, the man who, second only to the president, wielded the most power in influencing the policy and practice of nuclear testing.

In this final chapter we expand our scope and situate nuclear testing within the context of US nuclear policy during the period of atmospheric nuclear tests conducted by the United States (1945–1963). US nuclear policy evolved rapidly during that time in response to technological developments and the increasing nuclear capacities of the Soviet Union. In brief, the development was from viewing nuclear weapons as usable, indeed decisive, weapons for winning wars to the policy of Mutual Assured Destruction (MAD), which sought deterrence through a balance of terror. At first, nuclear bombs merely seemed to be more potent than conventional bombs. As its role in the Second World War seemingly showed, the atomic bomb was the winning weapon. For the advocates of MAD, the only sane use of a nuclear weapon is to prevent its use.[1]

For four years the United States was the only nation with atomic weapons. When, in September 1949, it was learned that the Soviet Union also had them, a new international situation emerged that would pose novel and deep challenges for strategic thinking and foreign policy. At first, though the Soviets had demonstrated a nuclear capacity, the United States held such a great advantage that a nuclear war still seemed winnable. With the acquisition of thermonuclear weapons by the USSR, in the mid-fifties, and with the development of Soviet rocket technology, as vividly demonstrated by the Sputnik launch in October, 1957, nuclear war came to look more like mutual suicide, and nuclear policy adapted accordingly.

In the nuclear age, conflicts between the superpowers were pushed into peripheral areas where involvement and sponsorship by the major players turned local conflicts into foci of the worldwide struggle. Our argument is that the people of the Marshall Islands were caught up in this global contest between East and West, just as much as the people of Korea and Vietnam. Their home was one more battlefield in a war that, for many millions, was not cold. At a deeper level, though nuclear war was often described as "unthinkable," such rhetoric belied the facts. From the beginning of the nuclear age to the emergence of MAD, except for an early and brief advocacy of international control, accepted American nuclear policy presumed or explicitly justified the use of nuclear weapons in warfare. In an ethical climate in which the possible use of nuclear weapons on human targets was not only thinkable, but was regarded as a winning strategy, concern about the incidental injury to indigenous people by nuclear tests was not a salient issue for policymakers.

THE FIRST POLICY: THE DECISION TO DROP THE BOMBS

On July 16, 1945, it became clear with the Trinity Test that the United States had two workable nuclear weapons, the "Little Boy" uranium bomb, and the "Fat Man" plutonium bomb. Once you have nuclear weapons, you have to decide what to do with them, and such decisions constitute nuclear policy. The initial policy decision, therefore, was how best to use this unprecedented destructive capacity to force Japan to surrender and so end the Second World War. The decision to drop the bombs on Hiroshima and Nagasaki remains deeply controversial and divisive to this day. In this section we will review that decision and its rationale, and see how those justifications bear on the later willingness to conduct atmospheric tests.

In order to understand the decision to use nuclear weapons in 1945, it is particularly important to emphasize both the strategic situation facing American leaders and the moral imperatives that had become paramount after four years of intensely bitter warfare. After the sudden forced entry of the United States into the war in December 1941, the first order of business was to halt the explosive Japanese expansion into the Pacific. This was done by the Navy at the Battle of Midway in June 1942, in which four Japanese fleet carriers were destroyed, and at Guadalcanal, where in savage fighting, the US Marines virtually annihilated repeated Japanese attacks. American forces went on the offensive with a series of "island hopping" invasions, beginning with Tarawa in November 1943 and ending with Okinawa in the spring of 1945. In addition to the island invasions, major operations conducted by the US Army steadily pushed back the Japanese, first in New Guinea and then in the Philippines. Meanwhile, American, Indian, and British forces, after suffering major setbacks, had halted and then repelled the Japanese advance in the China/ Burma/India Theater.

The effect of these campaigns, at huge human and material cost, was to push the front lines to the shores of the Japanese home islands, though Japan still held vast areas of mainland Asia and the southwestern Pacific. Japan was now exposed to devastating air attacks by land-based and carrier forces. Particularly destructive were the incendiary raids conducted by B-29 bombers under the command of General Curtis LeMay. In Tokyo alone, incendiary bombing on the night of March 9/10 killed approximately 100,000 and left millions homeless.[2] By this time, the US Navy had reduced the surface fleet of the Imperial Japanese Navy, formerly the pride of the Empire, to a useless relic (Japan was still capable of deadly submarine warfare, as shown by the sinking of the *USS Indianapolis*). The destruction of Japanese merchant shipping by American submarines had virtually blockaded the home islands, isolating them from the overseas possessions.

By V-E Day, May 8, 1945, when Nazi Germany surrendered, Japan had suffered defeat on all fronts and enormous civilian casualties, yet the truculence of the Japanese military leadership had not abated. Rather, as the war drew to a close, Japanese tactics became increasingly fanatical and desperate. Most famously, the kamikaze attacks, which were first employed in the Battle of Leyte Gulf in October and November 1944, were pursued with furious intensity during the Battle of Okinawa. This particularly terrifying form of warfare, in which a pilot intentionally sacrifices himself to kill his enemy, prefigured the suicide bombing tactics of terrorists in our day. To those who have suffered such attacks, nothing could more strongly inculcate the image of an implacable enemy who will not surrender and can only be destroyed. That image was reinforced by decrypts of ULTRA, the Japanese military code, which revealed the extensive preparations in anticipation of an American invasion of Kyushu, the southernmost of the Japanese home islands. These messages showed no weakening of resolve, but only a determination to go down fighting while inflicting as much damage as possible on the invader.[3]

Among America's enemies in the Second World War, the Japanese were loathed with particular vehemence. Commanders in Europe often complained that their soldiers did not hate the Germans enough. For those fighting in the Pacific, lack of rancor toward the Japanese was not a problem. American film, propaganda, and even children's cartoons, depicted the Japanese as yellow, squinting, buck-toothed sub-humans of unlimited cruelty and fanaticism. In 1944 the press broke the story of the Bataan Death March, in which American and Filipino prisoners of war had been murdered and brutalized by their Japanese captors in 1942. Public anger against the Japanese, already red hot, became incandescent, and US Senators led the call for genocidal retribution.[4]

When the United States acquired nuclear weapons, it therefore faced a hated and defiant enemy, one that had apparently adopted a policy of suicidal, last-ditch resistance. In this context, as Wilson D. Miscamble notes, there was never any serious question about *whether* to use the atomic bombs, but only *how* best to employ them.[5] The paramount goal was straightforward – how to defeat the Japanese as quickly as possible.[6] The decision to employ nuclear weapons against Japanese cities is examined and ably defended in two works, Richard B. Frank's *Downfall: The End of the Imperial Japanese Empire*, and Miscamble's *The Most Controversial Decision: Truman, the Atomic Bombs, and the Defeat of Japan*. We will follow the accounts presented in these works.

For President Harry Truman, who bore the ultimate responsibility, the decision to use the bombs did not require soul-searching. Mostly he just acquiesced with the assumptions that had held during the Roosevelt administration, and acceded to the trajectory of events already in motion:

Truman had to make no profound and wrenching decision to use the atomic weapon … the president showed no inclination to question in any way the guiding, if implied, assumption that had prevailed under his predecessor's administration that the bomb was a weapon of war and built to be used. His willingness to authorize the dropping of the atomic bombs placed him in a direct continuity with FDR ... [O]ne must acknowledge that Truman possessed neither the capacity nor the desire to question the logic of the bomb's use.[7]

For Truman and his Secretary of State, James F. Byrnes, the top priority was to end the war as quickly as possible in order to save American lives:

These two politicians [Truman and Byrnes] saw the matter clearly. Moral complexities or future diplomatic implications failed to complicate their straightforward thinking. The atomic bomb might possibly save American lives if it could be successfully tested and then delivered upon its Japanese targets. This remained, throughout, the essential motivation that guided the decision to use the horrific weapons on Hiroshima and Nagasaki in August of 1945.[8]

Their hope was that the shock of an unannounced attack with these terrifying new weapons would prompt the Japanese to surrender unconditionally without the need of a land invasion of the home islands.[9]

Why, though, was the decision so straightforward for Truman and his advisors? Why were alternatives not considered? The answer is that using the atomic bombs was not considered as just one among a number of possible options. *Nothing* was guaranteed to force the Japanese to surrender in a timely manner. The Japanese, both military and civilians, had clearly demonstrated a preference for suicide over surrender. Consequently, the military did not intend to put its eggs in any one basket:

Whatever the hopes for atomic weapons, the American military in no way built its strategy to defeat Japan on the successful testing and use of them. To achieve this ultimate goal the Americans forcefully pursued a number of strategies – tightening the naval blockade of the Japanese home islands, continuing a massive conventional bombing assault by General Curtis LeMay's B-29s, which rained incendiary napalm bombs on Japanese cities, and preparing for an invasion and subsequent ground war.[10]

The somber fact was that, despite the many setbacks and massive losses, in the summer of 1945, Imperial Japan was nowhere near to military defeat. American plans called for an invasion of Kyushu, called "Operation Olympic," in November 1945. Intelligence estimates based on ULTRA decrypts indicated that the American invasion force would be met by an equal number of Japanese troops, fighting in familiar terrain with a topography that favored defensive operations.[11] Further, approximately four thousand aircraft were available for kamikaze attacks, and these, operating with conventional torpedo planes, were predicted to knock out fifteen to twenty percent of the invasion force while still at sea.[12] The number of American casualties that would have been suffered in an invasion of Japan has been hotly debated for years.[13] No one can seriously maintain that these casualties would not have been very high, but with respect to the decision to drop the atomic bombs such casualty estimates are irrelevant. No American president could have proceeded with such an invasion without first using any means at his disposal to end the war beforehand. If dropping the atomic bombs had any chance of forcing surrender on their own, they had to be tried.

In the event, Japan did surrender, but only after the second bomb had been dropped on Nagasaki, and only after the personal intervention of Emperor Hirohito finally overcame the opposition of the military, which wanted to continue the war even after the second atomic bombing.[14] In his speech to the Japanese people broadcast on August 15, Hirohito called upon his subjects to "endure the unendurable" and end the war. He specifically mentioned that the enemy had begun to employ a "new and most cruel bomb." Frank and Miscamble forcefully argue that the use of the atomic bombs ended the war sooner than would otherwise have been the case. Other experts continue to question the bomb's efficacy in forcing surrender.[15] The important point is that the bomb was *perceived* as forcing the end of the war without the holocaust of a land invasion. To allied leaders, and especially to the soldiers who would have had to carry out the invasion, the atomic bombs appeared, in the words of Winston Churchill, as "a miracle of deliverance."

The first nuclear policy was therefore the decision to use the bomb in the hopes of ending the Second World War. The perception at the time was that this policy was a complete success. The civilians killed in Hiroshima and Nagasaki were the stakes in a gamble, a gamble that paid off abundantly for the victors – and for the vanquished as well, when you consider the Japanese casualties that would have been suffered in an invasion. The significance of Hiroshima and Nagasaki for the topic of this book is not that a moral line was crossed with the mass killing of civilians. That line had already been crossed repeatedly. The significance was that atomic weapons apparently worked; they were therefore regarded as feasible and practical weapons of war, and their use was a seemingly rational means of winning a war. At this stage, the use of nuclear weapons was very thinkable indeed.

HIATUS: THE INTERNATIONALIST INTERLUDE

With the end of the Second World War, by far the most destructive war in human history, and with the founding of the United Nations, many politicians, including President Truman, made hopeful speeches promising a new era of international cooperation. Remarkably, on the side of the

United States, at least, such pronouncements were not mere boilerplate, but were taken seriously. For a brief period extending well into 1946, the United States pursued a policy of international control of nuclear weapons. On November 15, 1945, the American, British, and Canadian governments signed an agreement that called for cautious openness in the sharing of information about atomic technology.[16] A specially created UN commission would oversee these exchanges, and would work toward the gradual elimination of nuclear weapons from national arsenals. This commission would be further charged with developing a program of inspections and rules for compliance. Initially, the Soviets also appeared willing to support a UN program for the international control of atomic energy.[17]

However, this was also a period of increasing tension and suspicion between East and West. It was during this period, in March 1946, that Churchill gave his famous "iron curtain" speech. Actually, at this stage the British were more alarmed than the Americans at the evidence of Soviet expansionism.[18] During the war, Stalin had successfully developed an image of himself as bluff, gruff "Uncle Joe," rather than the calculating, ice-cold mass murderer and manipulator that he was. Even President Roosevelt seemed to fall somewhat under his spell. As Miscamble notes, after the war the United States only slowly turned its perception of the Soviet Union "from difficult ally to potential foe."[19]

The short era of internationalist idealism came to a crashing end with the presentation of the Baruch Plan to the United Nations in June 1946. Bernard Baruch, a wealthy financier, was appointed as a special envoy to the United Nations to present a proposal for the international control of all aspects of nuclear energy, including atomic weapons. Baruch's plan was essentially one that had been formulated by Dean Acheson and David Lilienthal, but Baruch, with Truman's approval, added tougher sanctions and a more thorough system of inspections.[20] The Soviets flatly rejected the Baruch Plan, concerned, perhaps understandably, that it would compromise their national sovereignty, economy, and security. More basically, it would compromise Stalin's mania for secrecy behind his "iron curtain."[21] With the quick snuffing of Western internationalist idealism, both sides settled down into what John F. Kennedy called "the long twilight struggle" that would be the Cold War.[22]

WINNING THE NUCLEAR WAR

General Curtis LeMay was the prototype of the cigar-chomping, hard-driving, "iron-ass" commander. In 1948 he was placed at the head of the

Strategic Air Command (SAC), the unit of the US Air Force charged with delivering strategic nuclear weapons against the enemy. LeMay accepted the ruthless logic of a modern total war, which recognized that when you are fighting a highly industrialized and technologically sophisticated enemy, there can be no clear distinction between military and civilian targets. Civilians who produce the material and technological basis for modern war are just as essential to the war efforts as the armed and uniformed soldier. LeMay authorized the saturation incendiary bombing of Tokyo because manufacturing had been decentralized and dispersed throughout "civilian" areas. If children made bomb fuses, then children were legitimate targets.[23]

In a nuclear age, the goal of immediate and total destruction of the enemy was paramount. As envisioned by LeMay, in the event of war, hundreds of bombers would overwhelm Russian air defenses and the entire atomic arsenal would be emptied in one massive strike.[24] This was not just LeMay's opinion, but was widely accepted among senior Air Force officers.[25]

It is important to realize that the Air Force at this time did not see its mission as essentially different from its strategic bombing role in the Second World War. As historian Edward Kaplan puts it:

The atomic bomb was revolutionary in many ways, yet strategic airpower practitioners added it to their prewar ideas and wartime experience in incremental fashion … The strategic air campaign sought to paralyze the enemy through massive shock, a prospect made more realistic by the new weapon, but hardly a new concept.[26]

Lawrence Freedman confirms the persistence of a strategic bombing ideology into the atomic age:

Among airmen, an ideology had been created around a single weapon of war – the heavy bomber. They could not contemplate a truly effective defense against the bomber, nor accept that airpower had value in any role other than strategic bombardment.[27]

The USAF's Emergency War Plan of 1950 projected a war with the Soviet Union in which strategic bombardment would play a vital role, but one not substantially different from the one it had played in the Second World War:

The plan specified how, if successful, these operations would affect the war. Destruction of Delta targets [those vital to Soviet war-making capacity] would stop critical war-supporting industries by cutting their electric power, disrupting related, but less critical, industries, and "by the chaos and possible panic

occasioned by the industrial damage, the disruption of urban services, the inter-
ference with control channels, and the insecurity and fear on the part of the people." This was a classic attack on the industrial web.[28]

Air Force strategists of course recognized that you get a much bigger
bang from an atomic bomb, but the basic purpose of strategic bombing
and its role in warfare was not initially changed.

Even when the US nuclear capacity became so great that killing
nations by air power alone became feasible, nuclear war was still seen
as winnable. Before the development of ICBMs, the only means of delivering an atomic bomb was by bomber, so this period was known as the
"air atomic" era. As Kaplan notes, during the entire air-atomic age war
victory was still regarded as achievable:

> Before victory became impossible, it was plausible. Strategic Air Command could
> have destroyed the USSR throughout the air atomic period, while the latter could
> scarcely strike back at first. The casualties would have been horrendous in the
> Soviet Union and its allies, while its retaliatory capacity was small.[29]

So, for years into the nuclear age, atomic weapons were viewed by US
military planners as practical, usable weapons and incorporated the use
of those weapons into their plans for winning wars. As DeGroot succinctly puts it, "Soldiers could not conceive of a weapon not meant to be
used."[30]

But if US war plans at the beginning of the 1950s included using
atomic weapons to win wars, why were they not used in Korea? In fact,
soon after the war began on June 25, 1950, possible use of the bomb was
mooted at the highest levels. President Truman asked the Joint Chiefs of
Staff to consider going nuclear if the Soviets began to participate in the
conflict. In that eventuality, General Douglas MacArthur, the commander
in Korea, wanted to strike with atomic bombs at the routes leading from
Manchuria and Vladivostok into North Korea. B-29s with unassembled
nuclear weapons were sent to Guam, and, though the bombs were never
used, they stayed there through 1951.[31]

When the war seemed to be dragging on with no end in sight, Truman
began to imagine issuing an ultimatum to Stalin and Mao, and then, if
the threat were not heeded, to hit multiple targets in Russia and China.
As DeGroot notes, these fantasies probably are more indicative of a high
level of frustration than of an actual intent.[32] However, the fact that such
chilling scenarios were entertained at all shows how "thinkable" the use
of nuclear weapons was at the time.

According to John Lewis Gaddis, there were three reasons that the atomic bomb was not used in Korea. First, was the lack of suitable targets in the Korean peninsula:

The atomic bomb had been developed for use against cities, industrial complexes, military bases, and transportation networks. Few of these existed on the Korean peninsula, where United Nations forces were confronting an army that advanced mostly on foot, carrying its own supplies, along primitive roads and even improvised mountain paths. "What would it be dropped on?" one American general wanted to know. The answer was not clear, nor was the evidence that dropping one, several, or even many bombs under these circumstances would be decisive.[33]

Second, if Chinese cities were bombed, this risked a full-scale conflict with the Soviet Union and the very distinct danger that the war would spread to Europe, where NATO forces at the time were quite weak.[34] Finally, by the spring of 1951, the United Nations forces in Korea had counterattacked and had stabilized the military situation there.[35] In short, atomic weapons were not used in Korea because in that war at that time and place it would not likely have been a winning weapon. So, though the atomic bomb was not the right weapon in Korea, its usefulness in other situations was not discounted.

THE "NEW LOOK" VERSUS "FLEXIBLE RESPONSE"

Dwight David Eisenhower became the thirty-fourth president of the United States on January 20, 1953. As Eisenhower came into office, the world was entering the thermonuclear age. The Mike test occurred in the November of his election year, and the Bravo test just over a year into his presidency. The Soviets exploded their *sloika* device in August 1953, and tested their "true" H-bomb – which they delivered by bomber – in November 1955. As noted in Chapter 2, the advent of thermonuclear devices meant that no one could pretend anymore that nuclear weapons were not instruments of genocide.

Critics often regarded Eisenhower as a lightweight who read mostly Western novels and played a lot of golf while leaving the deep thinking to others. Gaddis strongly disagrees with this assessment. National leaders both in the United States and the Soviet Union had to face the emerging prospect of both sides possessing virtually unlimited destructive capacity, and to plan how to balance the hopes and fears generated by this situation. According to Gaddis:

Eisenhower did so exquisitely but terrifyingly: he was at once the most subtle and brutal strategist of the nuclear age. The *physical* effects of thermonuclear explosions appalled him at least as much as they did [Soviet leader Georgii] Malenkov and Churchill: "Atomic War will destroy civilization," he insisted several months after the BRAVO test. There will be millions of people dead ... If the Kremlin and Washington ever lock up in a war, the results are too horrible to contemplate." When told, early in 1956, that a Soviet attack on the United States could wipe out the entire government and kill 65 percent of the American people, he acknowledged that it "It would literally be a business of digging ourselves out of the ashes and beginning again."[36]

When he first came into office, Eisenhower held that nuclear weapons could be used as military weapons against military targets.[37] Gaddis says, "But by the time Eisenhower made that statement, the physics of thermonuclear explosions had shattered its logic," and he refers to the Bravo test as proof.[38] According to Gaddis, Eisenhower's response to the developing prospect of a world with opposing sides both possessing thermonuclear weapons was to develop the policy that has been termed "The New Look."

As we note below, however, it was hardly clear to every strategist that the development of thermonuclear weapons had "shattered" the "logic" behind their actual military use. Actually, the motivation behind The New Look was largely economic. It was a strategy for meeting the continuing menace of communist aggression and expansionism in an era of tightening budgets.[39] Protracted and piecemeal engagements such as Korea were indecisive and very expensive. Further, the Soviets maintained a huge conventional force in Europe, and to match them in manpower and matériel would also be ruinously costly. The New Look therefore placed nuclear weapons at the front and center of American defense policy. If America or its allies were attacked, by either conventional or nuclear means, there would be one response – all-out, massive retaliation with thermonuclear weapons. Aggression would be met with annihilation. The New Look therefore ratcheted up the terror and brought down costs.

Though it aimed at deterrence, and despite his personal qualms, Eisenhower's policy was bellicose, threatening "massive retaliation" against Soviet instigation of general war. As Freedman notes the term "massive retaliation" is not journalistic or academic hyperbole, but was the actual language used in a 1953 paper presented by the Joint Chiefs of Staff that advocated "New Look" doctrine.[40] At this point, the United States and its allies did not yet perceive a stalemate in the nuclear confrontation; the parity of the capacity for overkill that led to MAD had not yet emerged. Secretary of State John Foster Dulles opposed what he regarded as a psychological taboo against the use of nuclear weapons and advocated that, like any other weapon, they be used where and when appropriate.[41] That nuclear weapons were intended for *use* in the face of aggression was stated unequivocally in 1954 by Field Marshall Bernard Law Montgomery, who was the Deputy Supreme Allied Commander of Europe:

I want to make it absolutely clear that we at SHAPE are basing all our planning on using atomic and thermonuclear weapons in our defense. With us it is no longer "they may possibly be used"; it is very definitely: "They will be used if we are attacked."[42]

Montgomery no doubt meant what he said; nevertheless, no sane person would unleash thermonuclear weapons over just *any* aggression, but only for a major and significant threat such as a Soviet attack on Western Europe. Therefore, opponents of the United States might be tempted into a betting game, gambling that they could get by with modest or peripheral aggressions without provoking "massive retaliation." By patiently deploying a strategy of limited and piecemeal aggressions, no one of which is sufficient to bring down the nuclear hammer, the enemy might inflict a slow death by a thousand small cuts.

Nuclear strategists therefore devised the doctrine of "flexible response" as a critique of the all-or-nothing nature of The New Look. The best-known defender of the flexible response was Henry Kissinger, who articulated that view in his 1957 book *Nuclear Weapons and Foreign Policy*. This work is the classic statement of the new strategic situation of the late 1950s and its implications for American foreign policy. The book was widely read and highly influential at the time, and it remains in print in abridged form today.

Two dominant themes emerge in the first chapter of the book: (1) the implacable hostility and aggressiveness of the communist powers, and (2) the paradox that possession of ultimate destructive power by the United States has led to a paralysis of the ability to project and use that power.

Kissinger sees the communist leaders as cynical opportunists and credits them with a sinister aptitude for exploiting any vacillation or irresolution by the West. The expansionism of communist states is firmly rooted in ideology, and the only way to contain such aggression is by determined and forceful opposition:

we are confronted by two revolutionary powers, the U.S.S.R. and Communist China, which pride themselves on their superior understanding of "objective" forces and to which policies unrelated to a plausible possibility of employing force seem either hypocrisy or stupidity. Because harmony between different social systems is explicitly rejected by Soviet doctrine, the renunciation of force will create a vacuum into which the Soviet leadership can move with impunity. Because the Soviet leaders pride themselves on their ability to "see through" our protestations of peaceful intentions, our only possibility for affecting their actions resides in the possession of superior force. For the Soviet leadership has made every effort to retain its militancy. It has been careful to insist that no technological discovery, however powerful, can abolish the laws of history and that real peace is attainable only *after* the triumph of communism. "We will bury you," Nikita S. Khrushchev has said, and the democracies would have been spared much misery had they not so often insisted that dictators do not mean what they say.[43]

Put bluntly, the communists are rigid ideologues who respect only power.

Yet the possession of thermonuclear weapons has strangely diminished the influence of the United States and inhibited its ability to use its immense power effectively. Previously, the buffer of two great oceans had given the United States the luxury of abstaining from conflicts or, once in, of being protected from attack until overwhelming force could be developed. Both the First and Second World Wars had been raging for over two years before the United States entered, and in both cases considerable time was required to build up the human and material resources that ultimately delivered victory. In a nuclear war, the oceans would provide no protection, and the destruction would be immediate and horrific. Even the "winner" in a nuclear conflict will suffer loss on an unprecedented scale. Before the era of parity, thermonuclear war would have meant the utter destruction of the Soviet Union and a terrible, but lesser, price to be paid by the United States and Western Europe. The United States and its allies would still have suffered many millions of casualties and trillions of dollars of property damage. In a thermonuclear world, the difference between winning and losing is a difference in degree of catastrophe.

The policy of "massive retaliation" promised ferocious retribution, and its defenders like Dulles regarded it as a more offensive strategy compared to the perceived reserve and caution of the Truman years.[44] Kissinger argues that, on the contrary, fear of fomenting the apocalypse had fostered a dangerous passivity toward communist provocations and accounted for the West's record of fecklessness in the face of communist gains.[45] Further, as Kissinger notes, the more Soviet nuclear capacities advance, the higher the bar will be set for a *casus belli*, and the more "peripheral" provocations will be tolerated.[46] Hence, there is an urgent need to rethink how power is to be matched with goals in a thermonuclear world. A middle course must be found to escape the dilemma between all-out war on the one hand and appeasement on the other:

The dilemma of the nuclear period therefore can be defined as follows: the enormity of modern weapons makes the thought of war repugnant, but the refusal to run any risks would amount to giving the Soviet rulers a blank check. At a time when we have never been stronger, we have had to learn that power that is not clearly related to the objectives for which it is to be employed may merely paralyze the will. No more urgent task confronts American policy than to bring our power into balance with the issues for which we are most likely to have to contend.[47]

If fear of nuclear holocaust paralyzes us, the communists will win. They will exploit each instance of weakness with aggression, confident that any show of resistance can be dispelled by rattling the nuclear saber. So, US foreign policy will have to run risks, and the question Kissinger seeks to answer in his book is how to deploy power effectively and run risks intelligently.

In making his case for a flexible response and limited nuclear war, Kissinger first notes the fatal flaw in a policy of massive retaliation against any aggression. Since the consequences of total nuclear war are so mutually destructive, the decision to attack will be clear-cut only if the nation is directly attacked in a way that threatens its national existence.[48] If the provocation is anything less, all of the pressures will favor hesitation and paralysis. Would even a Soviet invasion of Western Europe be sufficient to provoke the United States into total war? There therefore must be a range of responses to aggression that do not take a path leading to all-out war.

Short of total war, how should the United States respond to the Soviet threat? First, Kissinger notes that the East/West conflict is likely to be long-term. Hopes for a spontaneous internal transformation in Soviet ideology or intentions are just that – hopes. In the meantime, policy must deal with worst cases and focus on what it can control, not what it hopes.[49] To that end, Kissinger says that both military and diplomatic policy must combine patience with firmness.[50] If done adroitly, a policy of graduated response could turn the tables on communist aggressors. When their aggression is met with an appropriately firm response, the pressure would then be on them to decide on running the risks of escalation. Kissinger thinks that the Soviets and Chinese will not risk total war to prevent adverse developments unless their national survival is at stake.[51] Even when they threaten war, Kissinger recommends calling their bluff when both history and doctrine indicate that such threats are bluster.[52]

Kissinger holds that the policy of graduated response must encompass a limited war, and even a limited nuclear war. For instance, if one side uses only low-yield tactical nuclear weapons, the other side could respond in kind and refrain from using the cataclysmic, megaton-yield strategic weapons.[53] He realizes that a limited response is risky and that a limited nuclear war could escalate.[54] However, he argues that in an age when nuclear-armed powers confront each other, technological developments have imposed stark conditions upon us.

If, for instance, the Soviets were to employ tactical nuclear weapons on the battlefield, the United States would have only two choices: total war or a limited response. Since these are the circumstances forced on us, we should make realistic and workable plans. He argues that highly mobile and independent nuclear-armed strike forces could attack any invading troop concentrations with devastating results. Couple this with rapid thrusts by ground troops deep into the aggressor's territory, and his situation will soon be untenable for the enemy.[55] In such a case, and realizing that further escalation will lead to national annihilation, Kissinger bets that the aggressor would quit. The purpose of limited war is to inflict losses on the enemy or make them face risks that are just not worth their objectives in waging war.[56] Kissinger thinks that this can be successfully accomplished. Kissinger's recommendation of flexible response therefore explicitly encompasses the possibility of winnable nuclear war, one that he hopes will remain limited.

DeGroot notes that the decisive rejection of the concept of winnable nuclear war came after the Cuban missile crisis. At the time of the crisis, the United States had the capacity to annihilate the Soviet Union, while the Soviets could launch only a relative handful in retaliation.[57] However, even a few dozen thermonuclear bombs would cause calamitous destruction and kill millions. Secretary of Defense Robert McNamara therefore proposed the doctrine of MAD.[58] MAD represented a sea change in nuclear policy. When it was recognized that both sides would retain the capacity to inflict devastating retaliation if attacked, the concept of winning a nuclear war was revealed as mad. Paradoxically, it took a doctrine with the acronym MAD to introduce a modicum of nuclear sanity.

CONCLUSION: WAR PLANS AND TESTING

Our brief survey of the development of American nuclear policy during the period of nuclear testing in the Marshall Islands shows that, with the exception of an early and short-lived period of internationalist idealism, these policies were war plans, plans for the *use* of nuclear weapons. These policies stand in sharp contrast to the policy of MAD, where the aim of continued weapons and delivery system development was *solely* to maintain a credible deterrent. In short, during this period, nuclear war was regarded as winnable, and so long as it was regarded as winnable, it was not unthinkable.

That American leaders and planners seriously entertained the prospect of nuclear war as a realistic and rational option is best shown by evidence that we have not so far mentioned – the extensive program of civil defense pursued by the US government during the 1950s and early 1960s. Millions of Americans grew up with "duck and cover" drills at school. Television programs, even Saturday morning cartoons, often carried public service reminders that we should all get busy on our fallout shelters. Whole cities participated in practice evacuations and many buildings were designated as public shelters, and were supplied with drinking water and concentrated food rations. Government films indicated that well-maintained properties with uncluttered yards were more likely to survive atomic attack.

The government's explicit message was that you could most definitely survive a nuclear war, if you recognized that survival was your responsibility and took the appropriate steps. The tacit aim of the messages was to inure the public to the idea of nuclear war. So long as war with strategic nuclear weapons was considered winnable, even if at terrible cost, planners planned for it, and it was easier to plan with a hopeful and trusting public than a terrified and possibly recalcitrant one. Actually, a more accurate reading of the implicit civil defense message is that it was the same as the one explicitly conveyed in *Strategic Air Command*: We are already at war, and we have to be ready for an attack that could literally come at any minute.

It eventually became obvious, particularly after the Cuban Missile Crisis of 1962, that defense against megaton weapons delivered by ICBMs was a futile fantasy.[59] Talk about fallout shelters and ducking and covering quickly trailed off. Humanity's only hope was never to use such weapons. The rise of the doctrine of MAD represented a significant shift in the view of strategic nuclear weapons, both in the eyes of policymakers and for the public. Their only use was to prevent their use.

When viewed in the context of evolving American nuclear policy during the period of testing in the Marshall Islands, the decision to conduct those tests can hardly be surprising. Those policies had approved of the actual use of nuclear weapons in 1945 and continued to project their use as a winning strategy. The atmospheric testing of nuclear weapons was simply an unremarkable corollary and extension of those policies. If blowing up the Soviet Union seemed feasible, blowing up Bikini certainly did. Further, the victims of atmospheric testing in the Pacific and the United States were collateral damage in a war that, though it was called "cold," was a real war with real casualties.

Putting things in the broadest perspective, we may note that humans, either individually or collectively, tend to move between two poles of ethical thinking, depending on state of mind. Philosophers classify ethical theories as "consequentialist" or "deontological." Consequentialist theories, like John Stuart Mill's utilitarianism, assess the moral status of actions or norms on the basis of their consequences. The simplest version of utilitarianism, act utilitarianism, says that the morally right action is the one that, of the available alternatives, maximizes happiness or minimizes unhappiness. If no course of action is without risk, you base your decision on a realistic assessment of expected risks and benefits. Deontological theories, on the other hand, assess the value of actions by their intrinsic moral worth, and such theories do not regard inherently bad actions as redeemable by good consequences. For the deontologist, an inherently immoral act is always bad, even if, on occasion, its consequence is to promote happiness or well-being for the larger number. For instance, if it is inherently immoral to take an innocent life, such an action cannot be justified by appeal to beneficial consequences.

When individuals or groups are stressed, they tend toward act utilitarianism as the basis of their ethical decisions. When our survival is threatened, we naturally resort to "lifeboat ethics" whereby we save those who can be saved and, ruthlessly if need be, leave others in danger when the effort to save them would likely result in disaster for all. For instance, during the Second World War, the Allies recognized that the bombing campaign would inevitably kill many innocent people, including children, the sick, and the elderly. Yet, deliverance from Nazism and Japanese militarism required total war, and all of the dreadful consequences that followed. Even the most decent people can do terrible things when it seems to them that the alternatives are even more terrible.

Later, when the danger is not so imminent, we have time to be more reflective, and to assess our behavior in less starkly consequentialist terms. Under less urgent circumstances we can be more self-critical and ask ourselves hard questions about the justice or fairness of our actions. We might even say that over time a society moves from one moral regime into another, a transition from a consequentialist to a more deontological regime, where the dominant moral categories are rights and justice rather than utility. When this occurs, and if the transition is deep enough, the moral decisions of one generation may look harsh or even unconscionable to a later generation. Decisions that, at the time, appeared to be imposed by circumstance, will appear later on to have been gratuitously risky or insensitive. By contrast, to those of the generation that had to make these hard decisions, the moral qualms of later generations will appear sentimental and unrealistic.

Throughout this book we have seen that actions that appeared sensible, reasonable, and responsible to officials and policy-makers of the 1950s might now appear to have been excessively risky, irresponsible, or downright immoral. This divergence is best explained in terms of the dominant moral regimes of different times. We no longer feel the imminence of the nuclear threat or the communist menace, both of which were felt insistently in the 1950s, and so we do not feel the burden of hard choices as they did.

Were the planners of the nuclear tests in the Marshall Islands aware that atmospheric tests of megaton weapons posed great potential dangers? Yes, of course; that is why they took so many elaborate precautions. Were those precautions adequate? No, as events proved. Could more have been done to assure the safety and well-being of the Marshallese people during the period of atmospheric testing? Yes, undoubtedly. Were those tests an excrescence of paranoia, irrational obsessions, and racism? No; not at all.

As we noted at the beginning, historically sensitive understanding often denies us the luxury of simple good guy/bad guy scenarios. We have to understand the hard choices – as they were seen at the time by the people who had to make them. Further, we must face up fully to the harsh reality of the consequences of those choices, the human suffering that resulted. If we do any less, minimizing one side or the other, then we are lying to ourselves.

NOTES

1 The history of US nuclear policy is an intricate and daunting subject, and this chapter can only offer the barest sketch of those complex developments in the period studied. A number of excellent specialized works provide detailed histories of nuclear policy in the relevant time frame. These include the works by Herken, Freedman, and Kaplan listed in the bibliography.

2 Frank, *Downfall*, p. 18.

3 Miscamble, *The Most Controversial Decision*, p. 50.
4 Spector, *Eagle Against the Sun*. p. 398.
5 Miscamble, *The Most Controversial Decision*, p. 45.
6 Miscamble, *The Most Controversial Decision*, p. 43.
7 Miscamble, *The Most Controversial Decision*, pp. 45–46.
8 Miscamble, *The Most Controversial Decision*, p. 44.
9 Miscamble, *The Most Controversial Decision*, p. 44.
10 Miscamble, *The Most Controversial Decision*, p. 46.
11 Frank, *Downfall*, pp. 197–211.
12 Miscamble, *The Most Controversial Decision*, p. 81
13 Frank, *Downfall*, pp. 131–139.
14 Frank, *Downfall*, pp. 308–322.
15 Freedman, *The Evolution of Nuclear Strategy*, pp. 18–19.
16 Miscamble, *The Most Controversial Decision*, p. 139.
17 Miscamble, *The Most Controversial Decision*, p. 140.
18 Miscamble, *The Most Controversial Decision, p. 141.*
19 Miscamble, *The Most Controversial Decision*, p. 143.
20 Miscamble, *The Most Controversial Decision*, p. 144.
21 Miscamble, *The Most Controversial Decision*, p. 144.
22 Kennedy, Inaugural Address.
23 DeGroot, *The Bomb*, p. 66.
24 DeGroot, *The Bomb*, p. 153.
25 Kaplan, *To Kill Nations*, p. 30.
26 Kaplan, *To Kill Nations*, p. 17.
27 Freedman, *The Evolution of Nuclear Strategy*, p. 21.
28 Kaplan, *To Kill Nations*, p. 34.
29 Kaplan, *To Kill Nations*, p. 3.
30 DeGroot, *The Bomb*, p. 186.
31 DeGroot, *The Bomb*, p. 186.
32 DeGroot, *The Bomb*, p. 187.
33 Gaddis, *The Cold War*, p. 59.
34 Gaddis, *The Cold War*, p. 59.
35 Gaddis, *The Cold War*, p. 59.
36 Gaddis, *The Cold War*, p. 66; emphasis and ellipsis in original.
37 Gaddis, *The Cold War*, p. 64.
38 Gaddis, *The Cold War*, p. 64.
39 DeGroot, *The Bomb*, p. 189.
40 Freedman, *The Evolution of Nuclear Strategy*, p. 78.
41 DeGroot, *The Bomb*, p. 189.
42 Freedman, *The Evolution of Nuclear Strategy*, p. 79.
43 Kissinger, *Nuclear Weapons and Foreign Policy*, p. 3.
44 Freedman, *The Evolution of Nuclear Strategy*, pp. 84–85.
45 Kissinger, *Nuclear Weapons and Foreign Policy*, p. 8.
46 Kissinger, *Nuclear Weapons and Foreign Policy*, p. 11.
47 Kissinger, *Nuclear Weapons and Foreign Policy*, p. 4.
48 Kissinger, *Nuclear Weapons and Foreign Policy*, p. 115.
49 Kissinger, *Nuclear Weapons and Foreign Policy*, p. 76.

50 Kissinger, *Nuclear Weapons and Foreign Policy*, p. 79.
51 Kissinger, *Nuclear Weapons and Foreign Policy*, p. 79.
52 Kissinger, *Nuclear Weapons and Foreign Policy*, p. 79.
53 Kissinger, *Nuclear Weapons and Foreign Policy*, p. 147.
54 Kissinger, *Nuclear Weapons and Foreign Policy*, p. 146.
55 Kissinger, *Nuclear Weapons and Foreign Policy*, p. 151.
56 Kissinger, *Nuclear Weapons and Foreign Policy*, pp. 123–124.
57 DeGroot, *The Bomb*, p. 270.
58 DeGroot, *The Bomb*, p. 270.
59 Friedman, *The Evolution of Nuclear Strategy*, p. 237.

Epilogue

Back to Bikini?

Let's recap: From 1946 to 1958, the United States conducted sixty-seven nuclear tests at and in the waters near Eniwetok and Bikini Atolls in the Marshall Islands. The cumulative yield of those detonations was 108 megatons. Bikini was grossly polluted with radioactive fallout and remains uninhabited today, over seventy years after the "temporary" removal of its inhabitants. The inhabitants of Rongelap were returned in 1957, three years after the Bravo event, yet in 1985 they left again, due to fear of the effects of lingering radiation, and despite reassurances from the US government that the atoll was safe. They have not returned.

In this Epilogue we look at the fate of the Marshallese who were displaced by the nuclear tests. What has been the effect of that displacement on them? What have they suffered? What are their chances of ever going back to their ancestral homes? Has justice been done for the Marshallese? Most disturbing of all, were some of them victims of a conspiracy to expose them to radiation? We first look at this charge.

WAS THERE A CONSPIRACY?

We have explained the harmful results of the Castle Bravo test as a consequence of actions that frightened men took or failed to take as they labored under a self-imposed delusion that they were in control of fundamentally uncontrollable events. Their errors were generally "sins of omission," in particular, the adoption of an insufficiently cautious attitude toward potential dangers and a safety policy that was reactive rather than proactive. However, some have suggested a far darker and more sinister explanation of the fate of the Marshallese. Some have suggested that these events were intentional, not accidental, that is, that the irradiation of the Marshallese was not a chance occurrence, but had been planned all along as an integral part of the test. The Marshallese were intentionally and cold-bloodedly made test subjects for the study of the effects of radiation.

Needless to say, this is an inflammatory claim, and the temptation is to dismiss it out of hand. However, there is no question that in the testing era some terrible things were done intentionally and with the full approval of the highest authorities. We saw that American soldiers wearing no protective gear were involved in training exercises conducted in the immediate proximity of nuclear blasts. Many American service personnel suffered disease and premature death as a result of exposure to radiation.[1] Would a society that so willingly exposed so many of its own personnel to such dangers scruple to use a few hundred non-Americans as test subjects? Remember, these were desperate times and it was all too easy to justify desperate measures.

The case for conspiracy is taken up by anthropologist Holly M. Barker in her book *Bravo for the Marshallese: Regaining Control in a Post-Nuclear, Post-Colonial World*. She refers to the 1954 calculation by meteorologist N. M. Lulejian (cited in Chapter 3) that indicated that a multimegaton blast could produce fallout over the inhabited atolls.[2] Yet, says Barker, "U.S. Government documents also demonstrate that military commanders purposefully ignored or rejected predictions about exposure to inhabited atolls."[3] She also repeats the charge, addressed in Chapter 3, that the decision to proceed with the test was made despite the fact that six hours prior to the test meteorologists determined that winds were blowing from the direction of Bikini toward Rongelap and Rongerik.[4]

Barker's most serious charge concerns so-called Project 4.1:

On November 10, 1953, four months before the Bravo test, the headquarters of Joint Task Force 7 in Los Alamos distributed a document outlining the scientific tests to be performed in conjunction with the Bravo test. The document lists 48 scientific programs ranging from measuring the force of the winds produced by the blast to monitoring radiation in plankton throughout the Pacific Ocean. Also contained in his list of scientific studies was Project 4.1, entitled "Study of Response of Human Beings exposed to Significant Beta and Gamma Radiation Due to Fall-Out from High Yield Weapons." ... When the Bravo test exposed Marshallese populations downwind from Bikini Atoll on March 1, 1954, project 4.1 came to fruition. The U.S. government issued a preliminary report on Project 4.1 on April 29, 1954; the title was modified, and was called the "Study of Response of Human Beings *Accidentally* Exposed to Significant Fall-Out Radiation."[5]

Barker adds that some officials within the Marshallese government have cited this evidence as grounds for the charge that the exposure to the Marshallese was premeditated.[6]

In fact, the idea that the deposition of fallout from Castle Bravo on inhabited atolls was premeditated is highly implausible. A plan to use the Bravo shot to irradiate test subjects on distant atolls would not have been a procedure that any planner, however sinister, could rationally propose. It is one thing to say that the weather situation just prior to Bravo would *possibly* have deposited the fallout on those atolls. It is another thing entirely to say that the winds could be *depended upon* to transfer large amounts of radiation to the desired site (e.g., the inhabited atolls). The Bravo bomb was a very expensive and one-of-a-kind device of uncertain yield. Anyone who planned to use it to irradiate prospective test subjects on Rongelap and Utirik would have had to employ a much more dependable means of achieving the desired exposure than to trust fickle winds to blow the required amount to the right sites a hundred miles away or more. Also, a moment's thought would have indicated that the irradiation of innocent men, women, and children, even if successfully passed off as accidental, would be a PR disaster and high-octane fuel for the antitesting movement (both of which, of course, it turned out to be). Proponents of the conspiracy charge would therefore not only have to accuse the planners of Bravo of gross depravity, but also of rank stupidity.

If, indeed, the fallout from Bravo was intended to go east toward the inhabited atolls, then why was the task force fleet moved to a position where they would wind up in the fallout path, as, in fact, they did?[7] Why were the firing team on Enyu and the observation ship *Curtiss* both located to the east of the blast? The conspiracy theory must hold that all these people were intentionally and uselessly placed in harm's way. Considering that scientists essential to the testing program were on the *Curtiss*, it is hard to imagine that the planners would have wanted to expose them to fallout, even if the sailors and marines onboard were considered expendable. Conspiracy theories can always deal with contrary evidence by inflating the size, complexity, and wickedness of the alleged conspiracy, but this procedure quickly makes it evident that the theory bears no relationship to reality.

As for Project 4.1, Kunkle and Ristvet easily debunk the conspiracy theory, with copious reference to the archival records. The document Barker mentions as issued on November 10, 1953, was a revision of the *Outline of Scientific Programs*, listing the scientific programs associated with the Castle operations. An addendum to this document mentions the establishment of Project 4.1. However, the addendum can be traced to a memorandum dated April 16, 1954 – *after* Bravo – and was later attached to the original document. The memorandum that was the source of the addendum clearly states that the establishment of Project 4.1 is a change to the original document of November 10, 1953.[8] Further, none of the other versions of the *Outline* document (several are available online) lists any sort of biomedical research at all, and makes no reference to a Project 4.1. The Operation Castle *Handbook* (available online), issued by the Los Alamos Scientific Laboratory as a guide to the scientific programs associated with the operation, and dated January 1, 1954, refers to no biomedical experiments.

In short, the documentary evidence indicates that prior to Bravo there was no program of biomedical research, and certainly none devoted to the study of radiation effects on human beings.[9] On the contrary, these studies were begun only after the accidental exposure presented the opportunity to combine research with treatment.[10] This, however, does not mean that there were no ethical issues involved with these studies of radiation effects.

One fundamental rule of biomedical ethics is that the study of human subjects requires that they give informed consent. What would "informed consent" be when dealing with people who spoke no English, were provided with no translators, and had no understanding of radioactivity or the nature of the researchers' procedures? Barker describes other issues related to the Brookhaven studies:

From the Marshallese perspective, they knew that they were sick and assumed that the doctors were taking care of them. Over time, the patients complained to U.S. government officials that they felt like "guinea pigs." In some cases, communities protested the doctors' visits and refused to allow the doctors to examine them. U.S. government researchers used bribery or force to ensure that the doctors had access to the patients. The local police returned children who ran away from the doctors; during the trust territory, the police force was under the control of U.S. government administrators.[11]

The irradiation of the Marshallese was a tragic and terrible event, and the posttest studies of the radiation effects on human beings raise very serious issues with respect to biomedical ethics. However, it is counterproductive to muddy the waters by the promulgation of groundless and inflammatory conspiracy theories. Such theories do nothing to help the victims of Castle Bravo. On the contrary, the claim is a red herring that distracts from the real issues.

THE WANDERERS IN THE WILDERNESS

When Commodore Wyatt addressed the Bikinians in 1946, he compared them to the Biblical Children of Israel who had to wander in the wilderness for forty years. His words were prophetic. Those displaced by the tests are still in the wilderness, even though much more than forty years have passed. We have seen some of the health effects of the Bravo event, such as the thyroid cancers that resulted. Here we focus on the personal, social, and cultural disruption due to the tests. Anthropologist Barker, though she unfortunately endorses conspiracy theories, is on far more solid ground – her own area of expertise – when detailing such consequences of Bravo. She and others have compiled oral testimonies of those who lived through the nuclear tests and their aftermath. These testimonies reveal that the Marshallese were not the "simple," carefree natives of the ruling stereotype and government propaganda, but were deeply resentful of what they regarded as their exploitation and manipulation by the American government. They were quite aware of the condescending stereotypes and thought that Americans took them for idiots.[12]

To understand the sense of displacement and loss felt by those removed from their ancestral homes, it is essential to understand the attachment of the Marshallese to their land, a job Barker does well in her fifth chapter. The government propaganda film from 1946, dealing with the evacuation of the Bikinians before Crossroads, refers to the people of Bikini as a "nomadic group" who will, in fact, thank the "Yanks" for providing them with a change of scenery. The implication, of course, is that the people had no real attachment to the land and could just as easily call any other of the near-identical atolls their temporary "home." To Americans, no doubt, one coral atoll looked pretty much like another.

The propaganda film was a masterpiece of its genre in that it succeeded in creating an impression precisely the opposite of truth. To understand the relation of the Marshallese to their land, you have to begin by reflecting on how little there is of it. In all of the Marshall Islands there is only about seventy square miles of land, slightly over double the size of Manhattan Island. That means that each bit is important.

When outsiders look at a coral atoll, it looks like a barren and unproductive parcel of sand and palm trees, barely rising above the high-tide mark. To a native, such an atoll is a paradise of abundance, a cornucopia that, with proper management, will provide a perpetual bounty. Breadfruit, pandanus, coconuts, arrowroot, fish, shellfish, crustaceans, turtles and birds were all to be had. Chickens, goats, and pigs were easily

raised. For the inhabitants, the land and the surrounding seas were prov-
ident benefactors for whom they felt a sense of profound attachment and
reverence. In comparison with the Marshallese, modern Americans are
the nomads, people who must remain mobile in pursuit of distant jobs,
and who often have little sense of place or attachment to a locale.

For people like the inhabitants of Eniwetok, Bikini, or Rongelap,
during a residence of many generations they gained an intimate knowledge of their surroundings. A "simple" lifestyle is not one that requires
little thinking or knowledge. It is not a matter of occasionally getting out
of your hammock and picking a low-hanging breadfruit. On the contrary,
self-sufficiency requires acute observation, accurate memory, careful planning, and the mastery of various essential skills – and lots of plain hard
work. They had to know the details of topography and the distribution of
animals and vegetation. They had to be aware of winds, clouds, tides, and
ocean currents and innumerable other subtle details of the environment.
They had to know how to harvest the bounty of their islands in a sustainable way to make sure that it would always be plentiful. In short, the
Marshallese had a relation to their land that was close and personal in a
way that few now would understand. When they were moved from that
land, it was not merely a change of address, but a radical dispossession
and disruption, the loss of an intimate and beloved partner.

Marshallese social relations and customs were also closely attached
to the land. Your role in society depended upon your relationship to
the land:

Marshallese culture and society is tightly structured by its land rights. There are
three different tiers of society, each with distinct land and resource use rights ...
the three tiers or classifications of people are the *iroij* (chiefs), *alap* (managers of
the land), and the *ri-jerbal* (workers). Land rights exclusively define a person's
designation into one of three categories ... The fluid system of land rights and
access to resources provides an effective means of ensuring that the land is cared
for, and that everyone has access to the resources necessary for survival.[13]

With displacement from the land, all of these traditional social relations
and their associated customs are disrupted. A whole way of life is lost and
is hard to reconstruct in different settings.

Many of these points are succinctly summarized by Dr. Neal Palafox
in testimony before the US Senate Committee on Energy and Natural
Resources in 2005:

Cultural and social disruptions from the USNWTP [US Nuclear Weapons Testing
Program] are associated with adverse health outcomes and illness. Alienation

from the land and critical natural resources through radioactive contamination or forced evacuation destroyed the physical and cultural means of sustaining and reproducing a self-sufficient way of life. It also destroyed community integrity, traditional health practices and sociopolitical relationships. Furthermore, community history and knowledge is destroyed when there is not lineage land from which to pass on knowledge about the local environment.[14]

When they abandoned Rongelap in 1985, the people settled on the previously uninhabited island Mejatto, a tiny and inhospitable site. Resources on Mejatto were scarce and hard to get, and they became dependent on canned food provided by the US Department of Agriculture (USDA). The USDA food was higher in fat and carbohydrates, lower in fiber, and lacking vitamin A and iron. Poor diet was combined with a more sedentary lifestyle due to the loss of activity in getting and preparing food. The consequence was higher rates of diabetes, hypertension, and atherosclerosis.[15] Eventually, the former inhabitants of Rongelap dispersed into crowded and often squalid conditions in the two urban centers of the Republic of the Marshall Islands, the towns of Majuro and Ebeye.[16] So, the Rongelapese have gone from an atoll that provided for them and their ancestors through many generations to live in urban shantytowns. A way of life that had existed for two thousand years was gone.

Much more could be told about the effects of the nuclear tests on the Marshallese, and much of this detail is contained in the books by Holly Barker and Jane Dibblin. Here we will conclude with some words from the Bikinians themselves.

First is a statement made to Jack Niedenthal by Jukawa Jakeo, a former resident of Bikini, upon a visit back to Bikini made in 1987:

I want to speak about land and the reason we Marshallese treasure it so highly. The land we sit on now as we talk is like gold. The ground that you walk on, from time to time and from day to day, no matter where you are in the Marshall Islands, is also like gold. If you were Marshallese and you didn't have any land you would be considered a bum, a drifter or a beggar. But if you were an owner of vast amounts of land, you would be considered a very rich and wealthy man. Land is the Marshallese form of gold. To all Marshallese; land is gold. If you were an owner of land you would be held up as a very important figure in our society. Without land you would be viewed as a person of no consequence. But land here on Bikini is now poison land. When I think of that as a consequence for my family members, it frustrates me. I apologize to them because I don't quite understand the depth of the situation here on Bikini. I am an uneducated man. I am Marshallese and I can't quite understand or tell what is safe and what is unsafe here. I can only have faith in the U.S. government. They have the responsibility for telling us what is good for us and what is dangerous.[17]

Next is a portion of a 1997 interview by Niedenthal, of Dretin Jokdru, the *iroij*, or traditional leader of the people of Bikini:

Can you ever trust the Americans again with regard to the radiological status of Bikini, even with the latest developments in the technology that the scientists now say would permit a quick return to your homeland?

DRETIN JOKDRU: I don't understand some of these methods. They say the poison is still there, but we can live there if certain things are done. Some scientists have a hard time explaining this, and sometimes we have a hard time understanding them. If they ever came to us as a group – the president of the United States and the scientists – and all agreed about Bikini and that it was safe for us to live, I think we'd go back. We just have to wait, even though we want to go back and are still sad about what happened to our islands.

After the compensation money started coming via the trust funds in the 1970's, did your view of the U.S. government change? What do you think about the trust fund as a form of compensation … Do you feel that the money has adequately compensated you for your suffering?

The money is wonderful. Many people in the Marshalls are jealous of us now because we take care of ourselves so well …

Has money replaced your desire to return to your homeland?

Our Love for Bikini will never disappear, but the money is important, it is used to take care of our families. Bikini is a gift from God, it is not something that gets forgotten. Money comes and money goes …

How will you react if the United States does not live up to their promises in the future?

We will remind them of our history together, we will remind them of how we have sacrificed for them, then we will ask them to continue to take care of us. That was their promise and we will hold them to it.[18]

Finally, from the PBS program *The World's Biggest Bomb* from the series *Secrets of the Dead*, are the comments of Alson Kelen, Mayor of Bikini Atoll, on a trip back to Bikini, his first in two years:

According to the DOE [Department of Energy], they say that it's safe enough to come back. The more it rains the more the radiation goes out. But I actually was one of those kids that got relocated back in the 1970s. Some people say it's not safe yet. So I guess it's how you look at the picture.

Right now we are at the old graveyard site from before the testing was happening on Bikini. These graves are our grandfathers, great great grandparents. Bikini are all one family. So anybody dies here, we're all related.

NARRATOR: The United States has, over the years, paid almost 200 million dollars in compensation – and in its efforts to clean up Bikini. But it appears it will remain an island of ghosts.

ALSON KELEN: The children of Israel, they traveled for 40 years. But the children of Bikini – I really know don't know if we will ever come back to Bikini.[19]

CONCLUSION

All of the victims of nuclear testing, in the Marshall Islands and elsewhere, were casualties of the Cold War. Two superpowers threatened each other, and the whole world, with weapons of apocalyptic destruction. The advent of thermonuclear weapons created a situation unprecedented in history. With no rational hope of conquest, survival without surrender became the goal for each side. The only hope of achieving that goal was to create in the mind of your enemy a dread as terrible as that you felt in your own mind. The main battlefield of the Cold War was the minds of the leaders of the opposing powers.

For Strauss and others like him, saving America – and the world – was the matter of utmost urgency. If saving the world required deterrence and deterrence required thermonuclear weapons, and such weapons had to be tested, then those tests would go forward, and there could be no tests without risk. The planners of the test were not oblivious to risk; they just did not take it seriously enough. Their biggest failure was that they did not expect the unexpected. They let themselves think that they had anticipated and adequately prepared for every contingency when they did not.

Has justice been done for the Marshallese? Have they received adequate recompense? Compensation has been paid to the communities and individuals affected by the fallout from Bravo and the other tests. The website of the Embassy of the United States at Majuro, Marshall Islands summarizes the compensatory payments:

As referenced in the U.S. government's 2004 Report on the Republic of the Marshall Islands (RMI) Changed Circumstances Petition and data from the Department of Energy ... and Department of the Interior ... the United States provided a total of more than $604 million to the affected communities. Adjusting for inflation, this amount equals $1.055 billion in 2010 dollars, or $1.87 million per original inhabitant of the four affected atolls (Bikini, Enewetak, Rongelap, and Utirik) at the time of the testing, in funds and programs designed to support those impacted by the nuclear testing program. Among other programs, this compensation included direct financial settlement of nuclear claims, resettlement funds, rehabilitation of affected atolls, and radiation related health care costs.[20]

Further, the United States paid $150 million to the Republic of the Marshall Islands to establish a nuclear claims fund:

From 1991 to 2003, the RMI Nuclear Claims Tribunal awarded over $2 billion for personal injury, property loss, and class action claims. The amount of the claims awarded thus far exceeded the settlement amount, and payments from the Tribunal ceased in 2009 after having disbursed all existing funds.[21]

Is this compensation enough? What is adequate recompense for ending a way of life that had existed for countless generations? How do you quantify the degradation of once happy, healthy, and self-sufficient people? How much do you pay for bombing paradise? We cannot restore Bikini or Rongelap to a pristine state, and even if we could and even if the descendants of those displaced were to return, how could life ever again be like it was? Much time has passed, and those still alive who remember the old ways are now few.

Whatever healing can occur at this stage can occur only on the basis of absolute honesty. Americans and their government must be absolutely truthful to themselves and others about what was done to the victims, all of the victims, of the nuclear tests in the Marshall Islands. This book has endeavored to tell the truth about those tests. We have attempted to describe those events and explain their occurrence as objectively and accurately as possible. We have not downplayed the suffering of the victims. Neither have we demonized those responsible for the tests, rather, we have attempted to understand their actions in the light of the beliefs and fears prevailing at the time. While we are naturally appalled at the suffering of the victims of nuclear testing, we have not played the role of advocates, being confident that truth is the best advocacy. Our endeavor has been to inform, but if in giving understanding we also promote healing, then our work will be doubly rewarded.

NOTES

1 DeGroot, *The Bomb*, pp. 241–242.
2 Barker, *Bravo for the Marshallese*, p. 40.
3 Barker, *Bravo for the Marshallese*, p. 40.
4 Barker, *Bravo for the Marshallese*, 40.
5 Barker, *Bravo for the Marshallese*, p. 41; emphasis in original.
6 Barker, *Bravo for the Marshallese*, p. 41.
7 Hansen, *U.S. Nuclear Weapons*, p. 66.
8 Kunkle and Ristvet, *Castle Bravo*, p. 133.
9 Kunkle and Ristvet, *Castle Bravo*, p. 131.
10 Kunkle and Ristvet, *Castle Bravo*, p. 132.
11 Barker, *Bravo for the Marshallese*, p. 42.
12 Barker, *Bravo for the Marshallese*, p. 57.
13 Barker, *Bravo for the Marshallese*, pp. 61–62.
14 Palafox, "Testimony before U.S. Senate Committee on Energy and Natural Resources," p. 2.
15 Palafox, "Testimony before U.S. Senate Committee on Energy and Natural Resources," p. 2.

16 Barker, *Bravo for the Marshallese*, p. 67.
17 Niedenthal, *For the Good of Mankind*, p. 87.
18 Niedenthal, *For the Good of Mankind*, pp. 109–110.
19 "The World's Biggest Bomb," transcript.
20 "The Legacy of U.S. Nuclear Testing and Radiation Exposure in the Marshall Islands," p. 1. Website of the Embassy of the United States at Majuro, Marshall Islands.
21 "The Legacy of U.S. Nuclear Testing and Radiation Exposure in the Marshall Islands," p. 2. Website of the Embassy of the United States at Majuro, Marshall Islands.

Appendix 1

Ultimate Weapons

In order to understand the nature and impact of nuclear weapons, basic physical concepts are introduced in this first appendix, along with a discussion of nuclear weapon design and effects. Key terms encountered in the main text are highlighted in bold, while related terms are italicized. In the section "What Is Matter?" we will begin by introducing the concepts of matter and mass. This includes topics such as chemical elements, compounds, atoms, and nuclei. The next section, "What Is Energy?" introduces the concepts of energy and radiation, followed by a discussion on radioactivity and the fundamental forces in "Radioactivity and Nuclear Forces." Then, in "Nuclear Energy and Nuclear Reactions," nuclear fission and fusion are introduced. The next sections of this appendix, "The Fission Bomb," and "The Thermonuclear Bomb," focus on the motivation for and development of nuclear weapons. The physical characteristics of nuclear explosions are then described in the section "Nuclear Detonations." Finally, in "Hiroshima and Nagasaki" a brief summary is given of the destructive aftermath of the atomic bombing of Japan in the Second World War, the only actual case of the war-time use of nuclear weapons, to provide further insight into the devastating capability of these weapons. The biological effects of radiation are covered in Appendix 2.

WHAT IS MATTER?

In the strictest scientific sense, the term "matter" is vague. However, here we will simply take *matter* to mean the "stuff" of which objects are made. Any material is a particular type of matter. Matter occupies space and is composed of microscopic structural units called *atoms*.

The idea that matter is composed of atoms was proposed by the ancient Greeks based on philosophical arguments, most notably by the philosopher Democritus, but for over two thousand years, there was no way to test these ideas since atoms are so incredibly small.[1] However, in the seventeenth through the twentieth centuries, it was shown through a series of experiments that matter is indeed composed of atoms, and in fact, there are many kinds of atoms, each with its own unique properties.[2] Each type of atom corresponds to a simple substance known as an *element*. Based on the chemical properties of the elements, atoms combine together in definite ratios to form *molecules*, the constituents of chemical *compounds* such as H_2O, water.

Each element has unique chemical properties and consists of identical atoms of the same *mass*, an important property of matter. A loose definition of mass is that it is the amount of matter in an atom or other object. A more accurate definition of mass is that it is the amount of *inertia* an object has, which is the degree to which the object resists a change in its motion. The concept of inertia was introduced in the seventeenth century by the English physicist Sir Isaac Newton in his laws of motion.[3] The more massive an object is, the harder it is to change its velocity. For example, it is more difficult to stop a moving bowling ball than a moving tennis ball, since a bowling ball has more mass.

In the nineteenth century, many elements had been identified and they were then organized into the *periodic table* by the Russian chemist Dmitri Mendeleev according to their chemical properties and in order of increasing mass.[4] This arrangement of the elements even allowed Mendeleev to predict the existence of additional elements, along with their chemical properties, that had not yet been discovered, since there were locations on the periodic table where there appeared to be missing elements. Similar chemical properties were found to repeat themselves in a periodic fashion in the table, and this is where the periodic table gets its name. The interested reader may consult the periodic table in any chemistry textbook or online.

An atom consists of a massive *nucleus* at its center and a region around it where *electrons* are found as shown in Figure A1.1. The atomic nucleus was first discovered in the early twentieth century by the physicist Ernest Rutherford.[5] The nucleus consists of *protons* and *neutrons*, known collectively as *nucleons*. Each proton has a positive electric charge, neutrons have no electric charge, and each electron has a negative electric charge that exactly balances the charge of a proton. For an atom of a particular element, the sum of the number of neutrons and protons is referred to as

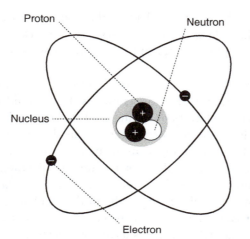

FIGURE A1.1 The structure of the atom.
Note: Sherman, "Atomic Diagram" (illustration).

the *mass number*. All atoms of a particular element have the same number of protons in their nuclei. The number of protons is known as the *atomic number*. For example, all carbon atoms have six protons in their nuclei, all oxygen nuclei have eight protons, and all uranium nuclei have ninety-two protons.

The number of protons is also equal to the number of electrons that an atom has in its natural state (not ionized), and the atom does not carry an electric charge in this state. The number of electrons is crucial to the chemical interactions of an atom, and thus to the chemical properties of an element and its location on the periodic table.

Whereas electrons are responsible for the chemical properties of matter, it is the atomic nucleus that will be of greatest interest to us. Of particular importance is the fact that all atoms of a particular element must have the same atomic number, but the number of neutrons in their nuclei can differ. These different forms of the same element are referred to as *isotopes* of the element. For example, the most abundant form of hydrogen in nature is hydrogen containing one proton in its nucleus and no neutrons. However two other isotopes of hydrogen are *deuterium*, containing one proton and one neutron, and *tritium*, containing one proton and two neutrons. These isotopes of hydrogen will be discussed later in connection with thermonuclear (hydrogen) bombs. The most abundant form of hydrogen has an atomic mass of one, deuterium has an atomic mass of two, and tritium has an atomic mass of three, hence the names of these isotopes. Other elements have higher atomic masses. Many metals in particular have large atomic masses. The heaviest elements, including uranium and plutonium, can have atomic masses of well above two hundred.

Matter is found to exist in three different states, also known as *phases*. These are the solid, liquid, and gas phases. In the solid phase, the constituent atoms or molecules of the material stay relatively fixed or locked together. In a liquid, atoms or molecules can slide past each other in a very crowded fashion. In a gas, atoms or molecules move freely, undergoing collisions with each other. Some materials, like the elements hydrogen and helium, are typically found in the gaseous state. Others, like most metals, are typically found to be in the solid state. Solids tend to be denser, that is, their mass tends to be more concentrated for a given volume of material, whereas gases have lower densities.

In general, materials may be found in any of the states of matter, depending on temperature and pressure conditions. A common example is water. At very low temperatures, water is found in solid form as ice, while at more moderate temperatures it is a liquid, and at higher temperatures it is a vapor. The concept of *vaporization*, the transformation of a solid or liquid into a gas, will be important when considering the nature of detonations.

WHAT IS ENERGY?

Another important property of matter is *energy*. A simple way to define energy is that it is the ability to cause an object or particle to move. In physics, energy is defined as the ability to do *work*. To do work is to exert a force on an object, displacing it in the direction of that force, resulting in motion or a change in motion. When a bowling ball is set in motion, a force is first exerted on it. When the ball is rolling, it has *kinetic energy*, energy due to its motion.

Energy takes on various forms. In nature, there are various types of force fields, such as electric, gravitational, and nuclear fields, which have the potential to do work on an object or particle by exerting forces on it. This potential to do work is called the *potential energy* and is the energy an object has because of its *position* in a field. If you hold a stone in your hand, it has potential energy in the earth's gravitational field, that is, it will fall toward the ground if you let go of it. When you let go of the stone, it starts to fall, acted upon by the downward force of gravity. The gravitational field does work on the stone. This work results in the falling stone acquiring kinetic energy, which is simply the energy it has due to its motion. Similarly, electric fields exert forces on electrically charged particles, giving them electric potential energy. In an electric circuit for example, an applied electric field, or *voltage*, exerts force on electrons, doing work and causing them to flow as electric current.

In the example of the falling stone, as it falls, the stone's potential energy decreases and its kinetic energy increases, but its total energy remains constant. This is an example of the principle of the *conservation of energy*, which is always satisfied for all forms of energy. If an object loses energy, that energy has to go somewhere else in the environment and cannot vanish into nothing. The conservation of energy will be of importance later when discussing nuclear reactions.

Yet another form of energy is *thermal* energy,[6] also referred to as *internal* energy since it is the total kinetic and potential energy of all the atoms or molecules in a substance due to their random motions and positions. At any temperature, the atoms or molecules vibrate or move around, and as the temperature of the substance is increased, they move more rapidly. Thermal energy that is actually being transferred from a hotter object to a cooler object is known as *heat*. When an ice cube is placed in a warm drink, thermal energy is transferred from the drink to the ice, the ice is heated and the internal energy of the ice increases. As thermal energy is transferred from the drink to the ice cube, molecules within the ice start to vibrate more rapidly, to the point of slipping by each other. At this point, the ice melts into liquid water. The melting of ice is an example of a *phase transition* from a solid to a liquid state.

After defining what energy is, we now come to the concept of radiation. *Radiation* is the transfer of energy, carried by waves or particles, from one point to another in space. *Electromagnetic radiation* consists of oscillating electric and magnetic fields that propagate through space together in the form of waves. These *electromagnetic waves* are characterized by their *wavelength*, or the distance between wave peaks: shorter wavelengths correspond to higher frequencies, with wave peaks closer together, and longer wavelengths correspond to lower frequencies, with wave peaks further apart. These waves travel through a vacuum at the speed of light or in a material at a speed slightly less than the speed of light in a vacuum. Electromagnetic waves were predicted to exist by the Scottish physicist James Clerk Maxwell who formulated the theory of electromagnetism in the 1860s.[7]

There is a vast spectrum of electromagnetic radiation corresponding to a very wide range of wavelengths, from the longest wavelengths (radio waves) to the shortest wavelengths (gamma radiation, or simply *gamma rays*). Visible light is in the middle of the electromagnetic spectrum. Red light has longer wavelengths while violet light has shorter wavelengths. Infrared radiation has wavelengths slightly longer than that of visible light and ultraviolet radiation has wavelengths shorter than that of light. Microwave radiation has a range of wavelengths longer than that of infrared radiation but shorter than radio waves. X-rays have even shorter wavelengths than ultraviolet light and gamma rays have the shortest wavelengths.

Any object with a temperature will emit radiation due to the random motions and vibrations of its constituent atoms or molecules. Such radiation is referred to as *thermal radiation*, and will be relevant when discussing nuclear detonations and fireballs. Infrared radiation, in particular, is readily absorbed and emitted by molecules, and is also emitted in large amounts by heated objects. It is therefore often associated with the sensation of heat, though more generally, heat can correspond to the transfer of any kind of radiation since all radiation transfers energy.

An important connection exists between the temperature of a perfectly radiating object and the wavelength of the radiation it emits. This is particularly important regarding the radiation emitted by the fireball formed in a nuclear detonation. A perfect radiating object emits radiation at all wavelengths as well as absorbs radiation at all wavelengths. Such an object, known as a *black body*, is actually an idealization, though some objects may be taken to closely approximate one. Examples include stars, nuclear fireballs, and heated metals. Black bodies emit the majority of their radiation at a particular wavelength with smaller amounts of radiation emitted at all other wavelengths. As the temperature of the radiator increases, the wavelength at which most of its radiation is emitted gets shorter. In other words, at higher temperatures this shorter wavelength at which radiation emission peaks corresponds to a higher frequency.

A simple example of black body radiation is in the heating of an iron rod. At lower temperatures, the rod will be hot yet emit most of its radiation in the infrared range, but as its temperature is raised, the rod will glow red and as the temperature is raised even higher, the rod will glow orange, and then white. Similarly, lower temperature stars are red in color, while hotter stars are yellow, then white, and at even higher temperatures, blue. The temperature of a nuclear fireball is so high that it emits "soft" x-rays. These are longer-wavelength (lower-frequency) x-rays.

Briefly, the *Kelvin* temperature scale, referred to later, is defined such that its lowest temperature, zero Kelvin (K), corresponds to *absolute zero*, the temperature at which atoms and molecules in a substance will be in their lowest possible energy state. These particles then cannot transfer heat to their surroundings so that absolute zero is the lowest possible temperature. The freezing point of water on this scale is 273.15 K and its boiling point is 373.15 K.[8]

Electromagnetic radiation can also be viewed as consisting of particles called *photons*. Some experiments with radiation demonstrate its wave-like properties while others demonstrate its particle-like properties. This dual wave-particle nature of radiation is known as *wave-particle duality*. Shorter wavelength radiation consists of photons that carry more energy, such as ultraviolet, x-ray, and gamma radiation. Longer wavelength radiation, such as radio waves, infrared, and visible light, consists of photons of lower energy.

When an electron in an atom or molecule absorbs a photon, it will be boosted from a lower energy to a higher energy. Emission of a photon occurs when an electron in a higher-energy state transitions to a lower-energy state. The excited energy state is said to *spontaneously* decay when the electron transitions to a lower energy. This decay process is entirely random and is the same principle behind radioactive decay, which will be mentioned shortly. This process also applies to atomic nuclei in excited energy states. In this case, excited nuclei emit excess energy in the form of gamma radiation as they transition to lower-energy states. Normally, electrons and other particles tend to reside in their lowest possible energy state in an atom or molecule, called their *ground state*, unless excited by a process such as a chemical reaction or absorption of radiation.

If the energy carried by a photon is sufficiently high, *ionization* occurs in which the photon is absorbed by an electron bound to an atom or molecule, and the electron is knocked out of its atom. Radiation that has the ability to remove electrons from atoms or molecules is referred to as *ionizing radiation*. X-ray and gamma radiations are ionizing electromagnetic radiations as is higher-energy ultraviolet radiation. Ionized atoms and molecules are electrically charged and can have altered chemical binding properties. In addition, the ejected electrons can cause further damage when traveling through materials by depositing energy in the material, which can cause additional changes in molecular structure. Also, additional x-rays can be emitted when the electrons are suddenly decelerated as they travel near atomic nuclei. Thus, with such effects on matter, ionizing radiation is dangerous to living organisms, resulting in damage to cells and tissues, with pathological effects, as will be discussed in more detail in Appendix 2.

RADIOACTIVITY AND NUCLEAR FORCES

Radioactivity occurs because radioactive nuclei are energetically unstable, that is they contain an excess of energy. Consequently, these nuclei, known as *radionuclides*, breakdown to other nuclei, known as *daughter nuclides*,[9] with the excess energy removed through the emission of radiation. If the daughter nuclides are also radioactive they too will decay, forming a series of radioactive nuclei, known as a *decay chain*, all of which decay in a sequence until a stable nuclide is finally reached. Each radionuclide has a characteristic *half-life*, which is the amount of time for half the nuclei of that species in a sample to decay. Over time, the number of original radioactive nuclei in a sample decreases: after one half-life, only half of them remain; after two half-lives, only one-quarter remain; and so on. These nuclei will decay to other nuclear species that may be stable or may be radioactive with a different half-life.

There are three types of ionizing radiation typically emitted in radioactive decays: alpha particles, beta particles, and gamma radiation. An *alpha particle* consists of two protons and two neutrons bound together in a very stable configuration, which is simply a helium 4 nucleus, while a *beta particle* is a high-energy electron. Emitted by energetic nuclei, *gamma radiation* is the most penetrating form of ionizing radiation, carrying so much energy that thick walls of lead are required to shield against it. Alpha and beta particles are charged particles whereas gamma radiation is electromagnetic radiation.

To further understand radioactivity as well as nuclear reactions, which will be discussed shortly, it is important to understand the forces acting within the atomic nucleus. Since electric charges of like sign repel one another, including the protons in a nucleus, all of which are positively charged, a force stronger than the electric force must exist within the nucleus to hold it together. First of all, there is the *strong force*, which is an attractive force, that acts between *quarks*, the constituents of protons and neutrons, with the result that there is an attractive *residual nuclear force* that acts over very short distances between neighboring nucleons within a nucleus. From here on we will refer only to this force between nucleons and call it the *nuclear force* to avoid confusion with the strong force that acts between quarks within a single nucleon.

The nuclear force between nucleons is largely responsible for the enormous energy changes in nuclear reactions and is indeed the stronger attractive force in the nucleus that overcomes the repulsive electric force between protons. The electric forces between protons are an example of the *electrostatic force*. Chemical reactions are also associated with electrostatic forces between electrons and atoms. Electrostatic forces are commonly known for causing the attraction of lint to laundry, and are much weaker than the nuclear force between nucleons, so the energy changes in chemical reactions are literally millions of times lower than those of nuclear reactions. The nuclear force results in the very tight binding between nucleons within the atomic nucleus, and therefore a significant amount of energy is required to break these bonds, that is, to break apart a nucleus.

However, there is a limit to how well the nuclear force can hold together larger nuclei, such as uranium 238, since this force acts over very short distances, becoming virtually nonexistent over longer distances. Consequently, the nuclear and electrostatic forces are together responsible for *alpha decay* in unstable nuclei, with the nuclear force tending to hold the nucleons together while the electrostatic force tends to push them apart. If there are too many protons in an unstable nucleus of high atomic number, the nuclear force will not be able to hold the nucleus together, and the electrostatic force will then result in the decay of the nucleus by the emission of alpha particles, each containing two protons and two neutrons. The electrostatic force also plays a part in nuclear fission.

Heavier radionuclides tend to decay by emitting alpha particles as illustrated in the following examples.[10] Uranium 238 undergoes alpha decay, with a half-life of about 4.5 billion years, to form thorium 234. Uranium 235 decays by alpha emission to thorium 231 with a half-life of over 700 million years. Plutonium 239 also undergoes alpha decay, with a half-life of over 24,000 years, to form uranium 235. Notice that by emitting an alpha particle, containing two protons and two neutrons, the mass number decreases by four and the atomic number decreases by two. Also note that with such long half-lives, these radionuclides will linger for long periods in the environment, posing significant health and environmental threats in a radiological emergency.

There is also the weak nuclear force, or *weak force*, which is responsible for *beta decay*, the decay of a neutron into a proton, a beta particle (an energetic electron), and another particle, the antineutrino. Neutrons undergo beta decay when alone in empty space, with a half-life of about eleven minutes,[11] or in nuclei where there is an excess of neutrons. The nucleus will then transform into a nuclide with one less neutron and one more proton so that the atomic number increases by one unit and the mass number remains unchanged. Neutrinos and their antimatter counterparts, antineutrinos, are particles emitted in nuclear reactions whenever a neutron transforms into a proton or vice versa. Neutrinos and antineutrinos have very little mass, have no electric charge, and only interact in nuclear reactions through the weak force. Since they are not important in nuclear weapons, neutrinos will not be discussed further.

An important example of beta decay is that of strontium 90, a major byproduct of the fission reactions of nuclear weapons. With its long half-life of 28.8 years, it accumulates in the environment and poses a significant health threat when ingested, for example, in contaminated milk.[12] Strontium 90 is among other fission products in a series of radioactive isotopes that undergo beta decay. Strontium 90 has the longest half-life in this series and decays to yttrium 90, which in turn undergoes beta decay, with a half-life of only sixty-four hours, to form stable zirconium 90.[13]

NUCLEAR ENERGY AND NUCLEAR REACTIONS

In nuclear physics, energy is often expressed in units of *electron volts* (eV). One electron volt is defined as the amount of energy gained by an electron that has moved through a potential difference, a *voltage*, of one volt. The electric potential energy changes when work is done in moving a charged particle from one point to another by or against an electric force, just as there is a change in gravitational potential energy when dropping or lifting an object. The potential difference is then the ratio of the change in electric potential energy to the electric charge carried by the particle. Typically in nuclear reactions, energies in the mega-electron volt range (MeV), in millions of electron volts, are released. In chemical reactions, such as combustion reactions, only a few electron volts of energy are released per reaction, so nuclear reactions can indeed release millions of times more energy.

The *binding energy* of a nucleus is the energy required to split the nucleus into its constituent nucleons so that they are all completely separated from each other. A plot of the average binding energy per nucleon with mass number is shown below in Figure A1.2. This plot is known as the *binding energy curve* and indicates the average amount of energy per nucleon needed to split a nucleus apart. A nucleus with a higher binding energy is more stable and therefore more difficult to break apart. Whereas it is often stated that iron 56 is the most stable nucleus, nickel 62 actually has the highest binding energy per nucleon, and so it is the most stable

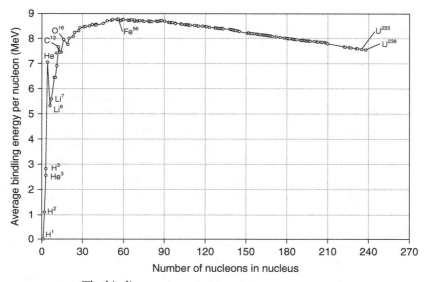

FIGURE A1.2 The binding energy curve.
Note: Mononomic, "Binding Energy Curve – Common Isotopes with Gridlines" (illustration).

nucleus.[14] For our purposes, we can take the peak of the curve to be at an atomic mass of about sixty.

In undergoing nuclear reactions, nuclei transform to configurations of higher binding energy by moving toward the peak on the curve. Nuclei of lower atomic mass favor the process of fusing together, nuclear *fusion*, to increase their binding energy, while nuclei of greater atomic mass favor splitting apart, nuclear *fission*. These reactions result in a more stable, tighter, configuration of the nucleons with a tremendous release of energy. In particular, the energies released per nucleon in fusion reactions tend to be greater than those released in fission as can be seen from the binding energy curve. This will be an important consideration in distinguishing between the types of nuclear weapons.

As mentioned before, the large energy changes in nuclear reactions are due to the incredible strength of the strong nuclear force (and also in part to the electrostatic force between protons). This results in the release of large amounts of energy and is ultimately responsible for the immense destructive force, heat, and radiation of nuclear weapons. The more energy released in a reaction, the greater the binding energy will be of the resulting nuclei. This release of energy also results in the product nuclei having a total mass less than that of the reacting nuclei.

This is because mass and energy are equivalent, mass is a concentrated form of energy, by Einstein's famous equation, $E = mc^2$, according to the theory of relativity.[15] Just as mass and energy are properties of matter, they are also properties of radiation: the released radiation carries away energy, and therefore, mass.

Typically, a nucleus is roughly a few tenths of a percent to about one percent lower in mass than the total mass of its nucleons if separated from each other. From Einstein's equation, this small difference in mass is equivalent to a large amount of energy as can be seen by noting that the square of the speed of light[16] ($c^2 = 8.988 \times 10^{20}$ cm²/s²) is a very large factor multiplying the mass. This large energy release associated with a small change in mass is certainly evident in a nuclear detonation. By contrast, the change in mass of an atom during a chemical reaction is exceedingly minute and undetectable.

As an example, in the fission of a single uranium 235 nucleus about 200 MeV of energy is released,[17] which is equivalent to about one-fifth the mass of a proton or neutron. Together, the resulting product nuclei and neutrons have a total mass less than the original uranium nucleus. The mass lost is released as energy, with about 85 percent in the form of heat, which is distributed as the kinetic energies of the fission products and neutrons released in the reaction.[18] The other 15 percent of the released energy is in the form of radiation.[19] As another example, in the fusion of hydrogen (deuterium + tritium → helium 4 + neutron), about 17.6 MeV of energy is released per fusion reaction, with about 14 MeV of it carried by the free neutron,[20] and the remaining energy released as radiation.

Nuclear reactions are similar in many ways to chemical reactions among atoms and molecules. Chemical reactions, as well as nuclear reactions, can occur as *chain reactions*, in which energy is released into the environment by an increasing number of reacting particles. Reacting particles interact to yield a set of excited atoms, molecules, or nuclei in part of the reacting material or "fuel." This initial set of reacting particles, the first *generation* of the chain reaction, consists of a relatively small number of particles or even just one particle. Energy from the first generation of reacting particles rapidly spreads to other atoms, molecules, or nuclei in the fuel to form subsequent generations of reacting particles. The number of reacting particles increases in each subsequent generation until the chain reaction is stopped through some mechanism (for example, in an explosion, the fuel is blown apart). The particles in the final product will be in a more stable state, having released energy to the environment. The

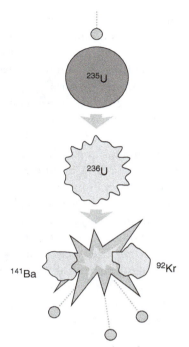

FIGURE A1.3 Nuclear fission.
Note: Sherman, *wpclipart.com*, "Nuclear fission" (illustration).

concept of the fission chain reaction was introduced by the Hungarian physicist Leo Szilard in 1934 in which he imagined a generic process of an incoming neutron splitting a nucleus into fragments with the emission of neutrons that could then go on to split other nuclei and continue the chain reaction.[21] Nuclear fission and fusion, and their associated chain reactions, which are vital to the operation of nuclear weapons, will now be discussed in detail here.

In the process of nuclear fission, illustrated in Figure A1.3, a heavy nucleus, such as uranium 235 or plutonium 239, splits apart into smaller nuclei after being struck by an incoming neutron. Not only does the original nucleus split into smaller nuclei, but neutrons are released along with a large amount of energy. Nuclear fission was first observed experimentally in Germany in late 1938 by chemist Otto Hahn and his assistant Fritz Strassmann.[22] They had been bombarding uranium nuclei with low-energy neutrons. It was initially thought that they would transform uranium into another element near uranium on the periodic table, such as radium, but they found instead that barium was formed.[23] Barium has a mass number of 137, which is about one hundred atomic mass units lower than uranium. Rather than transforming uranium to a neighboring element by absorbing neutrons, uranium was being transformed into barium through some other process. Austrian physicists Lise Meitner and Otto Frisch soon provided a theoretical interpretation of the experimental results. They reasoned that the uranium nucleus had been split when exposed to neutrons, with one of the fragments being a barium nucleus.[24]

Naturally occurring uranium is approximately 99.3 percent uranium 238 and 0.7 percent uranium 235.[25] Uranium 238 tends to absorb neutrons, without undergoing fission, transforming into uranium 239 with the emission of gamma radiation. It was realized by the Danish physicist Niels Bohr that the rare uranium 235 nuclei underwent fission in the experiment of Hahn and Strassmann, but not uranium 238.[26] If uranium could be produced, or *enriched*, consisting of a higher proportion of uranium 235 than is found in naturally occurring uranium, then a chain reaction could be sustained in which neutrons released in each fission process would subsequently fission additional uranium 235 nuclei which, in turn, would release more neutrons, and the process would continue.

Uranium 235 is said to be *fissile*, meaning that when bombarded by neutrons, it readily undergoes fission and can sustain a chain reaction, in contrast to naturally occurring uranium, consisting mostly of uranium 238. Uranium 238, on the other hand, is said to be *fissionable* in that it can undergo fission if struck by high-energy (fast) neutrons but it will not sustain a chain reaction. In the fission of uranium 235, a neutron strikes a uranium 235 nucleus and is absorbed, resulting in an unstable uranium 236 nucleus that splits into two nuclei known as *fission fragments*, typically barium and krypton. In this process, two or three neutrons on average are released along with a significant amount of energy, about fifty million times the amount of energy released by a typical combustion reaction of carbon. Per weight of fuel, uranium fission yields about 2.5 million times as much energy as carbon combustion.[27]

Plutonium 239 is another fissile material that can be used, releasing three neutrons on average and roughly the same amount of energy as the fission of uranium 235.[28] The fission discussed so far is *induced* fission, meaning that a neutron must be made to strike a nucleus to cause fission. However, there is also *spontaneous* fission that can occur automatically within the fissile material as a rare decay process of certain nuclides, emitting neutrons at random, which poses a problem when incorporating plutonium in a bomb, as will be discussed in more detail later.

In nuclear fusion, illustrated in Figure A1.4, light nuclei, such as those of hydrogen, combine to form more massive nuclei, such as helium. Fusion is the process that occurs in the cores of stars, first realized by the German American physicist Hans Bethe in 1938.[29] Hydrogen nuclei in stars fuse together to form helium nuclei, and further fusion reactions lead to the formation of heavier nuclei, such as carbon. As mentioned before, the energy released per nucleon in fusion tends to be greater than that released in fission, as can be seen from the binding energy curve. The steep increase in binding energy per nucleon at lower atomic mass between hydrogen and helium indicates this large difference in binding energies between helium and hydrogen (deuterium) nuclei as compared to the difference in binding energies of uranium nuclei and a typical fission product, such as barium.

Due to the greater release of energy per nucleon in fusion reactions, they can be utilized in the construction of weapons that are even more powerful than fission devices. Fusion reactions include, among others, those between deuterium nuclei, $H_2 + H_2 \rightarrow H_3 + H_1 + 4.0$ MeV, or between deuterium and tritium nuclei, $H_2 + H_3 \rightarrow He_4 + n + 17.6$ MeV.[30] In the first reaction, two deuterium nuclei fuse to yield one tritium nucleus and one regular hydrogen nucleus with the release of energy. In the second reaction, a deuterium nucleus and a tritium nucleus fuse yielding helium 4, an energetic neutron, and a large amount of energy. Per weight, deuterium can release about three times as much energy in fusion as can uranium 235 in fission.[31]

In order for nuclear fusion to occur, atomic nuclei must be brought very close together so that they may bind under the influence of the strong force. However, since the nuclei are each positively charged they will normally repel each other electrically before fusion can occur. Energy must be supplied to overcome this repulsion. Under high temperature and pressure, this energy can be supplied to the nuclei by compressing the material significantly. In stars, these conditions are initiated by gravitational collapse of hydrogen gas in star formation and they persist during a star's lifetime in its core. In a nuclear weapon, these conditions can be established by use of a fission reaction. Radiation from the fission reaction, in the form of x-rays, heats and compresses the material to undergo fusion. Such weapons are referred to as *thermonuclear* weapons since a state of high temperature must first be established by a fission chain reaction in order for the fusion chain reaction to occur. The first man-made

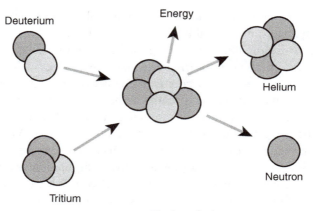

FIGURE A1.4 Nuclear fusion.
Note: Sherman, *wpclipart.com*, "nuclear fusion" (illustration).

fusion reactions occurred in the detonation of the first thermonuclear device in 1952, developed by the United States.[32]

The explosive power of a bomb is referred to as its *yield*, and for nuclear weapons this is typically expressed in *kilotons* or *megatons*. The yield is the amount of energy released in an explosion, with a single "ton" equaling the amount of energy released in the explosion of one ton of TNT. Hence a yield of one kiloton is equal to the amount of energy that is released by one thousand tons of TNT and one megaton is equivalent to the energy released by one million tons of TNT.

Having introduced the basic physical concepts, the following two sections will next discuss how nuclear weapons work and why they were pursued. To understand how they work, it will be necessary to describe how they were developed, including problems encountered during their development. The resolution of these problems ultimately influenced their design. Also, the motivation for these weapons will be discussed within an historical context in order to make clear why such a tremendous effort would be undertaken to acquire such destructive weapons.

THE FISSION BOMB

The first nuclear weapons utilized only nuclear fission for their destructive power. These bombs were relatively simpler in design than thermonuclear devices like the one tested at Castle Bravo. Both nuclear weapons that were dropped on Japan were fission devices. As soon as fission had been discovered, it was realized that it could be used for energy or military purposes as a powerful weapon many times more powerful than a conventional explosive. At this point, it should be noted that although Hahn and Strassmann induced the first fission reactions, they did not create a fission chain reaction. If a fission chain reaction could be sustained, a high-yield bomb could be constructed.

The discovery of fission was made in the same year as Hitler's annexation of Austria and almost a year before the invasion of Poland that started the Second World War.[33] This sparked a panic that Nazi Germany may obtain the first nuclear weapons. That same year, Leo Szilard, along with two other physicists, Eugene Wigner and Edward Teller, the latter of who would later be instrumental in hydrogen bomb development, discussed the Nazi threat with Albert Einstein who then wrote a letter to President Franklin Roosevelt, warning of the possibility that Germany may be first in acquiring nuclear weapons.[34]

In October 1941, two months before the bombing of Pearl Harbor, Roosevelt established the American effort to develop nuclear weapons, which would come to be known as the Manhattan Project.[35] Many new techniques and technologies would have to be discovered for adequate nuclear fuel production, as well as developing and testing the components needed to construct these bombs. These techniques would include the enrichment of uranium, formation of plutonium, understanding the chemistry of these and other rare metals, precision manipulation of high explosives, and determining the optimal configuration of bomb designs. These efforts would in turn require novel techniques in analyzing the components under assembly and testing the components in trial runs.

Several laboratories were built at various undisclosed locations throughout the United States for this enormous effort. These included the laboratories in Los Alamos, New Mexico, where bombs were to be tested, Oak Ridge, Tennessee, where uranium would be enriched, and Hanford, Washington, where plutonium would be produced.[36] In December 1942, Enrico Fermi was successful in producing the first fission chain reaction in the nuclear reactor he constructed at the University of Chicago.[37] Fermi worked at Los Alamos soon afterward.[38]

One of the most important undertakings in the Manhattan Project was the process of enrichment, in which the amount of uranium 235 in the nuclear fuel is increased. As mentioned before, uranium 235 is fissile, that is, its nuclei will readily undergo nuclear fission, whereas uranium 238 is fissionable, meaning it can undergo fission but only by high-energy neutrons and it cannot sustain a fission chain reaction. Thus, uranium 235 is favorable in nuclear reactors and weapons as a fuel since it can sustain a fission chain reaction. Enrichment requires the separation of the more commonly occurring isotope uranium 238 from the fissile isotope uranium 235. Weapons-grade uranium is about 90 percent uranium 235,[39] whereas slightly enriched uranium, used in commercial nuclear reactors, is about 5 percent uranium 235.[40]

Isotopes of an element are identical chemically since they have the same number of protons and electrons, so they cannot be separated through chemical means. Separation must be achieved through some other means by taking advantage of the difference in the isotopes, that is, the difference in their mass numbers. There are five principle methods for achieving this separation: centrifugal separation, gaseous diffusion separation, thermal diffusion separation, electromagnetic separation, and laser separation,[41] though the fifth method is a very recent development and was not available during the Manhattan Project or the Cold War. The gaseous diffusion, thermal diffusion, and electromagnetic separation methods were employed in the Manhattan Project at Oak Ridge.[42] We refer the reader elsewhere for the details of these methods.

The other fissile material used in nuclear weapons, plutonium 239, is formed in nuclear reactors. In fact, nuclear reactors were first built for the purpose of producing plutonium, and only later were they applied to power production.[43] In order to ensure success in a timely manner to end the war more quickly, both uranium-based and plutonium-based bombs were researched in parallel, along with the various methods of uranium enrichment and plutonium production.[44] In this way, if one method failed, others may still succeed. Plutonium 239 is formed in the following way. Uranium 238 in a reactor is first bombarded with neutrons, forming uranium 239. Uranium 239 undergoes beta decay to form neptunium 239. Neptunium 239 then undergoes beta decay, transforming into plutonium 239 which accumulates in the reactor. Plutonium has many advantages over uranium as a nuclear fuel. It is readily formed from uranium 238, which is much more abundant than uranium 235. Plutonium can therefore be produced in larger quantities.

Despite the uranium enrichment effort carried out, due to the difficulty in separating uranium 235 from uranium 238 on account of their atomic masses being nearly identical, there would only be enough enriched uranium to construct one uranium-based fission weapon by the summer of 1945.[45] It was realized that more bombs could be created using plutonium if only the proper design for such bombs could be determined. Ultimately, two plutonium-based bombs were constructed by the summer of 1945, the bomb tested at Trinity on July 16, and the bomb dropped on Nagasaki on August 9.[46]

Uranium 235 and plutonium 239 are invaluable as nuclear fuels. With the right amount of fissile material and with the right design of the reactor or bomb, a fission chain reaction can be sustained. Some neutrons released during fission will escape from the nuclear fuel to the environment and not induce further fission reactions, while others will be absorbed by nuclei in nonfission processes. In a nuclear weapon, a certain amount of mass of fissile material, for a given shape and volume of the fissile material, is needed to maintain an adequate number of neutrons to sustain a fission chain reaction. This mass of fissile material needed to sustain a chain reaction is known as the **critical mass**. If the chain reaction is controlled so that one neutron is released on average per fission event, and each of these neutrons in turn causes one fission event, then the chain reaction can be used in a nuclear reactor for harnessing the energy released during fission. In this case the amount of energy released per generation of the chain reaction will be nearly constant and the chain reaction is said to be *critical*. If the chain reaction is not controlled, then the amount of energy released in each generation can be greater than the energy released in the previous generation. This will happen if more than one neutron is released per fission and more than one neutron from each fission event causes fission.

Whereas uranium 235 releases about 2.5 neutrons on average per fission, that is it releases typically two or three neutrons at a time, plutonium 239 releases slightly more neutrons at a time, about three on average.[47] When summed up over a large number of nuclei undergoing fission, this difference in the number of neutrons released is significant. At their normal densities, the critical mass of plutonium 239 is significantly lower than that of uranium 235. Thus, plutonium 239 is a more efficient fission fuel. For a given shape of fissile material, such as a sphere, increasing the material's density will decrease the critical mass necessary to sustain a chain reaction. This concept will be important later when discussing the implosion design of the fission weapon. It should be noted that enriching uranium fuel lowers its critical mass, whereas natural uranium by itself can never become critical since a large number of neutrons are absorbed in nonfission processes.

In a nuclear weapon, more energy will be released in each subsequent generation of the chain reaction and the chain reaction will be *supercritical*, that is, it will become a runaway chain reaction, resulting in a violent explosion. As mentioned before, not every neutron released in a fission reaction necessarily results in a subsequent fission reaction. Some neutrons may for example be absorbed by uranium 235 but not result in fission, others may be absorbed by other materials, including uranium 238, that have a tendency to absorb neutrons, and still other neutrons may escape to the environment without affecting any nuclei in the fuel. Neutron absorption and escape lead to some of the most difficult problems that must be taken into consideration when designing a bomb.

A fissile nucleus like uranium 235 has a distinct probability of undergoing fission when a neutron of a given kinetic energy is projected in its direction. This probability is expressed by the fission **cross section**, which is essentially the target area in which the nucleus and the neutron must enter for fission to occur. The cross section is larger (fission more probable) when the kinetic energy of the incoming neutron is lower. A nucleus is more likely to react with a slow neutron that approaches it in comparison to a fast neutron. A fast neutron approaching a nucleus must make a "direct hit" to induce a reaction. With a slow neutron, however, the target area is two hundred times bigger and the target nucleus will react even without a direct hit due to the quantum mechanical properties of the neutron.[48]

The construction of a bomb with highly enriched nuclear fuel ensures a higher probability of fission reactions so that a chain reaction can be maintained. A *tamper* is a material used to encase fissile or other nuclear material in a bomb. Tampers can be made of materials such as natural uranium, depleted uranium,[49] or beryllium. This material slows the expansion of the nuclear fuel during the initial explosion to lengthen the time interval over which the fuel can remain supercritical and the fission chain reaction can occur. Then, more of the nuclei in the fuel can undergo fission, maximizing the yield, with less material going to waste. This time interval is on the order of a microsecond.[50]

The tamper also reflects escaping neutrons released during a fission chain reaction back into the bulk of the nuclear material, increasing the number of neutrons that can induce fission reactions. By reflecting escaping neutrons, the tamper reduces the critical mass needed to sustain a chain reaction. For example, without a tamper, a sphere of uranium 235 at its normal density will be critical with a diameter of seventeen centimeters and mass of forty-nine kilograms.[51] With a tamper surrounding the uranium, the sphere would need to be just under twelve centimeters in diameter and have a mass of seventeen kilograms to be critical.[52]

One important requirement in the design of these weapons is that they must be kept subcritical prior to detonation otherwise a stray neutron could set off the chain reaction during storage or transport of the bomb if the nuclear fuel were kept at or above critical mass. The nuclear fuel must be kept at lower density or separated into smaller pieces that are each unable to sustain a chain reaction unless brought together. For an efficient explosion that uses as much of the fissile material as possible, it is desirable for the subcritical pieces, when completely joined together, to form a supercritical mass, a mass of fissile material larger than the critical mass. Indeed, the critical mass is merely a threshold required for a minimal chain reaction. As a result, difficulties arise in devising a means of obtaining the supercritical mass at the moment when the bomb is to be detonated. This involves the proper placement of high explosives within the bomb that will force the subcritical masses of nuclear fuel to join together into the supercritical mass where the fission chain reaction can be optimally sustained. In addition, the shape and constituent materials of the bomb must be such that the number of neutrons that escape to the environment is minimized, otherwise a chain reaction will not be possible.

When the subcritical masses are brought together by the blast of the high explosive, a neutron strikes a nucleus within the nuclear fuel and initiates the chain reaction. This neutron can be a stray neutron originating from a uranium or plutonium nucleus in the fuel that has spontaneously fissioned. However, a neutron source known as a neutron initiator may also be used for delivering a burst of neutrons exactly when the subcritical masses of nuclear fuel combine to form the critical mass. This burst of neutrons guarantees that the chain reaction will be initiated.

The fission bomb dropped on Hiroshima, on August 6, 1945, "Little Boy," consisted of the simpler of the two designs for fission weapons (see Figs. AI.5 and AI.6). Although the exact details of bomb designs are classified, we can discuss the basic principles and components. The method of this bomb was known as the *gun method*. Little Boy consisted of a long cylindrical bomb approximately three meters long and 0.75 m in diameter with an explosive charge on one end of its interior.[53] At this end a subcritical cylindrical "bullet," consisting of rings of 80-percent enriched uranium, was placed prior to detonation.[54] On the other end of the bomb's interior was a series of target rings composed of subcritical 80-percent enriched uranium.[55]

When the gun bomb was to be detonated, the high explosive would first detonate and shoot the cylindrical uranium bullet toward the uranium target rings. The bullet would then meet the target rings, resulting in the formation of a larger supercritical mass of uranium, and a neutron

FIGURE A1.5 Little Boy and Fat Man (inset).
Notes: Image of Little Boy: National Archives website, ARC 519394 (illustration).
Image of Fat Man: Australian War Memorial website, #045196 (illustration).

would initiate the fission chain reaction. The supercritical mass of uranium
was surrounded by an encasing composed of tungsten carbide and steel
to serve as a tamper and to reflect neutrons back into the supercritical
uranium.[56] Although a neutron initiator was incorporated in Little Boy,
the initiator was not actually necessary since stray neutrons from spontaneous fission of uranium 238 would have been sufficient to initiate the
fission chain reaction.[57]

A full-scale test prior to the bombing of Hiroshima was not imple-
mented since the gun design was assumed very likely to succeed, and
also there was not enough uranium 235 to build more than one bomb
of this type.[58] The yield of Little Boy was about fifteen kilotons[59] and the
detonation occurred at an altitude of about 1,900 feet.[60] Although Little
Boy was simpler in design, it was also very inefficient. A total of forty-two
kilograms of uranium was used with only about 2 percent of the uranium

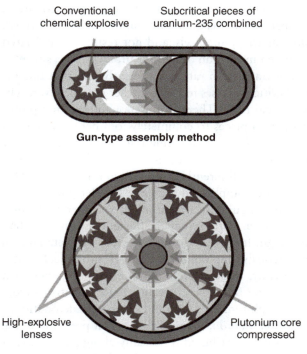

Conventional chemical explosive   Subcritical pieces of uranium-235 combined

Gun-type assembly method

High-explosive lenses   Plutonium core compressed

Implosion assembly method

FIGURE A1.6 Assembly methods for obtaining the critical mass needed for fission chain reaction in each design.
Notes: Fastfission, "Fission bomb assembly methods" (illustration). Atomic Archive website, "Cold War: A Brief History – The Soviet Atomic Bomb."

contributing to the explosion.[61] A more efficient design is possible with plutonium but a different bomb configuration is required, as will be discussed next.

The simple gun design worked with enriched uranium, but not with plutonium. In the formation of plutonium 239 in reactors, some amount of plutonium 240 inevitably forms with it, and since the two differ by only one atomic mass unit, it would be even more difficult to separate them than it already is to separate the isotopes of uranium. The problem with plutonium 240 is that it has a very high rate of spontaneous fission, releasing neutrons at random and very rapidly. As a result, a gun design would not work for a plutonium-based device because as the two pieces of subcritical plutonium begin to join together, but have not yet completely joined, a partial chain reaction called a *fizzle* could occur that would result in a lower-yield explosion of the device, a predetonation, before the optimal supercritical mass of plutonium could be formed. The bomb would blow apart prematurely and not result in the desired yield. This does not happen in the gun design for uranium 235, since for this nuclide, the spontaneous fission rate is sufficiently low that there is enough time for the subcritical masses to join together completely, reaching the optimal supercritical mass. There is not enough time in a plutonium gun device for the two pieces to completely join before a neutron initiates a predetonation, so the optimal configuration of supercriticality would not be reached, and the gun design is not feasible for plutonium.

A bomb must be configured differently if plutonium is to be used. This design is considerably more complicated than the simpler gun method. The method of bringing the subcritical plutonium together to form a supercritical mass has to occur within a much shorter time interval than is typical in the gun design. It was proposed by John von Neumann in 1943, that by simultaneously imploding wedges of subcritical plutonium distributed spherically, they could be compressed together in a much shorter time, achieving full supercriticality, before neutrons from the spontaneous fission of plutonium 240 could cause a predetonation.[62] This method, the *implosion method*, requires the utmost precision in the detonation of high explosives distributed spherically along the outside of the subcritical masses.

The implosion bomb design is basically spherical in shape, consisting of layers of components from the outside in as follows: high explosive "lenses" – block-like segments of high explosive that generate and focus their resulting explosive shock waves to converge inward – which are arranged around the outermost layers of the bomb along with a detonator that is activated electrically to ignite the explosives; these surround a tamper which may consist of natural uranium as in the original design; and at the center of the bomb is the plutonium core which, when the bomb is inactive, consists of subcritical plutonium that is compressed to the supercritical state by the inward-bound shock wave from the high explosives during detonation.

Plutonium cores can consist of various configurations, such as a subcritical solid sphere of plutonium that, when compressed to higher density, become supercritical, making a chain reaction possible. The original core developed during the Manhattan Project consisted of two solid subcritical hemispheres of plutonium roughly the size of a softball that, when compressed by the shock wave to about the size of a tennis ball, formed a supercritical sphere.[63] In the center of a plutonium core is a neutron initiator that when activated will release a burst of neutrons at the same time that the plutonium is supercritical, initiating the chain reaction. This occurs when the plutonium is maximally compressed. Timing is absolutely crucial: the events of maximal compression and the burst of neutrons have to coincide within a time on the order of one ten-millionth (10^{-7}) of a second.[64] Since the plutonium is compressed into a smaller volume, neutrons travel shorter distances when initiating fission reactions and the chain reaction occurs faster and more efficiently, that is, more of the plutonium fuel gets used before the bomb blows itself apart.

A neutron initiator consists of a combination of beryllium and polonium. From the work of James Chadwick, who first discovered the neutron, it is known that polonium 210 releases alpha particles as it undergoes radioactive decay.[65] When bombarded with alpha particles, neutrons are ejected from beryllium nuclei. Thus, a burst of neutrons can be delivered when these materials are mixed together. Metal foils can be used to separate the polonium and beryllium and therefore stop alpha particles emitted from polonium from reaching the beryllium prior to detonation. The inward compression wave from the high explosive will then mix polonium and beryllium together during detonation, exactly when the plutonium is supercritical. The neutron initiator, when active, releases about ninety five million neutrons per second, so in one ten-millionth of a second, about nine or ten neutrons are released, more than enough to initiate a chain reaction.[66] More exact details of the neutron initiator are classified, but the above description is sufficient to illustrate the basic principles.

In addition to lowering the critical mass of plutonium needed in the bomb by reflecting neutrons back into the fuel, as well as slowing its expansion, allowing more fission reactions to take place, in the implosion design, the tamper is also necessary for smoothing the symmetry of the inward shock wave so that it will be perfectly spherical in shape when it strikes the plutonium. This is crucial so that all of the plutonium moves symmetrically inward, resulting in the maximum yield.

The original implosion bomb used about 6.2 kilograms of a plutonium–gallium metal alloy with a natural uranium tamper,[67] weighed over 4,600 kilograms (over 10,200 pounds),[68] was about 3.25 m long (nearly eleven feet),[69] and had a diameter of about 1.5 m (5 feet).[70] Unlike the gun design, which was certain to work, the implosion design was tested before being dropped on Nagasaki on August 9, 1945. Due to its more complicated design, it was decided one test would be necessary before using it. The implosion bomb dropped on Nagasaki was known as "Fat Man," based on its shape, and had a yield of about twenty-one kilotons.[71] Little Boy and Fat Man were dropped on Japan, ending the Second World War.

It is also possible to produce more efficient designs of fission weapons using cores consisting of a combination of uranium and plutonium, or by boosted fission, where small amounts of the gases deuterium and tritium are contained within the core of the bomb. After fission reactions have been initiated, conditions are obtained whereby fusion reactions can occur in the gases, and these fusion reactions enhance the fission chain reaction by releasing neutrons. These modifications greatly enhance the efficiency of fission weapons, particularly those used as thermonuclear primaries, as will be discussed next.

THE THERMONUCLEAR BOMB

With the development of the fission bomb and the conclusion of the Second World War, it was already realized by many physicists that even more powerful weapons could be developed, as the nuclear arms race unfolded between the United States and the Soviet Union. In the summer of 1945, the United States succeeded in detonating and using the first fission bombs in history. The Soviet Union soon followed with its first detonation of "Joe-1" on August 29, 1949 with a yield of twenty-two kilotons.[72] As far back as the early 1940s the idea of a thermonuclear bomb, or *hydrogen bomb*, was already of great interest to the Hungarian American physicist Edward Teller when he joined the Manhattan Project.[73] He is considered the father of the hydrogen bomb[74] though Enrico Fermi had suggested the concept of a fusion-based bomb to Teller in September 1941.[75] This new super bomb would be the ultimate in destructive power and both the United States and Soviet Union sought to possess it.

One crucial step toward developing the thermonuclear bomb was the "Cylinder" design tested in Operation Greenhouse in the George shot, detonated on May 9, 1951, with a yield of 225 kilotons.[76] This test was essentially a physics experiment for investigating the initiation of thermonuclear reactions from a fission detonation.[77] The shape of the Cylinder design was basically a disk with a small hole running through its center.[78] The disk was about eight feet in diameter and about two feet in height.[79] Uranium in the disk, when imploded, would fission, and x-rays emitted as thermal radiation from the fission reactions would then travel through the central hole to a small chamber that contained a cryogenic mixture of liquid deuterium and a small amount of liquid tritium, from here on referred to as a *DT mixture.*

The thermal radiation, traveling at the speed of light and arriving first, would then compress and heat the chamber, initiating fusion reactions within the DT mixture for a very short time before the mixture was destroyed by the heated gases and materials of the fission explosion that would then arrive soon after. The yield of the fusion reactions was insignificant compared to that of the fission reactions, but the occurrence of fusion reactions was indicated by the detection of x-rays emitted from them. The x-rays traveled through metal pipes to detectors, shielded from the radiation produced by the fission reactions. Of the 225 kilotons yield, fission contributed about 200 kilotons, and fusion contributed about twenty-five kilotons.[80]

Another important step to a true thermonuclear bomb was the "Booster," tested on May 25, 1951, in the Bikini Atoll.[81] This was the "Item" shot of Operation Greenhouse.[82] The design was first conceived by Edward Teller in December 1945.[83] The Booster was the first *boosted fission* device,[84] containing a small chamber of cryogenic DT mixture.[85] When the fission reactions were initiated, high temperature and pressure were established, and a small number of fusion reactions were initiated in the DT mixture. These fusion reactions in turn released neutrons which then served to induce further fission reactions, thus enhancing the explosive yield of the detonation. The resulting yield was 45.5 kilotons, estimated to have been double the yield that would have been obtained if the device were only fission-based.[86]

For many years after the Manhattan Project, Teller pursued theoretical studies to develop the first thermonuclear weapon, working with the Polish mathematician Stanislaw Ulam on complicated calculations.[87] Teller and Ulam would finally arrive at the Teller-Ulam design, shown in Figure A1.7, which incorporates staged nuclear devices. A fission device, the **primary**, would detonate first, releasing vast amounts of thermal radiation in the form of soft x-rays. This radiation could then be channeled to a fusion device, or **secondary**, where the radiation could be focused inward, in a process known as "radiation implosion," to compress and heat the fuel that would then undergo nuclear fusion.

The fuel would have to be compressed to a density thousands of times greater than its natural density.[88] The amount of energy carried by the x-rays is tremendous and would result in this degree of compression. Also, the radiation from the fission device would arrive at the secondary first, compressing the fusion fuel before it was destroyed by the fireball

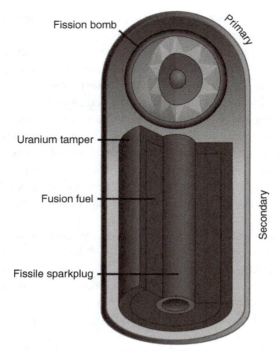

Fission bomb

Primary

Uranium tamper

Fusion fuel

Secondary

Fissile sparkplug

FIGURE A1.7 The Teller-Ulam design.
Note: Fastfission. "Teller-Ulam device 3D" (illustration).

from the primary detonation. The compression and heating would be necessary since nuclei normally repel each other due to their positive electrical charges. Compression would bring the nuclei close enough to each other that the short-ranged nuclear force could cause them to bind, thus establishing nuclear fusion. Compressing the nuclear fuel would also increase the reaction rate of the fusion reactions.

In the Teller-Ulam design, the fusion fuel may be liquid deuterium mixed with tritium, or the solid compound lithium deuteride. A tamper, consisting of natural uranium or depleted uranium for example, surrounds the fusion fuel, slowing its expansion during detonation. A lining of lead and polyethylene plastic on the periphery of the tamper serves as the x-ray channel.[89] In the process of channeling x-rays to the secondary, the polyethylene and outer tamper are vaporized by the incoming x-rays, forming a high-temperature ionized state of matter, or *plasma*, which also emits x-rays. These x-rays then travel inward toward the center of the secondary, exerting pressure, heating and compressing it. In addition, fission reactions will then occur in the uranium 238 as it is bombarded by high-energy neutrons released from the fusion reactions.

A narrow column of plutonium with a chamber of tritium gas is placed along the center of the tank within the secondary. Fission reactions also occur within this "fission spark plug" as it is imploded by the x-rays mentioned before, and the tritium enhances its explosive yield. The spark plug then exerts outward pressure on the deuterium so that, between this outward pressure and the inward pressure from the inward traveling x-rays, the deuterium will be heated and compressed even further, leading to the establishment of nuclear fusion.

The first true thermonuclear device, the Mike device, was detonated on November 1, 1952, by the United States in the Bikini Atoll with a yield of 10.4 megatons[90] and a fireball over three miles in diameter.[91] This was the first device to incorporate the Teller-Ulam design.[92] The particular design of Mike, known as the "Sausage" design, essentially consisted of a cylindrical steel tank containing liquid deuterium, with a fission bomb on one end of it.[93] The tank was nearly seven feet in diameter and over twenty feet tall.[94]

The deuterium was kept separate from the fission device so that the fusion reactions could be observed outside of the fission detonation via instrumentation around the tank.[95] To maintain its liquid state, the deuterium had to be kept cryogenically cooled to very low temperatures near absolute zero. The tank containing the deuterium was a large thermally insulated flask, or "dewar."[96] Liquid deuterium was again chosen as the thermonuclear fuel since its properties were better understood than other potential fuels, in particular, the details of the fusion reaction between deuterium nuclei. The Sausage was not a deliverable weapon but was intended as an experiment to see if fusion reactions could be initiated on a large scale and to study their properties.

The use of liquid deuterium as the fusion fuel is impractical for the purposes of deliverable thermonuclear bombs. For a practical weapon design, certain compounds must be used to obtain the hydrogen needed for fusion reactions. Lithium deuteride, incorporated in the Teller-Ulam design, is the fusion fuel used in thermonuclear weapons. The two isotopes lithium 6 and lithium 7 are found naturally in lithium deuteride, the majority of the lithium being lithium 7. When lithium 6 nuclei are bombarded with neutrons, helium 4 and tritium are produced with the release of about 4.8 MeV of energy per reaction (the energy that an electron will gain when accelerated through 4.8 million volts).[97] The tritium will then undergo fusion with the deuterium if the lithium deuteride material is compressed and heated. This is the fusion reaction mentioned before, $H_2 + H_3 \rightarrow He_4 + n +$ energy, which releases neutrons and a large amount of energy.

A lithium deuteride device is often referred to as a "dry bomb," since it does not use liquid deuterium as fuel. The Soviets first incorporated lithium deuteride, as well as lithium tritide, into their "*sloika*," or "layer cake" thermonuclear design.[98] Conceived by Andrei Sakharov, often considered the father of the Soviet thermonuclear bomb, the layer cake was a single stage device consisting of alternating layers of uranium and lithium deuteride/tritide, imploded by high explosives, not utilizing radiation implosion.[99] On August 12, 1953, the Soviet Union detonated its first thermonuclear weapon, Joe-4, with a yield of about 400 kilotons, based on the layer cake design.[100] This device was not a true thermonuclear weapon, only about 20 percent of its yield came from fusion.[101] It was actually a boosted fission device, but it was deliverable by aircraft, unlike the Mike device, and this gave the Soviets a temporary advantage which, at the time, was a major concern to the United States.[102] The first dry bomb developed by the United States was the "Shrimp," tested at Castle Bravo on March 1, 1954, having the largest yield of any US detonation at an unexpected fifteen megatons.[103] It used lithium deuteride that was enriched to 40 percent lithium 6.[104] As mentioned in the main text, when bombarded with high-energy neutrons, lithium 7 forms tritium, and in fact, another solid fusion fuel is the compound lithium 7 hydride, formed by the lithium 7 isotope bound to the lightest hydrogen isotope.

NUCLEAR DETONATIONS

In conducting nuclear tests, vast amounts of scientific data were gathered through the use of instruments designed to measure various physical properties of nuclear detonations, as well as by observing the effects of detonations on the environment, animals, exposed structures, buildings, equipment, and electronics. Most of the destruction from a nuclear weapon is due to its blast and the shock wave it generates. The blast generated by these weapons can be thousands or millions of times more powerful than that of conventional weapons, but in addition, a large amount of thermal radiation is released in the form of heat and light, along with nuclear radiation, the latter being unique to nuclear weapons. Radioactive materials are left afterward as well.

Almost all energy from a conventional weapon takes the form of blast. On the other hand, for a nuclear weapon detonated in the atmosphere, about half of the total energy released is in the form of blast, while more than a third is in the form of thermal radiation, and the rest is in the form of nuclear radiation.[105] Nuclear radiation is released during the chain reaction, as well as in the radioactivity of leftover fission products. The exact manner in which energy is distributed depends on the yield, altitude of detonation, and design of the bomb.[106]

The violent release of energy in a detonation is due primarily to the kinetic energy of fission fragments being transferred in the form of heat to particles of the bomb constituents. This accounts for about 85 percent of the total energy released in the detonation.[107] Fission fragments collide with bomb materials, heating them, and a high temperature ionized gas, or plasma, is formed, generating x-rays. The energy of this radiation is then transformed into intense heat and blast energy as the surrounding air in the environment is rapidly heated, with about 50 percent of the total energy released in the form of blast energy, and another 35 percent in the form of heat.[108] Roughly 5 percent of the total energy is released in the form of gamma radiation and neutron kinetic energy immediately from nuclear reactions during detonation, while the remaining 10 percent of the energy will be released over time as radiation from the radioactive decay of fission products.[109] In a thermonuclear device in particular, radiation from these radioactive decays accounts for roughly 5 percent of the total energy from detonation.[110] Also, in this case, fission and fusion reactions may contribute roughly equally to the yield.

Immediately after an atmospheric detonation, an extremely hot, glowing, nearly spherical air mass forms, the fireball. Whereas a conventional explosion may reach temperatures of thousands of degrees, a nuclear explosion can result in temperatures of tens of millions of degrees.[111] At these temperatures, all materials, including metals, the weapon's materials, and fission products, are vaporized. Pressures in the range of millions of pounds per square inch are generated in a nuclear fireball.[112] X-rays are emitted in less than a microsecond,[113] heating the surrounding air. This heated air and the gases from the vaporized bomb materials form the hot and bright fireball.

Approximately one millisecond after detonation, the fireball from a one megaton device will appear many times brighter than the sun even when viewed fifty miles away.[114] Most of the x-rays emitted by the fireball will be absorbed in the air within a few feet, rapidly heating it, contributing to the fireball.[115] Thermal energy will then be radiated at longer wavelengths, mainly in the form of UV, visible, and infrared radiation, at lower temperatures than the actual detonation.

During its rapid formation, the fireball emits two pulses of intense thermal and optical radiation.[116] The first is shorter and hotter, lasting a fraction of a second, consisting mostly of UV radiation. The second is longer, lasting up to ten seconds for high yield weapons, consisting mostly of visible and infrared radiation, lower in temperature than the first pulse.[117] The duration of these pulses will depend on the yield of the detonation and the size of the fireball. The observed intensity and duration of these pulses can actually be used to measure the explosive yield. The first pulse delivers roughly 1 percent of the thermal and optical radiation because it is very short in duration, while the second pulse delivers the other 99 percent.[118]

Much of the UV radiation from the first pulse is absorbed in air and may not necessarily be significant in causing skin burns, but it is a danger to unprotected eyes. This UV radiation is more of a problem to skin at closer range, but other thermal damage will be more significant at these close distances. Intense heat will be felt from the fireball before the blast and shock wave arrive. The second pulse is responsible for severe skin burns, as well as causing fires, out to about twelve miles for a one megaton bomb.[119] The flashes associated with these pulses are so bright that they can cause temporary or permanent blindness to anyone looking directly at the fireball without adequate eye protection.

As the fireball rises and grows in size, it cools. The brightness of the fireball and the pressure inside it also decrease as it expands. After about a minute, the fireball of a one megaton detonation will have cooled sufficiently that it will no longer appear visible and no longer glow.[120] At this point, the fireball will have risen several miles into the atmosphere at a rate of a few hundred feet per second due to its buoyancy.[121] In nearly a tenth of a second, the fireball of a one megaton explosion will be about 500 feet in diameter, and after about ten seconds, will reach nearly 6,000 feet in height.[122]

The blast wave, or *shock wave*, is the high-pressure wave of compressed air that rapidly travels outward from the detonation, having been formed as an immediate result of the high temperature and pressure of the rapidly expanding fireball. As the expanding fireball emits energy and cools, its expansion slows to the speed of sound and the shock wave forms on its outer edge. In fifty seconds, moving slightly faster than the speed of sound, the shock wave will have traveled about twelve miles.[123]

Pressure in the shock wave of a one-megaton detonation can reach well over 100 pounds per square inch (psi) above atmospheric pressure at half-a-mile from the center.[124] This amount of pressure above atmospheric pressure is known as *overpressure*. Whereas one-half of a psi of overpressure can cause window damage, a few pounds per square inch of overpressure can cause significant damage to a building.[125] The pressure in the shock wave diminishes with distance as the wave travels away from the blast and spreads outward. Another form of damaging pressure from the shock wave is *dynamic pressure* due to the drag force of air as it rushes by a structure. The damage caused by the shock wave alone is comparable to that of an earthquake or a hurricane. This is particularly true closer to the site of detonation.

Traveling away from the fireball, the shock wave heats air as it compresses it, and immediately after it passes, the air cools and spreads out. This air behind the shock wave is rarefied to a pressure below atmospheric pressure. As a result, objects at a point will first be blown outward from the detonation due to the overpressure of the shock wave, and then sucked inward to a lesser extent as the rarefied air behind the shock wave passes. This cooling of the air also results in the formation of a visible cloud of condensation just behind the shock wave when it has reached a distance far enough away from the fireball that temperatures become low enough for condensation to occur. This effect tends to be more pronounced in detonations over water where there is higher humidity.

The propagation of a shock wave from a nuclear blast can be altered by meteorological conditions.[126] Normally, air temperature in the atmosphere decreases with altitude. However, weather conditions can be such that temperature actually increases with altitude in the lower atmosphere (above a certain height however, temperature will again decrease with altitude). This can be caused, for example, in the winter or at night when the ground is cold so that air closer to the ground is cooler and denser than the air above it. This is known as a **temperature inversion**, and can result in an enhancement of a shock wave's overpressure at ground level. If instead temperature decreases quickly with altitude, the overpressure at ground level will be attenuated. The shock wave can also be deflected downward off of jet-stream winds at high altitude, leading to a more intense shock wave on the ground.

The fireball takes on a doughnut shape as it rises and expands due to the lowering of its temperature and drag from the surrounding air. Gases formed from the vaporization of bomb and other materials circulate in the doughnut-shaped cloud, and updrafts into the bottom of the cloud result in further cooling, leading to the formation of the characteristic mushroom cloud.[127] Compounds formed from these gases, water vapor, and the air result in a brownish or reddish color of the cloud initially,

FIGURE A1.8 The mushroom cloud from the Castle Bravo test.
Note: Operation Castle, BRAVO Event. n.d. Photo courtesy of National Nuclear Security Administration / Nevada Field Office.

and then as the gases cool and condense, water droplets give the cloud a white color. The mushroom cloud from the Castle Bravo test is shown in Figure A1.8. Dust and debris from the ground are also sucked up into the cloud by windy updrafts.[128] After traveling upward for a time, particles in the cloud start to settle to the ground due to gravity. This includes the settling of radioactive particles that have mixed in with materials from the environment. This radioactive mix of material that settles to the ground is known as **fallout**.

In a fission weapon, sources of fallout include fission products from weapon debris as well as any remaining uranium or plutonium that did not undergo fission. There are over 300 isotopes of nearly forty different elements found in fission products and their decay products.[129] Some nuclear tests have even resulted in the formation of newly discovered elements, such as einsteinium and fermium, which had never been observed before in nature.[130] About two ounces of fission product material are formed for every kiloton of yield.[131] Within the first few hours after an explosion, radioactivity is particularly high and decreases over time as radionuclides decay further. The first day after the explosion is the most dangerous with regard to fallout, as a much higher radiation dose is received than in the days that follow.[132] Fallout also tends to accumulate in precipitation. Plants will then absorb radioactive contaminants, and if these plants are consumed by animals, the entire food chain will become contaminated.

Early fallout, also called **local fallout**, reaches the ground within twenty-four hours.[133] It is a more immediate, short-term threat in the first few weeks after detonation. Early fallout tends to be found closer to the detonation site, within 100 km.[134] Delayed fallout, or **global fallout**, is fallout that is distributed over much larger areas, or even worldwide, and reaches the ground more than twenty-four hours after the explosion.[135]

Global fallout will have had more time to decay further along the decay chain to other radionuclides not found in local fallout. These include strontium 90, with a half-life of nearly twenty-eight years, and cesium 137, with a half-life of over thirty years.[136] These nuclides can continue to collect in the environment for years or decades. Some of their ancestors, that is, precursor nuclides that decay to them in their decay chain, are gaseous, so they readily disperse in the atmosphere, and accordingly, upper atmospheric properties ultimately determine the distribution of global fallout. Global fallout from higher-yield weapons can become stored in the upper atmosphere for months or even years since there is virtually no precipitation in the stratosphere. Over time, very fine fallout particles, less than a few microns in radius, will descend very slowly from the atmosphere.[137]

Radioactive materials may also be formed by neutron interactions with weapon material as well as materials in the environment, such as air, earth, water, and within living organisms. This is of particular concern in thermonuclear detonations since fusion reactions release large quantities of high-energy neutrons. Neutrons are captured by nuclei in these materials, and the nuclei become excited, emitting their excess energy in the form of gamma rays. In fact, at detonation, a very short burst of gamma rays is emitted in this way in addition to gamma rays emitted directly from nuclear reactions. This burst lasts less than a microsecond. Some nuclei emit beta particles upon absorbing neutrons.

The fireball formed in an underwater burst, such as that of the Baker shot, is smaller than it would be if it were an air burst of the same yield.[138] The fireball results in a large gas bubble of vaporized water that expands and rises to the surface. As it expands, the fireball generates a powerful shock wave, and a large column of radioactively contaminated water spray then shoots upward above the surface. Most or all of the thermal and nuclear radiation in an underwater blast is absorbed by water, but fission products mixed in the water reach the surface and rise into the air, posing a major radiological threat.[139] Water waves of around 100 feet can be produced and flooding of beaches can result.[140] Also, the height of the resulting mushroom cloud is considerably less than it would be for an air burst.[141]

HIROSHIMA AND NAGASAKI

There were approximately seventy thousand killed in Hiroshima and forty thousand killed in Nagasaki in the immediate bombings of August 1945.[142] There were roughly seventy-six thousand injuries in Hiroshima and twenty-one thousand in Nagasaki.[143] More people died later due to injuries and radiation effects. Approximately thirty thousand more people in Hiroshima died by the end of 1945.[144] In Nagasaki, another twenty-five thousand died in this same period.[145] More than 80 percent of the population of either city was killed within a 0.6 mile radius of ground zero.[146] Within this 0.6 mile radius, each of the following three factors was more than sufficient to cause death: blast, thermal radiation, and nuclear radiation. Beyond a 1.6 mile radius, more people survived, and more people between 0.6 and 1.6 miles probably would have survived with proper medical attention.[147]

Burns were a significant cause of death in addition to blast injury. About two-thirds of the deaths in the first day were due to severe burns.[148] More deaths occurred over the next week from burns.[149] A small percentage of people within 0.6 mile of ground zero survived initially, but many died within about two weeks from radiation sickness (see Appendix 2). Up to 30 percent of the fatalities in Hiroshima were due to lethal doses of radiation, though in some cases, they died from other causes such as burns or blast injuries.[150] People outside of buildings during the bombing were most susceptible, whereas a greater proportion of people indoors survived the initial bombing.[151] Roughly 20–30 percent of the casualties in Hiroshima and Nagasaki were due to flash burns from the thermal radiation of the fireball.[152] Out to about 1.1 miles from ground zero, flash burns were generally fatal unless the person was wearing heavy clothing.[153]

The bombings in Japan occurred in the summer when lighter clothes would have been worn and fewer people would have been indoors.[154] The weather in Hiroshima was particularly clear, contributing to the degree of exposure to thermal radiation.[155] In mild cases, erythema occurred (see Appendix 2), and in more severe cases, charring of the outer skin occurred. Infections were often a problem with severe burns, as medical services, sanitation, and transportation were severely disrupted making proper medical care difficult or impossible.[156]

The incidence of injuries among survivors was the following: 70 percent were due to blast (mechanical injuries), 65 percent were due to burns from flash or flames, and 30 percent were due to initial nuclear radiation.[157] These percentages add to more than 100 percent since many survivors experienced more than one of these types of injuries.[158] Blast injuries were due for the most part to projectiles, particularly in or around buildings. The reported incidence of fractures in the skull, back, or legs was very low presumably because those people who experienced these injuries were trapped under rubble and unable to get medical attention, and consequently died.[159] Casualties among people in buildings correlated with the degree of damage to the buildings and the type of building. More people survived in reinforced concrete buildings than in wooden buildings.[160]

NOTES

1   Asimov, *Understanding Physics*, Vol.3, pp. 2–4.
2   Asimov, *Understanding Physics*, Vol. 3, pp. 4–13.
3   Asimov, *Understanding Physics*, Vol. 1, pp. 23–24.
4   Asimov, *Understanding Physics*, Vol. 3, pp. 13–15.
5   Asimov, *Understanding Physics*, Vol. 3, pp. 58–59.
6   The term *thermal energy* is vague in physics but we use it for simplicity here and identify it with *internal energy*.
7   Asimov, *Understanding Physics*, Vol. 2, pp. 236–237.
8   Oxtoby, Freeman, and Block, *Chemistry: Science of Change*, p. 191.
9   A nuclide is a "species" or specific type of nucleus with its own atomic mass and atomic number.
10 Chu, Ekstrom, and Firestone, "The Lund/LBNL Nuclear Data Search."
11 Friedlander, Gerhart, et al. *Nuclear and Radiochemistry*, pp. 21, 77.
12 Chu, Ekstrom, and Firestone, "The Lund/LBNL Nuclear Data Search." Glasstone and Dolan, *The Effects of Nuclear Weapons*, pp. 604–606.
13 Glasstone and Dolan, *The Effects of Nuclear Weapons*, pp. 604–606.
14 Fewell, "The atomic nuclide with the highest mean binding energy."
15 Mass and energy are equivalent, but it is not correct to say that matter and energy are equivalent. Mass and energy are *properties* of matter.
16 Friedlander, Gerhart, et al. *Nuclear and Radiochemistry*, p. 25.
17 Glasstone and Sesonske, *Nuclear Reactor Engineering*, pp. 15–16.
18 Glasstone and Dolan, *The Effects of Nuclear Weapons*, p. 64.

19 Glasstone and Dolan, *The Effects of Nuclear Weapons*, pp. 7–8.
20 Grace, *Nuclear Weapons: Principles, Effects, and Survivability*, p. 11.
21 Bernstein, *Hitler's Uranium Club*, p. 12.
22 Bernstein, *Hitler's Uranium Club*, pp. 8–10. Friedlander, Gerhart, et al. *Nuclear and Radiochemistry*, p. 12.
23 Bernstein, *Hitler's Uranium Club*, p. 9.
24 Bernstein, *Hitler's Uranium Club*, pp. 10–11.
25 Glasstone and Sesonske, *Nuclear Reactor Engineering*, pp. 4–5.
26 Bernstein, *Hitler's Uranium Club*, pp. 13–14.
27 Glasstone and Sesonske, *Nuclear Reactor Engineering*, p. 15.
28 Grace, *Nuclear Weapons: Principles, Effects, and Survivability*, p. 20.
29 Asimov, *Understanding Physics*, Vol. 3, pp. 207–208.
30 Glasstone and Dolan, *The Effects of Nuclear Weapons*, p. 21.
31 Glasstone and Dolan, *The Effects of Nuclear Weapons*, p. 21.
32 Rhodes, *Dark Sun: The Making of the Hydrogen Bomb*, pp. 482, 505.
33 Bernstein, *Hitler's Uranium Club*, p. 9. Rhodes, *The Making of the Atomic Bomb*, p. 309.
34 Bernstein, *Hitler's Uranium Club*, pp. 14–17. Newhouse, *War and Peace in the Nuclear Age*, pp. 20–21.
35 Newhouse, *War and Peace in the Nuclear Age*, p. 10.
36 Newhouse, *War and Peace in the Nuclear Age*, p. 26.
37 Bernstein, *Hitler's Uranium Club*, p. 26.
38 Newhouse, *War and Peace in the Nuclear Age*, p. 38.
39 Grace, *Nuclear Weapons: Principles, Effects, and Survivability*, p. 14.
40 U.S. Nuclear Regulatory Commission website, "Uranium Enrichment."
41 U.S. Nuclear Regulatory Commission website, "Uranium Enrichment." Rhodes, *Dark Sun: The Making of the Hydrogen Bomb*, pp. 71–72, 108.
42 Rhodes, *Dark Sun: The Making of the Hydrogen Bomb*, pp. 71–72, 108, 137.
43 Friedlander, Gerhart, et al. *Nuclear and Radiochemistry*, p. 525.
44 Rhodes, *The Making of the Atomic Bomb*, pp. 387, 406–407.
45 Newhouse, *War and Peace in the Nuclear Age*, p. 39.
46 Asimov, *Understanding Physics*, Vol. 3, p. 205. Rhodes, *The Making of the Atomic Bomb*, p. 740.
47 Grace, *Nuclear Weapons: Principles, Effects, and Survivability*, p. 20. Serber, *The Los Alamos Primer*, p. 16.
48 This is due to the wave-like properties of the neutron, which at low velocity has a long wavelength, resulting in a high cross-section.
49 Depleted uranium is the uranium 238 leftover in the enrichment process that has been depleted of uranium 235.
50 Grace, *Nuclear Weapons: Principles, Effects, and Survivability*, p. 16. Serber, *The Los Alamos Primer*, p. 10.
51 Grace, *Nuclear Weapons: Principles, Effects, and Survivability*, p. 16.
52 Grace, *Nuclear Weapons: Principles, Effects, and Survivability*, p. 16.
53 Grace, *Nuclear Weapons: Principles, Effects, and Survivability*, p. 23.
54 Grace, *Nuclear Weapons: Principles, Effects, and Survivability*, p. 23. Rhodes, *The Making of the Atomic Bomb*, pp. 541, 702. Sublette, "Section 8.0 The First Nuclear Weapons." Nuclear Weapon Archive website.

55 Sublette, "Section 8.0 The First Nuclear Weapons." Nuclear Weapon Archive website.
56 Sublette, "Section 8.0 The First Nuclear Weapons." Nuclear Weapon Archive website.
57 Sublette, "Section 8.0 The First Nuclear Weapons." Nuclear Weapon Archive website.
58 Newhouse, *War and Peace in the Nuclear Age*, p. 39.
59 Malik, "The Yields of the Hiroshima and Nagasaki Nuclear Explosions." Atomic Archive website, p. 25.
60 Malik, "The Yields of the Hiroshima and Nagasaki Nuclear Explosions." Atomic Archive website, p. 9.
61 Grace, *Nuclear Weapons: Principles, Effects, and Survivability*, p. 23.
62 Rhodes, *The Making of the Atomic Bomb*, pp. 479–480.
63 Sublette, "Section 8.0 The First Nuclear Weapons." Nuclear Weapon Archive. Atomic Heritage Foundation website, "Little Boy and Fat Man."
64 Rhodes, *The Making of the Atomic Bomb*, pp. 578–579.
65 Rhodes, *The Making of the Atomic Bomb*, p. 578.
66 Rhodes, *The Making of the Atomic Bomb*, p. 578.
67 Sublette, "Section 8.0 The First Nuclear Weapons." Nuclear Weapon Archive website.
68 Atomic Archive website, "Model of the Fat Man Bomb."
69 Atomic Heritage Foundation website, "Little Boy and Fat Man."
70 Grace, *Nuclear Weapons: Principles, Effects, and Survivability*, p. 23. Atomic Heritage Foundation website, "Little Boy and Fat Man."
71 Malik, "The Yields of the Hiroshima and Nagasaki Nuclear Explosions." Atomic Archive website, p. 25.
72 Atomic Archive website, "Cold War: A Brief History – The Soviet Atomic Bomb."
73 Rhodes, *Dark Sun: The Making of the Hydrogen Bomb*, p. 207.
74 Newhouse, *War and Peace in the Nuclear Age*, p. 6.
75 Rhodes, *Dark Sun: The Making of the Hydrogen Bomb*, pp. 207, 248.
76 Rhodes, *Dark Sun: The Making of the Hydrogen Bomb*, pp. 456, 473–474.
77 Rhodes, *Dark Sun: The Making of the Hydrogen Bomb*, pp. 457, 473.
78 Sublette, "Operation Greenhouse." Nuclear Weapon Archive website.
79 Sublette, "Operation Greenhouse." Nuclear Weapon Archive website.
80 Rhodes, *Dark Sun: The Making of the Hydrogen Bomb*, p. 474.
81 Rhodes, *Dark Sun: The Making of the Hydrogen Bomb*, pp. 456, 474.
82 Rhodes, *Dark Sun: The Making of the Hydrogen Bomb*, p. 456.
83 Rhodes, *Dark Sun: The Making of the Hydrogen Bomb*, p. 252.
84 U.S. Department of Energy. Nevada Operations Office website. *United States Nuclear Tests: July 1945 through September 1992.*
85 Sublette, "Operation Greenhouse." Nuclear Weapon Archive website.
86 Rhodes, *Dark Sun: The Making of the Hydrogen Bomb*, p. 474.
87 Rhodes, *Dark Sun: The Making of the Hydrogen Bomb*, pp. 462–474.
88 Rhodes, *Dark Sun: The Making of the Hydrogen Bomb*, p. 464.
89 Rhodes, *Dark Sun: The Making of the Hydrogen Bomb*, p. 492.
90 Rhodes, *Dark Sun: The Making of the Hydrogen Bomb*, p. 510.
91 Rhodes, *Dark Sun: The Making of the Hydrogen Bomb*, p. 508.

92   Sublette, "Operation Ivy." Nuclear Weapon Archive website.
93   Rhodes, *Dark Sun: The Making of the Hydrogen Bomb*, pp. 485, 486.
94   Sublette, "Operation Ivy." Nuclear Weapon Archive website.
95   Rhodes, *Dark Sun: The Making of the Hydrogen Bomb*, p. 501.
96   Rhodes, *Dark Sun: The Making of the Hydrogen Bomb*, pp. 488, 490.
97   Grace, *Nuclear Weapons: Principles, Effects, and Survivability*, p. 21.
98   Atomic Archive website, "The Soviets' 'Joe-4' Bomb Makes Its Mark."
99   Atomic Archive website, "The Soviets' 'Joe-4' Bomb Makes Its Mark."
100   Atomic Archive website, "The Soviets' 'Joe-4' Bomb Makes Its Mark."
101   Atomic Archive website, "The Soviets' 'Joe-4' Bomb Makes Its Mark."
102   Atomic Archive website, "The Soviets' 'Joe-4' Bomb Makes Its Mark."
103   Rhodes, *Dark Sun: The Making of the Hydrogen Bomb*, p. 541.
104   Rhodes, *Dark Sun: The Making of the Hydrogen Bomb*, p. 541.
105   Glastone and Dolan, *The Effects of Nuclear Weapons*, pp. 7, 277.
106   Glastone and Dolan, *The Effects of Nuclear Weapons*, pp. 7, 277.
107   Glastone and Dolan, *The Effects of Nuclear Weapons*, pp. 7, 64.
108   Glastone and Dolan, *The Effects of Nuclear Weapons*, p. 7.
109   Glastone and Dolan, *The Effects of Nuclear Weapons*, p. 7.
110   Glastone and Dolan, *The Effects of Nuclear Weapons*, p. 8.
111   Glastone and Dolan, *The Effects of Nuclear Weapons*, pp. 6–7.
112   Glastone and Dolan, *The Effects of Nuclear Weapons*, p. 27.
113   Glastone and Dolan, *The Effects of Nuclear Weapons*, p. 27.
114   Glastone and Dolan, *The Effects of Nuclear Weapons*, p. 27.
115   Glastone and Dolan, *The Effects of Nuclear Weapons*, p. 27.
116   Glastone and Dolan, *The Effects of Nuclear Weapons*, pp. 40–41, 68–70.
117   Glastone and Dolan, *The Effects of Nuclear Weapons*, pp. 40–41.
118   Glastone and Dolan, *The Effects of Nuclear Weapons*, pp. 40–41.
119   Glastone and Dolan, *The Effects of Nuclear Weapons*, p. 41.
120   Glastone and Dolan, *The Effects of Nuclear Weapons*, p. 28.
121   Glastone and Dolan, *The Effects of Nuclear Weapons*, p. 28.
122   Glastone and Dolan, *The Effects of Nuclear Weapons*, p. 28.
123   Glastone and Dolan, *The Effects of Nuclear Weapons*, p. 38.
124   Glastone and Dolan, *The Effects of Nuclear Weapons*, pp. 108–109.
125   U.S. Department of Commerce/National Oceanic and Atmospheric Administration (NOAA)/ National Ocean Service. Office of Response and Restoration website. "Overpressure Levels of Concern."
126   Glastone and Dolan, *The Effects of Nuclear Weapons*, pp. 93–94.
127   Glastone and Dolan, *The Effects of Nuclear Weapons*, pp. 28–29.
128   Glastone and Dolan, *The Effects of Nuclear Weapons*, pp. 29–31.
129   Glastone and Dolan, *The Effects of Nuclear Weapons*, pp. 18–19, 390.
130   Asimov, *Understanding Physics*, Vol. 3, p. 177.
131   Glastone and Dolan, *The Effects of Nuclear Weapons*, p. 390.
132   Glastone and Dolan, *The Effects of Nuclear Weapons*, p. 404.
133   ICRP Publication 60. Ann. ICRP 21 (1–3), pp. 255, 257. Glastone and Dolan, *The Effects of Nuclear Weapons*, pp. 37, 387–388.
134   ICRP Publication 60. Ann. ICRP 21 (1–3), pp. 255, 256–257.
135   ICRP Publication 60. Ann. ICRP 21 (1–3), pp. 255–256.

136 Glasstone and Dolan, *The Effects of Nuclear Weapons*, p. 443.
137 Glasstone and Dolan, *The Effects of Nuclear Weapons*, pp. 445–450. ICRP Publication 60. Ann. ICRP 21 (1–3), pp. 255–256.
138 Glasstone and Dolan, *The Effects of Nuclear Weapons*, p. 48.
139 Glasstone and Dolan, *The Effects of Nuclear Weapons*, p. 55.
140 Glasstone and Dolan, *The Effects of Nuclear Weapons*, p. 52.
141 Glasstone and Dolan, *The Effects of Nuclear Weapons*, p. 52.
142 Glasstone and Dolan, *The Effects of Nuclear Weapons*, p. 544.
143 Glasstone and Dolan, *The Effects of Nuclear Weapons*, p. 544.
144 Wheaton, *You and the Atomic Bomb: History of Nuclear Bombs*, p. 79.
145 Wheaton, *You and the Atomic Bomb: History of Nuclear Bombs*, p. 80.
146 Glasstone and Dolan, *The Effects of Nuclear Weapons*, p. 544.
147 Glasstone and Dolan, *The Effects of Nuclear Weapons*, pp. 544–545.
148 Glasstone and Dolan, *The Effects of Nuclear Weapons*, p. 545.
149 Glasstone and Dolan, *The Effects of Nuclear Weapons*, p. 545.
150 Glasstone and Dolan, *The Effects of Nuclear Weapons*, p. 545.
151 Glasstone and Dolan, *The Effects of Nuclear Weapons*, pp. 545–546.
152 Glasstone and Dolan, *The Effects of Nuclear Weapons*, p. 566.
153 Glasstone and Dolan, *The Effects of Nuclear Weapons*, p. 566.
154 Glasstone and Dolan, *The Effects of Nuclear Weapons*, pp. 567–568.
155 Glasstone and Dolan, *The Effects of Nuclear Weapons*, p. 566.
156 Glasstone and Dolan, *The Effects of Nuclear Weapons*, p. 569.
157 Glasstone and Dolan, *The Effects of Nuclear Weapons*, p. 546.
158 Glasstone and Dolan, *The Effects of Nuclear Weapons*, p. 546.
159 Glasstone and Dolan, *The Effects of Nuclear Weapons*, p. 546.
160 Glasstone and Dolan, *The Effects of Nuclear Weapons*, pp. 547–548.

Appendix 2

Radiation Exposure, Dosage, and Its Biomedical Effects

Ionizing radiation has various damaging effects on living organisms. Ionization is dangerous because as electrons are removed from atoms and molecules, the ionized atoms and molecules become electrically charged and altered in their chemical binding properties. The removed electrons may themselves ionize additional atoms and molecules leading to further alterations in chemical bonds. These changes can lead not only to structural damage, but to changes in the normal functioning of tissues and cells. This second appendix focuses on the biological effects of radiation and the resulting pathological conditions. In the first section, "Radiation Passage Through Matter" the passage of radiation through matter is described with emphasis on how the three types of ionizing radiations, alpha, beta, and gamma, deposit energy in materials. A couple of examples of biological damage due to these radiations are included in this section. In the second section, "Dose, Exposure, and Units," the concepts of radiation exposure and dose are defined as well as the associated units of measure and additional related concepts. Next, in "Biomedical Effects," specific biological effects and pathologies are described. Then, in the section "Exposure from Nuclear Testing," estimates are presented of the exposure of the general population to global and local fallout from nuclear testing. In the last section, "Background Radiation," data are presented of the exposure levels due to background radiation from natural and artificial sources.

RADIATION PASSAGE THROUGH MATTER

Alpha particles, being massive compared to beta particles, travel relatively slowly, at speeds of roughly a few percent of the speed of light, depositing all of their energy within a very short distance and do not travel very far within a material. Alpha particles can be stopped by a sheet of paper or by the outer layer of dead skin cells on the body. If these cells absorb alpha radiation there is no harm done, but if alpha-emitting materials are ingested, inhaled, or otherwise introduced into the body, their absorption by living cells and accumulation inside the body will be extremely hazardous and damaging. For example, when alpha-emitting radio nuclides are inhaled, injury to the respiratory system will tend to result, and when they are ingested, there will tend to be injury to the gastrointestinal tract. Alpha emitters may also enter the body through wounds.

Beta particles travel further through a material than alpha particles since they travel near the speed of light and have lower mass, giving up their energy over a longer distance. They can travel a few millimeters through solid material or a few meters through air. Beta particles can be stopped with a thin piece of metal, such as aluminum foil. Even if their source is outside the body, they are still problematic, particularly to skin. They will tend to be absorbed within the layers of living skin tissue, resulting in skin burns known as *beta burns*.

Gamma rays are much more penetrating than alpha or beta particles, requiring a thick layer of lead or other material of high atomic number to absorb them. The entire body is susceptible to gamma rays as they may travel through any thickness or type of tissue with their high penetrating capability. Unlike alpha and beta particles, which lose energy gradually in a material by interactions with multiple electrons, gamma rays lose their energy in a single, very energetic, interaction with one electron. As a result, gamma photons may travel through a considerable thickness of material before being absorbed, and this is why thick heavy materials are needed to shield against them.

Radiation cannot be felt so detectors must be used to detect it. A basic detector, such as a Geiger counter, consists of a chamber of air or other gas connected to a voltage in an electric circuit. When gas particles are ionized by radiation, the ionized electric charge forms an electric current under the influence of the voltage and is registered as a signal. A signal from a single particle of radiation is referred to as a "count" and can be heard as a click or a beep on the detector or otherwise counted and recorded.

DOSE, EXPOSURE, AND UNITS

The damaging effects of radiation are the result of energy being deposited in a material when the radiation is absorbed. The nature and degree of damage will in turn depend on the type of radiation, the energy of the radiation, the type of material absorbing the radiation, and in the case of living organisms, the type of tissue or organ absorbing the radiation, as well as the location of the radiation source relative to the tissue. These considerations lead to the definitions of various types of radiation *dose*. This can indeed be a very confusing subject, so we will only speak of the definitions that are most relevant for our purposes.

The amount of energy absorbed per mass of any absorbing material from ionizing radiation is called the *absorbed dose*. This concept applies to all types of radiation and any type of material, living or nonliving. The absorbed dose can be measured and forms the basis of all dose assessments and calculations. The international unit of measure for absorbed dose is the *gray* (Gy), equal to one joule per kilogram. Another commonly used unit is the *rad*, for "radiation absorbed dose." One gray is equal to 100 rad. The millirad (mrad), equal to 1/1,000 of a rad, is often used for smaller doses, as is the milligray (mGy).

When referring to x-rays or gamma rays, for photon energies below 3 MeV, the amount of radiation present is quantified by the *exposure*, which is the amount of electrical charge per mass of *air* that results from ionization of the air by the radiation. This is typically used, for example, in medical applications. The common unit for exposure is the *roentgen* (R), named for Wilhelm Conrad Roentgen who discovered x-rays in 1895.[1] A chest x-ray, for example, results in approximately 10–25 milliroentgens (mR) of radiation exposure (this exposure being *entrance skin exposure* – exposure at the skin's surface where x-rays enter the body).[2]

Before proceeding further, an important distinction must be made between two general classes of biological effect. First, there are the *deterministic (nonstochastic) effects*, which are biological effects whose severity is proportional to the amount of radiation exposure. They are given the name deterministic because they are certain to occur after exposure in contrast to other effects, to be mentioned shortly, that are randomly occurring. Deterministic effects occur above a *threshold dose*, a minimum absorbed dose below which the effect does not occur. For example, the doses for the onset of the various forms of acute radiation syndrome, to be mentioned shortly, are threshold doses, as are doses at which the populations of various cell types are significantly affected, such as blood cells. In the assessment of deterministic effects, doses are expressed as absorbed doses in rad or gray since the severity of the effect is correlated with absorbed dose.

Second, there are randomly occurring effects, known as *probabilistic (stochastic) effects*, which can occur theoretically at any radiation dose, even low doses, and include cancers of various forms as well as genetic aberrations in future offspring. The severity of such an effect will not depend on dose. For example, either cancer occurs or it does not. However, the probability for the condition to occur increases with radiation dose. Very low doses of radiation carry a very low risk of causing probabilistic effects while very high doses carry a very high risk of causing such effects. Such effects tend to occur later in life, many years after exposure. Whereas it is not impossible for a single chest x-ray, a very low radiation exposure, to cause cancer many years later, it is not very likely to, and furthermore, it is not possible to state with certainty that such a cancer would have been due to that single x-ray exposure of such low dose instead of it being due to some other cause, such as a genetic predisposition to cancer.

Effects that occur immediately after exposure, within hours, to days, to weeks, are known as *early effects*, for example, acute radiation syndrome, a deterministic effect, while those that occur months to years later, are known as *late effects*, for example, cancer, a probabilistic effect, cataracts, a deterministic effect, and genetic effects, which are probabilistic, affecting future offspring.

Beta particles, x-rays, and gamma rays have very similar biological effects, but since alpha particles deposit large amounts of energy in very short distances, they are even more ionizing. In addition, the degree of biological damage of neutrons depends on their energy. The absorbed dose mentioned earlier does not take into account these differences in biological damage, or *relative biological effectiveness* (RBE) of a specific type of radiation. For this reason, another dose quantity, known as the *dose equivalent* is defined, which is the absorbed dose multiplied by the RBE expressed as a numerical factor whose value is dependent on the type of radiation and energy. RBE values are listed for various types of radiation in Table B.1.[3]

The RBE specifies how much more effective a given type of radiation is in causing a biological effect or type of damage as compared to x-rays with an energy of 250 KeV. For example, the RBE is twenty for alpha particles and one for gamma rays. So 100 rad of alpha radiation is twenty times more damaging than 100 rad of gamma rays. As an example, a 100 rad dose of fast neutrons will kill a rat, but 100 rad of x-rays will not.[4] This is because the neutrons are stopped within very short distances inside tissue that absorbs all of their energy, whereas only some x-rays

TABLE B.1

Type of radiation	RBE
Beta, gamma, x-rays	1
Neutrons, fission fragments	2–11
Alpha, fission fragments	20

may be stopped in the tissue, with the rest exiting the rat, resulting in the absorption of less energy. This is analogous to a bullet that is stopped in the body causing more damage than one that penetrates and exits the body. The products of the rad and the gray with the RBE do not have official names as units but are sometimes referred to respectively as the rad-equivalent (RadEq) and gray-equivalent (GyEq).[5]

Still, another dose quantity is *equivalent dose*, distinct from dose equivalent.

The equivalent dose is used to estimate the risk of developing probabilistic effects from radiation exposure, for example, from disasters or occupational settings. There are also tissue weighting factors that can be specified for various parts of the body when assessing probabilistic effects, since different tissues or organs are more sensitive to radiation than others, but the tissue weighting factor will not be discussed here.

The equivalent dose is equal to the absorbed dose in a tissue or organ multiplied by a factor known as the *radiation weighting factor*, a numerical quantity that also is dependent on the type and energy of the radiation. The radiation weighting factor quantifies the risk of developing certain randomly occurring effects caused by a particular type of radiation. Also, the value of the radiation weighting factor will generally differ from the corresponding RBE value for a given type of radiation and energy.[6] The difference in these values is often seen in neutrons for example.[7] The radiation weighting factor of x-rays, gamma rays, and beta particles is one, for neutrons it varies with energy between about five and twenty, and for alpha particles and fission fragments it is twenty.[8]

The international unit for equivalent dose is the *sievert*, equal to one joule of energy absorbed per kilogram of tissue mass multiplied by the radiation weighting factor. Typically the millisievert (mSv), one-thousandth of a sievert, is used to express common doses, for example medical doses. Another commonly used unit is the *rem*, for "radiation equivalent man," equal to the rad multiplied by the radiation weighting factor. One sievert is equal to 100 rem. The millirem (mrem) is also used in medicine and other applications.

BIOMEDICAL EFFECTS

In our following discussion on specific doses and their health effects, doses will be given in rad. By using the rad we are referring to the amount of energy absorbed per mass of tissue. However, it must be emphasized that a given amount of absorbed energy will cause differing degrees of damage for differing types of radiation and in differing types of tissue.

Under the action of ionizing radiation, water, DNA, and protein molecules become altered in their chemical binding properties. Chromosomes, the fundamental units of heredity, when damaged, may result in cellular damage, mutations, birth defects, and cancer. This leads not only to structural damage, but to changes in the normal functioning of tissues and cells. Parts of a cell, such as the nucleus, may swell, and entire cells may die. The cell division process, *mitosis*, can also be halted, leading to a failure to properly replace dead cells with healthy cells. This is particularly the case for blood cell formation.

Radiation may directly ionize biological macromolecules, including DNA, RNA, enzymes, and protein molecules, in a process called *direct action*.[9] This is more likely to occur with alpha particles and neutrons which are stopped over very short distances, which can transfer all of their energy to a single molecule within a cell. Alternatively, radiation may ionize the water molecules in which cellular structures are distributed, forming excited and extremely reactive molecular fragments, called *free radicals*, which can then interact with the biological macromolecules in a process known as *indirect action*. Free radicals are excited molecular fragments that carry extra energy, formed in this case from the *radiolysis*, the radiation breakdown, of water or organic molecules. Thus, molecules like DNA are damaged indirectly by radiation through their interaction with free radicals.[10]

Free radicals are so reactive that they will break already existing chemical bonds in their reactions. Hydrogen peroxide, a particular byproduct formed in the radiolysis of water, is toxic to cellular structure. In oxygenated tissue, free radicals may bind with oxygen, leading to the formation of still other free radicals, causing irreversible processes and damage, but in deoxygenated tissues, the damage can be reversed since free radicals can reassemble to form their original organic molecules without having bonded with oxygen.[11]

Chemical bonds in DNA molecules can be broken by radiation exposure. The DNA molecule consists of strands of molecular sequences. The breaking of these strands can lead to cell death. Chromosomes themselves consist of long DNA chains and if these are disrupted, chromosomes will break apart. If damaged chromosomes partake in cell division, improper amounts of genetic material will be passed on to the newly formed cells, resulting in their death or malfunctioning. When the base sequence of DNA is damaged, mutations occur, and the precise genetic information that is to be passed on to daughter cells becomes corrupted. Yet another effect of ionizing radiation is *cross-linking*: the creation of abnormal chemical bonds, resulting in bonding between molecules or within a complex molecule, such as between DNA or protein molecules, in abnormal arrangements.[12]

There are many consequences for cells as a result of radiation damage. An x-ray or gamma ray dose of 100,000 rad can kill a significant cell population within seconds or minutes as cellular structure and chemistry are severely damaged and disrupted.[13] Much lower doses of 100–1,000 rad may not kill a cell, but its ability to reproduce will be lost.[14] Cell division can be delayed by doses as low as 1 rad.[15] At lower doses, cells can recover their normal functioning if the radiation damage can be repaired by enzymes.[16]

The degree to which a type of cell is sensitive to the effects of radiation is known as *radiosensitivity*. Cells with higher reproductive activity are more radiosensitive. These are cells that are undergoing cell division at a higher rate. Being young cells that have not yet specialized in function, these cells are also referred to as immature, nonspecialized, or undifferentiated.[17] This is in contrast to cells that are slowly dividing or nondividing cells which are then less radiosensitive. Radiosensitive cells include the *germ* cells, the sperm and ovum that fuse to form the embryo after conception, and also many of the *somatic* cells, the cells comprising the body. Radiosensitivity is particularly significant when considering the development of the embryo and fetus, which contain vast quantities of reproductively active, immature cells.

Equal doses of radiation can result in different effects in different types of tissue based on the type of tissue and radiosensitivity of its cells, which depends on the metabolic and reproductive activity, and the specialization (maturity) of its cells. The most sensitive systems and tissues of the body are the *hematopoietic* or blood-forming tissues, including bone marrow and blood cells, as well as the lymphatic system.[18] The gastrointestinal tract and the reproductive system, including germ cells, are also highly radiosensitive. The moderately sensitive areas are skin and epithelial tissues, which form membranes and linings, as well as the lungs and liver. The least radiosensitive tissues are muscle and nerves.

There are two types of radiation exposure: *acute* exposure and *chronic* exposure.[19] In an acute exposure, the radiation is received in a relatively short time period or all at once. This happens, for example, with the initial nuclear radiation released from a detonation. Acute exposures by definition occur within a twenty-four-hour period or less, or in a single shot (a single instantaneous dose).[20] High enough doses result in *acute radiation syndrome*, often referred to simply as *radiation sickness*. Higher doses result in greater severity of symptoms, and doses experienced over a shorter period of time result in more severe effects than if they were experienced over longer periods of time or in multiple smaller doses. Chronic exposures occur over extended periods of more than twenty-four hours, for example, from fallout radiation. The part of the body exposed, type of radiation, and extent of exposure will determine the degree of injury. If a small area of the body is exposed, then there will be greater chance of recovery, whereas if the whole body is exposed, recovery will be much more difficult since multiple organs or all body systems will be affected and all will suffer a burden.

There are four stages of acute radiation syndrome: the initial (prodromal) stage, latent period, manifest illness, and either recovery or death. The initial stage begins within hours after exposure for a single whole-body dose of 100 rad or higher.[21] Symptoms include nausea, vomiting, diarrhea, fatigue, and leukopenia (abnormal depression of white blood cells).[22] The initial stage lasts between a few hours to a few days.[23] Following the initial stage the latent period lasts for about a week.[24] During this period there are no apparent symptoms and at this time either recovery or lethality begins. After this, is the manifest illness, when the syndromes of the hematopoietic, gastrointestinal, or neurovascular systems, occur.[25]

At relatively low radiation doses, the sickness experienced is not necessarily severe enough to require medical attention. In this range of doses, there will still be changes in the blood. Moderate doses will require medical attention that will tend to be more successful at the lower end of this range, but not as successful at the higher end. Early symptoms of vomiting, nausea, headache, and dizziness will set in fifteen minutes to six hours after exposure depending on the severity,[26] with more severe doses resulting in quicker onset.

Single doses of 200–300 rad are generally considered nonlethal and the victim will experience the first three stages of acute radiation syndrome with less severe symptoms.[27] Recovery can then occur over a period of a few months.[28] There may however be lingering effects of radiation damage and late effects after recovery, including cataracts and cancer.[29] Single whole body doses are lethal at about 600–1,000 rad,[30] with death occurring within ten days, and single doses above 1,200 rad are absolutely fatal.[31]

There are three subclasses of acute radiation syndrome: *hematopoietic, gastrointestinal,* and *neurovascular* syndromes.[32] Hematopoietic syndrome occurs with an onset at relatively lower doses. Gastrointestinal syndrome occurs at moderate to severe doses. At extremely high doses, neurovascular syndrome occurs. These are now discussed in more detail in the following.

The onset for hematopoietic syndrome occurs at lower doses since the hematopoietic system, including blood cells and the lymphatic system, is the most radiosensitive body system. This also includes the bone marrow, more specifically, the red bone marrow, where most blood cells are produced, as well as the spleen, tonsils, lymph nodes, and tonsils, all of which are also involved in blood cell production. The onset for hematopoietic syndrome is at about 100 rad.[33] However, even a single dose of twenty-five rad can yield a detectable decrease in the number of these cells.[34]

There is the immediate occurrence of leukopenia, a decrease in the number of white blood cells, *leukocytes*, which fight infection and illness as part of the immune system. Therefore, a reduction in the number of white blood cells leads to a weakened immune response of the body and higher susceptibility to infection. Lymphocytes, an important type of white blood cell, are actually the most radiosensitive cells in the body.[35] A decrease in the number of red blood cells, *erythrocytes*, will also occur but tends to be less severe than the drop in leukocytes.[36] This lowered number of erythrocytes can cause anemia. In addition, there will also be a steady decline in platelet number, resulting in an increased risk of hemorrhaging (including internal bleeding) due to a compromised ability of blood to clot. Platelet count starts to decline noticeably at about fifty rad, and higher doses of 100–1,000 rad result in more severe reductions in platelet counts, which will slowly recover over the course of a few months.[37]

Over time, blood cell and platelet counts will gradually recover for moderate doses. However, at high doses, chances of survival are poor. Doses above 500 rad can result in death within one to two months due to complications resulting from severe reduction in the number of hematopoietic stem cells, namely infection and hemorrhaging.[38] The lethal dose for humans, without medical attention, is between 300 and 400 rad,[39] but can be higher with medical care. Death can occur six to eight weeks after exposure for whole body doses above 200 rad, with death occurring sooner for higher doses up to about 1,000 rad.[40] For doses up to 100–200 rad, bone marrow and blood cells can usually regenerate and return to adequate levels within one to six months.[41]

Gastrointestinal syndrome has an onset at about 600 rad, and an individual will typically die within three to ten days after acute irradiation at 600–1,000 rad.[42] The initial stage begins within hours of exposure, which includes nausea, vomiting, and diarrhea for about twenty-four hours.[43] The latent period follows, lasting for a few days, after which the manifest stage occurs, with more severe nausea, vomiting, and diarrhea.[44] In addition to these symptoms, as well as those associated with hematopoietic syndrome, other symptoms include dehydration, electrolytic imbalance, and gastrointestinal bleeding due to impaired clotting of blood.[45]

Death from gastrointestinal complications usually follows from damage of the cells of the gastrointestinal lining due to infection, dehydration, diarrhea, and electrolytic imbalances, which result in emaciation.[46] The small intestine is the most sensitive part of the gastrointestinal tract. The breakdown of cells lining the intestines is essentially a breakdown in a vital protective barrier within the intestines, making the victim susceptible to infection from even their own intestinal bacteria.

Membranous tissues in general, known as epithelial tissue, for example, those found in blood vessels, the lungs, gastrointestinal tract, along vital organs, and skin, are highly radiosensitive since they regenerate constantly, undergoing cell division regularly. Reddening of the skin, also known as *radiodermatitis* or *skin erythema*, can result in lesions that may become cancerous. Since skin regenerates regularly, it is very radiosensitive. A dose of 200 rad can induce skin erythema within one or two days of exposure.[47] The erythema will worsen over the next week or two until it peaks.[48] Shedding of the skin will occur at higher doses.[49] Hair loss, also known as *epilation*, results from damage to hair follicles.[50] For more moderate doses, hair loss is often temporary, but at much higher doses it may become permanent.[51]

For doses of 5,000 rad and above, the cardiovascular and nervous systems suffer.[52] Death may occur within a few hours or days after such severe irradiation.[53] Initial symptoms include agitation, confusion, extreme nervousness, nausea, vomiting, diarrhea, visual loss, burning sensations in the skin, and unconsciousness.[54] The latent period lasts for about twelve hours during which symptoms appear to resolve.[55] However, the manifest stage follows with similar symptoms as before but much more severe, and also accompanied by shock, disorientation, loss of muscle coordination and balance, extreme weakness and exhaustion, electrolytic imbalance, inflammation of blood vessels, meningitis, respiratory distress, and coma.[56] Due to the damage of cerebral capillaries and blood vessels, fluid accumulates in the brain, increasing intracranial pressure, resulting in failure of the nervous and cardiovascular systems.[57] Death may occur in minutes, before the effects from radiation damage of the gastrointestinal and hematopoietic systems will have had time to develop.

In an embryo, cells are rapidly developing and dividing, so they are very radiosensitive. The first trimester is the period during which the developing embryo is most radiosensitive.[58] Doses to the embryo of above twenty rem, in the first trimester, will likely lead to death or congenital defects.[59] If an embryo is exposed to radiation during organ development, congenital conditions may result, such as intellectual disability, and microcephaly, where the head is of abnormally small circumference. These effects were observed among survivors of the atomic bombings of Japan. The fetus appears to be less radiosensitive in the second and third trimesters, though still susceptible to later development of leukemia and sterility, as observed in children who were exposed in utero in the atomic bombings in Japan.[60]

Reproductive (germ) cells are also very radiosensitive. Irradiated germ cells, containing damaged chromosomes, can still fuse, passing on mutations that can result in congenital defects and disorders in offspring. A single radiation dose of 200 rad to the testes can cause temporary sterility for up to one year and a dose of 500 rad or more will result in permanent sterility.[61] A much smaller dose of only ten rad can result in depression of sperm count.[62] Similarly in women, a single dose of about 200 rad to the ovaries can cause temporary sterility, while a dose of 500 or more rad results in permanent sterility.[63] Doses as low as ten rad can result in irregularities in menstruation.[64]

As mentioned before, late effects of radiation are those that may occur later in life, typically years after exposure. These late changes are due to damage in cells and tissue that survive radiation exposure. Although cell division and replacement continue, the cells will be mutated due to damage of chromosomes and DNA. Late effects can be deterministic, which are correlated with dose and certain to occur after exposure, or probabilistic, which occur randomly and unpredictably.

Examples of late nonstochastic effects are organ atrophy, cataracts, lowered fertility, and sterility. Doses as low as about 200 rad can induce cataracts, for example.[65] Late stochastic effects include cancers, particularly leukemia, birth defects, and genetic effects on future generations. Ten to fifteen years after the atomic bombings of Japan, there was a major increase by about 100 times in the incidence of leukemia among survivors who had received a dose of about 100 rad or more.[66] Other forms of cancer that have been found among Japanese survivors include cancers of the thyroid, lung, breast, gastrointestinal tract, and salivary glands.[67] Late stochastic effects do not necessarily depend on dose and can even occur as a result of low doses, particularly those given repeatedly or over long periods of time. Repeated radiation exposure has cumulative effects.

Radioactive materials from fallout can enter the body through wounds, to the lungs through breathing of contaminated air, and to the digestive tract through ingestion of contaminated food or water. Most are removed gradually from the body as they undergo radioactive decay and are eliminated in body wastes, but elimination takes time. While in the body, organs are continually exposed to radiation. Some forms of damage may only become noticeable much later, not immediately during or after exposure. In addition, different elements are chemically active in different regions of the body and will concentrate in various organs. As a result, radioactive isotopes of those elements will be metabolized and incorporated into different organs or tissue.

In place of the usual stable isotopes of elements such as cesium, strontium, and iodine in milk, radioactive isotopes can substitute since they are chemically identical. These include cesium 137, strontium 90, and iodine 131. In the first few weeks after a detonation, considerable quantities of radionuclides with fairly short half-lives will be contained in fallout and will descend via precipitation. Radionuclides of this kind include iodine 131, with a half-life of eight days.[68] Iodine 131 has been found in rain that has fallen onto farmland where cows graze, thousands of miles from a detonation, and the iodine 131 is then distributed in milk. Iodine accumulates in the thyroid, so thyroid cancer may result from the uptake of radioactive iodine. Thyroid cancer can develop from exposures of less than 100 rad.[69] A significant number of cases in Japan occurred among survivors that were within a half-mile of ground zero in Hiroshima and Nagasaki.[70] Also, children of the Marshall Islands received significant doses to the thyroid due to both external and internal exposure (internal ingestion) of radioiodine, developing thyroid cancer over a ten- to twenty-year period.[71]

Still other chemical elements are not normally found in the body except in trace amounts. If they enter, they will behave chemically like neighboring elements on the periodic table that are normally found in the body, such as calcium. Strontium and barium fission products will tend to be deposited in bone since their chemical properties are similar to calcium. These elements that get deposited in bone are called *bone seekers* and also include cerium, another fission product, and plutonium.[72] These two elements are less like calcium and are not deposited in bone to the same extent as strontium and barium. There are two reasons bone seekers are harmful: (1) damage of bone marrow results in a decrease in the formation of blood cells, significantly impacting the entire body; and (2) the bone itself may develop cancer due to severe radiation damage from alpha and beta particles. One effect of strontium 90 accumulation in bone is the development of leukemia.

EXPOSURE FROM NUCLEAR TESTING

In this section on exposure from nuclear testing, doses associated with global and local fallout from nuclear testing are given and discussed. Unless cited otherwise, all information in this section was obtained from a 2008 report by the United Nations Scientific Committee on the Effects of Atomic Radiation.[73]

The annual exposure to global fallout radiation from all nuclear tests worldwide, in the early 2000s, was estimated to be below 0.005 mSv. This is about the same as the exposure to cosmic radiation from about a half-hour of airline flight. The exposure from one chest x-ray is about sixteen times this, 0.08 mSv.[74] This is a decrease from the maximum value in 1963 of around 0.11 mSv. External doses contribute about 53 percent of fallout exposure, which was initially from short-lived radionuclides, particularly zirconium 95 (a beta emitter with a half-life of about sixty-four days[75]), and later mainly from cesium 137 due to its long half-life. Internal doses contribute about 47 percent of fallout exposures, due mostly to ingestion of food and water contaminated with radioactive material. Some internal exposure is due also to inhalation of radioactive particles in air.

From 1967 to 1980, strontium 90 was the greatest contributor to internal exposure via ingestion due to its accumulation in food and the body. With the end of atmospheric nuclear testing in 1980, the amount of strontium 90 and other radionuclides in the atmosphere decreased, and in turn, their concentrations in food diminished. At present, the dose from the ingestion of the carbon 14 produced from nuclear testing is greater than that of any other radioisotope, contributing about 30 percent of total fallout exposure. This does not include naturally occurring carbon 14. Another radionuclide contributing a small degree of internal exposure through ingestion is tritium, which easily disperses in water globally. Weeks or months after a test, radionuclides with shorter half-lives, like iodine 131 and barium 140, contribute to exposure through ingestion during this period of time.

We next discuss two examples of local fallout associated with American nuclear test sites, starting with the Nevada Test Site (NTS), followed by the Marshall Islands. A total of eighty-six atmospheric tests were conducted at the NTS between 1951 and 1962. In addition, 800 underground tests were conducted, thirty-eight of which released small quantities of radioactive material that could be detected at locations away from the NTS. From measurements taken at 300 communities within a 300-km radius of the NTS in Nevada and southwest Utah, it was determined that the effective dose was above 3.0 mSv in one-fifth of the population of 180,000. The maximum effective dose was 60.0–90.0 mSv and the average dose, weighted over the population, was about 2.8 mSv. Most exposures were due to gamma-emitting radionuclides of shorter half-lives of less than 100 days.

The United States conducted a total of sixty-seven nuclear tests in the Marshall Islands from 1946 to 1958. Approximately 72 percent of the total yield from all of these tests originated from those conducted at the Bikini Atoll alone, with the greatest amount of local exposure resulting from Castle Bravo. Effective doses were due primarily to radionuclides with shorter half-lives and ranged from 0.1 Sv on Utirik Atoll to 1.9 Sv on Rongelap Island and 1.1 Sv on Ailinginae Atoll near Rongelap Island. Estimates for the average equivalent doses to the thyroid due to isotopes of iodine and tellurium, as well as by external exposure to gamma radiation were 12, 22, and 52 Sv for adults, nine-year-old, and one-year-old children, respectively. The maximum thyroid doses caused by these same agents to these same three age groups were 42, 82, and 200 Sv. When residents returned between 1954 and 1957 to Utirik and Rongelap Atolls, it is estimated that they received exposures of about 20–30 mSv from external exposure and 20–140 mSv from internal exposure over the next twenty years due to radioactive material in the environment.

In addition to the residents exposed to fallout from the Castle Bravo test, there were also US military personnel and Japanese fishermen who were exposed. The US military personnel were located on Rongerik Atoll and received an external exposure of 0.8 Sv. The Japanese fishing boat *Lucky Dragon*, with a crew of twenty-three, was also near this location. On deck, the crew received an external exposure around 1.7–6 Sv due to fallout, predominantly within the first day, with subsequent exposure lasting for fourteen days until they reached port. Thyroid doses for the crew, due to uptake of iodine 131, were estimated at around 0.2–1.2 Gy, but with the consideration of other iodine isotopes with shorter half-lives that were inhaled over the course of several hours, the total thyroid dose estimate was actually 0.8–4.5 Gy. The unit of gray was used in these estimates in accordance with the measurements taken.

From 1958 to 1968, radiological surveys were conducted of the Bikini Atoll, and Bikinian people started to resettle in 1968. Debris was removed in 1969. However, radiation studies in 1978 revealed that the amount of cesium 137 in the bodies of these residents had increased ten times, due to their consumption of contaminated coconut water and no supply of freshwater. The residents were relocated again. The annual whole-body exposure of these residents between 1971 and 1978 was around 2–3 mSv.

BACKGROUND RADIATION

In our everyday lives we are exposed to low levels of radiation that are not considered to be harmful. There are *natural sources* of radiation which together result in an annual dose of about 3.1 mSv per year per person.[76] These natural sources, and their typical contributions to the average annual dose to an individual are (expressed in mSv): radioactivity from *terrestrial radiation* – long-lived radionuclides such as uranium 238, thorium 232, and radium 226 within the crust of the earth (contributing about 0.2 mSv per year); *internal radiation* within our bodies from radionuclides such as carbon 14 (about 0.3 mSv); *cosmic radiation* from the sun and galaxy that interacts with the earth's atmosphere (about 0.3 mSv); and the largest contributor, *radon* (about 2.3 mSv), a radioactive gas that is the decay product of radium which also exists naturally in the earth's crust.[77] The total average dose per year from this natural background radiation is about 3.1 mSv per person, though the dose from terrestrial radiation varies with location on the earth.[78]

In addition to this natural background radiation, we are also exposed to *artificial* background radiation due mainly to medical imaging, which contributes another 3.1 mSv per year per person on average,[79] and about 0.1 mSv from various products, such as smoke detectors, cathode ray tubes, airport security, and even porcelain, which contains small amounts of potassium 40 (which is mainly a beta emitter).[80] Nuclear power plants contribute about 0.0005 mSv per year,[81] and once again fallout from nuclear testing contributes, on average, less than about .005 mSv per year per person.[82]

In total, one person receives about 6.2 mSv per year (620 mrem) from natural and artificial sources.[83] These numbers, on the order of one mSv and less than 10 mSv per year for one person (or about 600 mrem per year), are generally considered harmless. Once again, for comparison, an individual chest x-ray delivers a dose of about 0.08 mSv[84] and is also generally considered safe, though lead shielding is used to minimize radiation dose, particularly to sensitive areas of the body and for children and fetuses, in order to reduce the risks associated with probabilistic effects at low doses.

NOTES

1 Asimov, *Understanding Physics*, Vol. 3, pp. 34–35.
2 Statkiewicz-Sherer, Visconti, and Ritenour, *Radiation Protection in Medical Radiography*, p. 24.
3 Cember and Johnson, *Introduction to Health Physics*, p. 331.
4 Statkiewicz-Sherer, Visconti, and Ritenour, *Radiation Protection in Medical Radiography*, p. 63.
5 Sherbini, "Answer to Question #8933 Submitted to 'Ask the Experts.'" Health Physics Society website.
6 Sherbini, "Answer to Question #8933 Submitted to 'Ask the Experts.'" Health Physics Society website.
7 Cember, and Johnson, *Introduction to Health Physics*, p. 331.
8 Cember, and Johnson, *Introduction to Health Physics*, p. 331.
9 Statkiewicz-Sherer, Visconti, and Ritenour, *Radiation Protection in Medical Radiography*, p. 118.
10 Statkiewicz-Sherer, Visconti, and Ritenour, *Radiation Protection in Medical Radiography*, pp. 119–120.
11 Statkiewicz-Sherer, Visconti, and Ritenour, *Radiation Protection in Medical Radiography*, p. 117.
12 Statkiewicz-Sherer, Visconti, and Ritenour, *Radiation Protection in Medical Radiography*, pp. 122–123.
13 Statkiewicz-Sherer, Visconti, and Ritenour, *Radiation Protection in Medical Radiography*, p. 128.
14 Statkiewicz-Sherer, Visconti, and Ritenour, *Radiation Protection in Medical Radiography*, p. 128.
15 Statkiewicz-Sherer, Visconti, and Ritenour, *Radiation Protection in Medical Radiography*, p. 129.
16 Statkiewicz-Sherer, Visconti, and Ritenour, *Radiation Protection in Medical Radiography*, p. 129.

17 Statkiewicz-Sherer, Visconti, and Ritenour, *Radiation Protection in Medical Radiography*, p. 130.
18 Statkiewicz-Sherer, Visconti, and Ritenour, *Radiation Protection in Medical Radiography*, p. 144. Glasstone and Dolan, *The Effects of Nuclear Weapons*, p. 578.
19 Glasstone and Dolan, *The Effects of Nuclear Weapons*, p. 577.
20 Glasstone and Dolan, *The Effects of Nuclear Weapons*, p. 577.
21 Statkiewicz-Sherer, Visconti, and Ritenour, *Radiation Protection in Medical Radiography*, p. 142.
22 Statkiewicz-Sherer, Visconti, and Ritenour, *Radiation Protection in Medical Radiography*, p. 142.
23 Statkiewicz-Sherer, Visconti, and Ritenour, *Radiation Protection in Medical Radiography*, p. 142.
24 Statkiewicz-Sherer, Visconti, and Ritenour, *Radiation Protection in Medical Radiography*, p. 142.
25 Statkiewicz-Sherer, Visconti, and Ritenour, *Radiation Protection in Medical Radiography*, p. 142.
26 Glasstone and Dolan, *The Effects of Nuclear Weapons*, p. 582.
27 Statkiewicz-Sherer, Visconti, and Ritenour, *Radiation Protection in Medical Radiography*, p. 144.
28 Statkiewicz-Sherer, Visconti, and Ritenour, *Radiation Protection in Medical Radiography*, p. 144.
29 Statkiewicz-Sherer, Visconti, and Ritenour, *Radiation Protection in Medical Radiography*, p. 144.
30 Statkiewicz-Sherer, Visconti, and Ritenour, *Radiation Protection in Medical Radiography*, p. 145.
31 Statkiewicz-Sherer, Visconti, and Ritenour, *Radiation Protection in Medical Radiography*, p. 147.
32 Statkiewicz-Sherer, Visconti, and Ritenour, *Radiation Protection in Medical Radiography*, p. 141.
33 Statkiewicz-Sherer, Visconti, and Ritenour, *Radiation Protection in Medical Radiography*, p. 144.
34 Statkiewicz-Sherer, Visconti, and Ritenour, *Radiation Protection in Medical Radiography*, p. 131.
35 Statkiewicz-Sherer, Visconti, and Ritenour, *Radiation Protection in Medical Radiography*, p. 153.
36 Glasstone and Dolan, *The Effects of Nuclear Weapons*, p. 587.
37 Statkiewicz-Sherer, Visconti, and Ritenour, *Radiation Protection in Medical Radiography*, p. 133.
38 Statkiewicz-Sherer, Visconti, and Ritenour, *Radiation Protection in Medical Radiography*, p. 132.
39 Statkiewicz-Sherer, Visconti, and Ritenour, *Radiation Protection in Medical Radiography*, p. 132.
40 Statkiewicz-Sherer, Visconti, and Ritenour, *Radiation Protection in Medical Radiography*, p. 145.
41 Statkiewicz-Sherer, Visconti, and Ritenour, *Radiation Protection in Medical Radiography*, p. 145.
42 Statkiewicz-Sherer, Visconti, and Ritenour, *Radiation Protection in Medical Radiography*, p. 145.

43 Statkiewicz-Sherer, Visconti, and Ritenour, *Radiation Protection in Medical Radiography*, p. 145.
44 Statkiewicz-Sherer, Visconti, and Ritenour, *Radiation Protection in Medical Radiography*, p. 145.
45 Statkiewicz-Sherer, Visconti, and Ritenour, *Radiation Protection in Medical Radiography*, p. 145.
46 Statkiewicz-Sherer, Visconti, and Ritenour, *Radiation Protection in Medical Radiography*, p. 145.
47 Statkiewicz-Sherer, Visconti, and Ritenour, *Radiation Protection in Medical Radiography*, pp. 148–149.
48 Statkiewicz-Sherer, Visconti, and Ritenour, *Radiation Protection in Medical Radiography*, p. 149.
49 Statkiewicz-Sherer, Visconti, and Ritenour, *Radiation Protection in Medical Radiography*, p. 149.
50 Statkiewicz-Sherer, Visconti, and Ritenour, *Radiation Protection in Medical Radiography*, pp. 149–150.
51 Statkiewicz-Sherer, Visconti, and Ritenour, *Radiation Protection in Medical Radiography*, p. 150.
52 Statkiewicz-Sherer, Visconti, and Ritenour, *Radiation Protection in Medical Radiography*, p. 146.
53 Statkiewicz-Sherer, Visconti, and Ritenour, *Radiation Protection in Medical Radiography*, p. 146.
54 Statkiewicz-Sherer, Visconti, and Ritenour, *Radiation Protection in Medical Radiography*, p. 146.
55 Statkiewicz-Sherer, Visconti, and Ritenour, *Radiation Protection in Medical Radiography*, p. 146.
56 Statkiewicz-Sherer, Visconti, and Ritenour, *Radiation Protection in Medical Radiography*, p. 146.
57 Statkiewicz-Sherer, Visconti, and Ritenour, *Radiation Protection in Medical Radiography*, p. 146.
58 Statkiewicz-Sherer, Visconti, and Ritenour, *Radiation Protection in Medical Radiography*, p. 175.
59 Statkiewicz-Sherer, Visconti, and Ritenour, *Radiation Protection in Medical Radiography*, p. 175.
60 Statkiewicz-Sherer, Visconti, and Ritenour, *Radiation Protection in Medical Radiography*, p. 176.
61 Statkiewicz-Sherer, Visconti, and Ritenour, *Radiation Protection in Medical Radiography*, p. 135.
62 Statkiewicz-Sherer, Visconti, and Ritenour, *Radiation Protection in Medical Radiography*, p. 135.
63 Statkiewicz-Sherer, Visconti, and Ritenour, *Radiation Protection in Medical Radiography*, pp. 135–136.
64 Statkiewicz-Sherer, Visconti, and Ritenour, *Radiation Protection in Medical Radiography*, p. 136.
65 Statkiewicz-Sherer, Visconti, and Ritenour, *Radiation Protection in Medical Radiography*, p. 174.
66 Statkiewicz-Sherer, Visconti, and Ritenour, *Radiation Protection in Medical Radiography*, pp. 168–169.
67 Glasstone and Dolan, *The Effects of Nuclear Weapons*, pp. 592, 593.

68   Glasstone and Dolan, *The Effects of Nuclear Weapons*, p. 601.
69   Statkiewicz-Sherer, Visconti, and Ritenour, *Radiation Protection in Medical Radiography*, p. 171.
70   Glasstone and Dolan, *The Effects of Nuclear Weapons*, p. 592.
71   Glasstone and Dolan, *The Effects of Nuclear Weapons*, p. 603.
72   Glasstone and Dolan, *The Effects of Nuclear Weapons*, p. 599.
73   UNSCEAR, "Sources and Effects of Ionizing Radiation." pp. 255–258.
74   Statkiewicz-Sherer, Visconti, and Ritenour, *Radiation Protection in Medical Radiography*, p. 10.
75   Chu, Ekstrom, and Firestone, "The Lund/LBNL Nuclear Data Search."
76   U.S. Nuclear Regulatory Commission. "Fact Sheet on Biological Effects of Radiation."
77   Statkiewicz-Sherer, Visconti, and Ritenour, *Radiation Protection in Medical Radiography*, pp. 15–16. U.S. Nuclear Regulatory Commission. "Fact Sheet on Biological Effects of Radiation."
78   U.S. Nuclear Regulatory Commission. "Fact Sheet on Biological Effects of Radiation."
79   U.S. Nuclear Regulatory Commission. "Fact Sheet on Biological Effects of Radiation."
80   Statkiewicz-Sherer, Visconti, and Ritenour, *Radiation Protection in Medical Radiography*, p. 18.
81   Statkiewicz-Sherer, Visconti, and Ritenour, *Radiation Protection in Medical Radiography*, p. 14.
82   UNSCEAR, "Sources and Effects of Ionizing Radiation." p. 256.
83   U.S. Nuclear Regulatory Commission. "Fact Sheet on Biological Effects of Radiation."
84   Statkiewicz-Sherer, Visconti, and Ritenour, *Radiation Protection in Medical Radiography*, p. 10.

Bibliography

PUBLISHED BOOKS, ARTICLES, AND REPORTS

Anon. "Eyewitness Stories of the Bomb Test." *Bulletin of the Atomic Scientists* December 1952: 300.

Asimov, Isaac. *Understanding Physics* (New York: Barnes & Noble Books, 1993).

Baggott, Jim. *The First War of Physics: The Secret History of the Atom Bomb 1939–1949* (New York: Pegasus Books, 2010).

Barker, Holly M. *Bravo for the Marshallese: Regaining Control in a Post-Nuclear, Post-Colonial World* (Belmont, CA: Thomson Wadsworth).

Bernstein, Jeremy. *Oppenheimer: Portrait of an Enigma* (Chicago: Ivan R. Dee, 2004).

Bernstein, Jeremy. *Hitler's Uranium Club*, 2nd Ed. (New York: Copernicus Books, 2001).

Bird, Kai, and Sherwin, Martin J. *American Prometheus: The Triumph and Tragedy of J. Robert Oppenheimer* (New York: Vintage Books, 2006).

Blatt, John M., and Weisskopf, Victor F. *Theoretical Nuclear Physics* (New York: Dover Publications, 1991).

Boyer, Paul. *By the Bomb's Early Light: American Thought and Culture at the Dawn of the Atomic Age* (Chapel Hill, NC: University of North Carolina Press, 1985).

Bryson, Bill. *The Life and Times of the Thunderbolt Kid: A Memoir* (New York: Broadway Books, 2006).

Butterfield, Herbert. *The Whig Interpretation of History* (New York: W.W. Norton, 1965).

Cantelon, Philip L., Hewlett, Richard G., and Williams, Robert C., eds. *The American Atom: A Documentary History of Nuclear Policies from the Discovery of Fission to the Present*, 2nd Ed. (Philadelphia: University of Pennsylvania Press, 1991).

Cember, Herman, and Johnson, Thomas E. *Introduction to Health Physics*, 4th Ed. (New York: McGraw-Hill, 2009).

Clark, Ronald W. *Bertrand Russell and His World* (London: Thames and Hudson, 1981).

The Life of Bertrand Russell (New York: Alfred A. Knopf, 1976).

DeGroot, Gerald J. *The Bomb: A Life* (Cambridge, MA: Harvard University Press, 2004).

Dibblin, Jane. *Day of Two Suns: US Nuclear Testing and the Pacific Islanders* (New York: New Amsterdam, 1988).

Eisenbud, Merrill. "Monitoring Distant Fallout: The Role of the Atomic Energy Commission Health and Safety Laboratory during the Pacific Tests, with Special Attention to the Events Following Bravo." *Journal of Health Physics* 73(1) (1997): 21–27.

Fewell, M. P. "The Atomic Nuclide with the Highest Mean Binding Energy." *American Journal of Physics* 63 (July 1995): 653–658. doi: http://dx.doi.org/10.1119/1.17828

Figes, Orlando. *The Whisperers: Private Life in Stalin's Russia* (New York: Henry Holt and Company, 2007).

Fink, Carole. *The Cold War: An International History* (Boulder, CO: Westview Press, 2013).

Frank, Richard B. *Downfall: The End of the Imperial Japanese Empire* (New York: Penguin, 2001).

Freedman, Lawrence. *The Evolution of Nuclear Strategy*, 3rd Ed. (New York: Palgrave Macmillan, 2003).

Friedlander, Gerhart, et al. *Nuclear and Radiochemistry*, 3rd Ed. (New York: John Wiley & Sons, 1981).

Gaddis, John Lewis. *The Cold War: A New History* (New York: Penguin Books, 2005).

Glasstone, Samuel, and Dolan, Philip J. *The Effects of Nuclear Weapons*, 3rd Ed. (Washington, DC: US Department of Defense/US Department of Energy, 1977).

Glasstone, Samuel, and Sesonske, Alexander. *Nuclear Reactor Engineering* (New York: Van Nostrand Reinhold, 1967).

Grace, Charles S. *Nuclear Weapons: Principles, Effects, and Survivability*. Land Warfare: Brassey's New Battlefield Weapons Systems and Technology Series. Vol. 10 (London: Brassey's, 1994).

Hacker, Barton C. *Elements of Controversy: The Atomic Energy Commission and Radiation Safety in Nuclear Weapons Testing 1947–1974* (Berkeley: University of California Press, 1994).

Hansen, Chuck. *U.S. Nuclear Weapons, the Secret History* (New York: Orion Books, 1988).

Hecht, Eugene. *Optics*, 4th Ed. (New York: Addison-Wesley Publishing, 2002).

Herken, Gregg. *The Winning Weapon: The Atomic Bomb in the Cold War, 1945–1950* (New York: Alfred A. Knopf, 1980).

Holloway, David. *Stalin and the Bomb: The Soviet Union and Atomic Energy 1939–1956* (New Haven: Yale University Press).

International Commission on Radiological Protection (ICRP). "1990 Recommendations of the International Commission on Radiological

Protection." *Ann. ICRP* 60 (21) (1991). www.icrp.org/publication.asp?id= ICRP%20Publication%2060.

Kaplan, Edward. *To Kill Nations: American Strategy in the Air-Atomic Age and the Rise of Mutually Assured Destruction* (Ithaca and London: Cornell University Press, 2015).

Kissinger, Henry A. *Nuclear Weapons and Foreign Policy* (New York: W.W. Norton, 1969).

Kunkle, Thomas, and Ristvet, Byron. *Castle Bravo: Fifty Years of Legend and Lore a Guide to Off-Site Radiation Exposures* (Kirtland, NM: Defense Threat Reduction Agency, 2013).

Martin, Edwin J., and Rowland, Richard H. *Castle Series, 1954* (Washington, DC: Defense Nuclear Agency, 1982.

Meyerhof, Walter E. *Elements of Nuclear Physics* (New York: McGraw-Hill, 1967).

Miscamble, Wilson D. *The Most Controversial Decision: Truman, the Atomic Bombs, and the Defeat of Japan* (Cambridge: Cambridge University Press, 2011).

Nelson, Craig. *The Age of Radiance: The Epic Rise and Dramatic Fall of the Atomic Era* (New York: Scribner, 2014).

Newhouse, John. *War and Peace in the Nuclear Age* (New York: Alfred A. Knopf, 1989).

Niedenthal, Jack. *For the Good of Mankind: A History of the People of Bikini and Their Islands*, 2nd Ed. (Lexington, KY: A Bravo Book, 2013).

Ōishi Matashichi. *The Day the Sun Rose in the West: Bikini, the Lucky Dragon, and I* (Honolulu: The University of Hawai'i Press, 2011).

Oxtoby, David W., Freeman, Wade A., and Block, Toby F. *Chemistry: Science of Change*, 3rd Ed. (Philadelphia: Saunders College Publishing, 1998).

Rhodes, Richard. *The Making of the Atomic Bomb* (New York: Simon & Shuster, 1986).

    Dark Sun: The Making of the Hydrogen Bomb (New York: Simon & Schuster, 1995).

Ryfle, Steve. "Godzilla's Footprint." *Gojira: The Original Japanese Masterpiece.* DVD, Toho.

Russell, Bertrand. *Autobiography* (London: Routledge, 1975).

    "Man's Peril." In *The Basic Writings of Bertrand Russell*, ed. Egner, Robert E. and Dennon, Lester E. (New York: Simon and Schuster, 1961, 729–732).

Serber, Robert. *The Los Alamos Primer* (Berkeley: University of California Press, 1992).

Shurcliff, W. A. *Bombs at Bikini: The Official Report of Operation Crossroads* (New York: Wm. H. Wise & Co., 1947).

Simon, Steven L., Bouville, André, Land, Charles E., and Beck, Harold L. "Radiation Doses and Cancer Risks in the Marshall Islands Associated with Exposure to Radioactive Fallout from Bikini and Enewetak Nuclear Weapons Tests: Summary." *Journal of Health Physics* 99(2) (2010): 105–123.

Siracusa, Joseph M. *Nuclear Weapons: A Very Short Introduction* (New York: Oxford University Press, 2008).

Souder, William. "The Link between Castle Bravo and Modern Environmentalism." *Bulletin of the Atomic Scientists*, March 3, 2014.

Spector, Ronald H. *Eagle Against the Sun: The American War with Japan* (New York: Vintage, 1985).

Statkiewicz-Sherer, Mary Alice, Visconti, Paula J., and Ritenour, E. Russell. *Radiation Protection in Medical Radiography*, 6th Ed. (Maryland Heights, MO: Mosby, 2011).

Strauss, Lewis L. *Men and Decisions* (Garden City, NY: Doubleday & Company, 1962).

Symon, Keith R. *Mechanics*, 2nd Ed. (Reading, MA: Addison-Wesley, 1960).

Teller, Edward with Shoolery, Judith L. *Memoirs: A Twentieth-Century Journey in Science and Politics* (Cambridge, MA: Perseus Publishing, 2001).

United Nations Scientific Committee on the Effects of Atomic Radiation. "Sources and Effects of Ionizing Radiation." *UNSCEAR 2008 Report to the General Assembly with Scientific Annexes*, Vol. 1 (New York: United Nations, 2010). www.unscear.org/unscear/en/publications/2008_1.html.

US Arms Control and Disarmament Agency. *Worldwide Effects of Nuclear War: Some Perspectives* (Whitefish, MT: Kessinger, 2010).

Wheaton, James K. *You and the Atomic Bomb: History of Nuclear Bombs* (Hustonville, KY: Golgotha Press, 2010).

Weisgall, Jonathan M. *Operation Crossroads: The Atomic Tests at Bikini Atoll* (Annapolis, MD: Naval Institute Press, 1994).

INTERNET SOURCES AND DOCUMENTS

Brownlee, Robert R. "Learning to Contain Underground Nuclear Explosions." Nuclear Weapons Archive (June, 2002). http://nuclearweaponarchive.org/Usa/Tests/Brownlee.html.

Clark, John C. "We Were Trapped by Radioactive Fallout." www.sonicbomb.com/modules.php?name=News&file=article&sid=104.

Conard, Robert, Robertson, James S., Meyer, Leo M., Sutow, Wataru W., Wolins, William, Lowery, Austin, Urschel, Harold C., Barton, Johnnty M., Goldman, Morris, Hechter, Hyman, Eicher, Maynard, Carever, Russell K., and Potter, David W. *Medical Survey of Rongelap People, March 1958, Four Years after Exposure to Fallout*. Brookhaven National Laboratory, 1959. http://catalog.hathitrust.org/Record/011573393.

Conard, Robert A., Macdonald, Eugene H., Meyer, Leo M., Cohn, Stanton, Sutow, Wataru W., Karnofsky, David, Jaffee, A. A., and Riklon, Ezra. *Medical Survey of Rongelap People Seven Years after Exposure to Fallout*. Brookhaven National Laboratory, 1962. https://books.google.com/books/about/Medical_Survey_of_Rongelap_People_Seven.html?id=moYo9JsEsg8C.

Health Physics Society. *Doses from Medical X-Ray Procedures*. Accessed July 24, 2015. http://hps.org/physicians/documents/Doses_from_Medical_X-Ray_Procedures.pdf.

Hudson, Kate. "An Open Letter to President Loeak of the Marshall Islands." www.wagingpeace.org/an-open-letter-to-president-loeak-of-the-marshall-islands/.

Malik, John. *The Yields of the Hiroshima and Nagasaki Nuclear Explosions.* September 1985. Los Alamos National Laboratory. Accessed July 30, 2012. http://atomicarchive.com/Docs/pdfs/00313791.pdf.

Palafox, Neal A. "Statement of Neal A. Palafox, MD, MPH … to the Senate Energy and Natural Resources Committee," July 19, 2005. US Senate Committee on Energy and Natural Resources. www.energy.senate.gov/public/index .cfm/hearings-and-business-meetings?Id=3db96442-b31d-46eb-9b7f-d74ae31b88a6&Statement_id=a7d2f930-55e9-4542-923e-178619d20b61.

Skoog, Kim. "U.S. Nuclear Testing on the Marshall Islands: 1946 to 1958." www.uvu.edu/ethics/seac/US%20Nuclear%20Testing%20on%20the%20 Marshal%20Islands.pdf.

US Department of Energy. Nevada Operations Office. *United States Nuclear Tests: July 1945 Through September 1992.* December 2000, DOE/NV-209-REV 15. Accessed July 18, 2013. www.nv.doe.gov/library/publications/ historical/DOENV_209_REV15.pdf.

WEBSITES

Atomic Archive. "Cold War: A Brief History – The Soviet Atomic Bomb." Accessed September 19, 2013. www.atomicarchive.com/History/coldwar/ page03.shtml.

"Model of the Fat Man Bomb." Accessed September 21, 2013. www.atomicar chive.com/Movies/Movie3.shtml.

"The Soviets' 'Joe-4' Bomb Makes Its Mark." Accessed September 19, 2013. www.atomicarchive.com/History/hbomb/page_14.shtml.

Atomic Heritage Foundation. "Little Boy and Fat Man." Accessed September 10, 2015. www.atomicheritage.org/history/little-boy-and-fat-man.

Chu, S. Y. F., Ekstrom, L. P., and Firestone, R. B. "The Lund/LBNL Nuclear Data Search." Accessed August 3, 2015. http://nucleardata.nuclear.lu.se/toi/index .asp.

Embassy of the United States, Majuro, Marshall Islands. "The Legacy of U.S. Nuclear Testing and Radiation Exposure in the Marshall Islands." Accessed September 25, 2015. http://majuro.usembassy.gov/legacy.html

Federation of American Scientists. "Lithium Production." Accessed July 23, 2012. www.fas.org/nuke/intro/nuke/lithium.htm.

"Nuclear Weapon Design." Accessed July 23, 2012. www.fas.org/nuke/intro/ nuke/design.htm.

"United States Nuclear Tests July 1945 Through September 1992." Accessed July 18, 2013. http://fas.org/nuke/guide/usa/nuclear/usnuctests.htm.

Kennedy, John F. "Inaugural Address." The John F. Kennedy Presidential Library and Museum. January 20, 1961. Accessed September 2, 2016. www.jfklibrary .org/Research/Research-Aids/Ready-Reference/JFK-Quotations/Inaugural-Address.aspx.

Moltz, James Clay. "Global Submarine Proliferation: Emerging Trends and Problems." Accessed June 26, 2012. www.nti.org/analysis/articles/global-submarine-proliferation/.

Nuclear Weapon Archive. "Gallery of U.S. Nuclear Tests." Accessed July 18, 2013. http://nuclearweaponarchive.org/Usa/Tests/.

"Operation Greenhouse." Accessed September 25, 2015. http://nuclearweapon archive.org/Usa/Tests/Grnhouse.html

Sherbini, Sami. "Answer to Question #8933 Submitted to 'Ask the Experts.' " Health Physics Society. Accessed August 30, 2015. https://hps.org/ publicinformation/ ate/q8933.html.

Sublette, Carey. "Operation Castle." Nuclear Weapon Archive. Accessed April 25, 2017. http://nuclearweaponarchive.org/Usa/Tests/Castle.html.

"Operation Greenhouse." Nuclear Weapon Archive. Accessed July 19, 2013. http://nuclearweaponarchive.org/Usa/Tests/Grnhouse.html.

"Operation Ivy." Nuclear Weapon Archive. Accessed July 19, 2013. http:// nuclearweaponarchive.org/Usa/Tests/Ivy.html.

"Section 8.0 The First Nuclear Weapons." Nuclear Weapon Archive. Accessed September 9, 2015. http://nuclearweaponarchive.org/Nwfaq/Nfaq8.html# nfaq8.1.3.

The ABC's of Nuclear Science. "The Discovery of Radioactivity." Accessed June 21, 2012. www.lbl.gov/abc/wallchart/chapters/03/4.html.

US Department of Commerce/National Oceanic and Atmospheric Administration/ National Ocean Service. Office of Response and Restoration. "Overpressure Levels of Concern." Accessed September 13, 2015. http://response .restoration.noaa.gov/oil-and-chemical-spills/chemical-spills/resources/ overpressure-levels-concern.html.

US Nuclear Regulatory Commission. "Fact Sheet on Biological Effects of Radiation." Accessed September 18, 2015. www.nrc.gov/reading-rm/doc-collections/fact-sheets/bio-effects-radiation.html.

"Uranium Enrichment." Accessed July 29, 2015. www.nrc.gov/materials/fuel-cycle-fac/ur-enrichment.html#3.

Washington Nuclear Museum. "Radioactive Fallout to St. George, UT." Accessed September 25, 2015. www.toxipedia.org/display/wanmec/Radioactive+ Fallout+to+St.+George,+UT.

WikiQuotes. "Stalin." Accessed September 25, 2015.

Wellerstein, Alex, "The Spy, the Human Computer, and the H-Bomb." Accessed September 20, 2016. http://blog.nuclearsecrecy.com/2013/08/23/the-spy-the-human-computer-and-the-h-bomb/.

World Nuclear Association. "Plutonium." Accessed July 29, 2015. www .world-nuclear.org/info/Nuclear-Fuel-Cycle/Fuel-Recycling/Plutonium/ #.UaU2noBQHmQ.

DOCUMENTS FROM THE LEWIS L. STRAUSS ARCHIVES, HERBERT HOOVER PRESIDENTIAL LIBRARY, WEST BRANCH, IOWA

Address Before Virginia State Chamber of Commerce, April 14, 1950, Box 534, Tests and Testing, 1947–1954, p. 2.

Joint Committee on Atomic Energy, January, 27, 1953, Strauss Archives, Box 534, Tests and Testing, 1947–1954.

Letter to A. J. Muste, Strauss Archives, Box 534, Tests and Testing, 1955–57.

Memorandum, May 25, 1953, Strauss Archives, Box 534, Tests and Testing, 1947–1954.

Memorandum, May 26, 1953, Strauss Archives, Box 534, Tests and Testing, 1947–1954.

Notes About Natives, undated, Strauss Archives, Box 428, Castle Series I.

PBS TRANSCRIPTS

"Race for the Superbomb," *The American Experience.* www.pbs.org/wgbh/amex/bomb/.

"The World's Biggest Bomb," *Secrets of the Dead.* www.pbs.org/wnet/secrets/the-world%E2%80%99s-biggest-bomb-watch-the-full-episode/863/.

IMAGE CITATIONS

"A Model of the Atomic Bomb 'Fat Man' Dropped on Nagasaki." August 9, 1945. Australian War Memorial #045196. Accessed August 27, 2015. www.awm.gov.au/collection/045196/.

Fastfission. "Fission Bomb Assembly Methods." January 19, 2006. Accessed August 21, 2015. https://upload.wikimedia.org/wikipedia/commons/thumb/c/cb/Fission_bomb_assembly_methods.svg/880px-Fission_bomb_assembly_methods.svg.png.

"Teller-Ulam Device 3D." February 17, 2011. Accessed August 21, 2015. https://upload.wikimedia.org/wikipedia/commons/thumb/c/c1/Teller-Ulam_device_3D.svg/567px-Teller-Ulam_device_3D.svg.png.

LB (Little Boy) Unit on Trailer Cradle in Pit [bomb bay door in upper-right-hand corner]. August 1945 [Photographs and Other Graphic Materials]. Records of the Office of the Chief of Engineers, 1789–1999, Record Group 77; National Archives at College Park, College Park, MD. ARC Identifier 519394. Accessed August 27, 2015. https://catalog.archives.gov/id/519394.

Mononomic. "Binding Energy Curve – Common Isotopes with Gridlines." November 26, 2008. Accessed August 21, 2015. https://upload.wikimedia.org/wikipedia/en/thumb/7/7e/Binding_energy_curve_-_common_isotopes_with_gridlines.svg/1280px-Binding_energy_curve_-_common_isotopes_with_gridlines.svg.png.

"Operation Castle, BRAVO Event." n.d. Photo courtesy of National Nuclear Security Administration/Nevada Field Office. Image Number XX-92. Accessed August 27, 2015. www.nv.doe.gov/library/photos/photodetails.aspx?ID=1087.

Sherman, Paul. "Atomic Diagram." Accessed August 26, 2015. www.wpclipart.com/science/atoms_molecules/atom_diagram.png.html.

"Nuclear Fission." Accessed August 26, 2015. www.wpclipart.com/science/atoms_molecules/Nuclear_fission.png.html.

"Nuclear Fusion." Accessed August 26, 2015. www.wpclipart.com/energy/nuclear/nuclear_reaction/nuclear_fusion.png.html.

Index